APPLYING STRENGT
APPROACHES IN SO(

Edited by
Deanna Edwards and Kate Parkinson

ℙ

First published in Great Britain in 2023 by

Policy Press, an imprint of
Bristol University Press
University of Bristol
1-9 Old Park Hill
Bristol
BS2 8BB
UK
t: +44 (0)117 374 6645
e: bup-info@bristol.ac.uk

Details of international sales and distribution partners are available
at policy.bristoluniversitypress.co.uk

British Library Cataloguing in Publication Data
A catalogue record for this book is available from the British Library

ISBN 978-1-4473-6271-5 hardcover
ISBN 978-1-4473-6272-2 paperback
ISBN 978-1-4473-6273-9 ePub
ISBN 978-1-4473-6274-6 ePdf

Cover design: Robin Hawes
Front cover image: istock/simon2579
Bristol University Press and Policy Press use environmentally responsible
print partners.
Printed and bound in Great Britain by CPI Group (UK) Ltd, Croydon, CR0 4YY

In memory of

Dr Allister Butler

Ubuntu

Contents

List of tables   ix
Notes on contributors   x
Acknowledgements   xiii

1   An introduction to strengths-based approaches: inclusive and   1
    respectful practice
    Deanna Edwards and Kate Parkinson
        The aims of this book   1
        The organisation of the book   1
        An introduction to strengths-based approaches to social work practice   2
        The four elements of a strengths-based approach   3
        Twelve guidelines for a strengths-based assessment   4
        Types of strengths-based approaches   6
        What does the research tell us?   7
        The UK practice picture   9
        Characteristics of strengths-led practitioners   10

2   Theoretical context for the strengths-based approach   11
    Kate Parkinson and Deanna Edwards
        Origins of the strengths-based approach   11
        What is a strengths-based approach?   12
        Social constructionism   12
        Agency   14
        Social capital   14
        Resilience   15
        Social work theory   17
        Empowerment theory   17
        Ecological systems theory   18
        Culturally appropriate social work practice   19
        Key principles for social work practice   20
        Conclusion   22

3   Solution-focused practice   25
    Guy Shennan
        Introduction – a usable approach?   25
        A good fit?   26
        A little history, including some more usable ideas   26
        Formula first session task   26
        Exceptions and pre-session change   27
        The future focus and the miracle question   28
        Two ways   29
        The BRIEF version   29

Setting a direction   30
Describing preferred futures   31
Describing progress and what's working   32
Instances   32
Description and agency   32
Scaling questions   33
Listening with a constructive ear   34
Further practice examples and tips   35
Does it work?   35
Conclusion   36

4   Family Group Conferences   39
    Kate Parkinson, Deanna Edwards and Will Golden
    What are FGCs?   39
    FGCs as a strengths-based approach   42
    Empowerment theory   43
    Ecological systems theory   45
    Culturally sensitive social work practice   46
    Research findings   47
    Critical perspectives   49
    Conclusion   53

5   Signs of Safety   55
    Lauren Bailey and Steve Myers
    Introduction   55
    Development   55
    Principles   57
    Risk   58
    Step 2 Judgement: scaling questions   64
    Research   67
    Conclusion   68

6   Multisystemic therapy   71
    Simone Fox, Mhairi Fleming and Anne Edmondson
    Development of multisystemic therapy worldwide   71
    Overview of MST   72
    Theoretical orientation and principles   73
    Multisystemic therapy for child abuse and neglect (MST-CAN) 73
    Development of MST within the UK   76
    Workforce and social work context   77
    Referrals to MST   77
    MST's strengths-based approach in the context of UK social work 78
    Conclusion   82

Contents

7   A narrative approach to social work   85
    Michaela Rogers and Jennifer Cooper
        Introduction   85
        Narrative concepts and methods   86
        Master narrative and counter-narrative   87
        The development of narrative approaches in social work   89
        Using a narrative approach in practice   90
        Assessments   91
        Externalising the problem   92
        Narrative and biographical work   93
        Narrative approaches with adults   95
        Narrative approaches to social work with family and social networks 97
        Conclusion   97

8   Strengths-based approaches in adult social care   99
    Sarah Pollock and Alex Withers
        Introduction   99
        The history and development of strengths-based approaches   100
        The Care Act (2014): introducing the 'new' strengths-based approach 101
        The contemporary context   102
        Strengths-based framework for adult social work   103
        Strengths-based approaches in practice   104
        Focus on the Three Conversations approach   105
        Focus on Making Safeguarding Personal   106
        The case of Luke Davey: *R (Davey) v. Oxfordshire CC*   108
        Responsibilisation   109
        Care   110
        Community   111
        Conclusion   112

9   Strengths-based approaches in mental health services   115
    Emily Weygang
        Introduction   115
        The pathology of mental distress   115
        Personal is political   116
        Lost for words   117
        Punitive Personal Independence Payments   119
        All in the mind   121
        Arcs of resistance: 'opening the window'   121
        'A human-shaped space'   124
        Conclusion   127

10 People with lived experience of strengths-based approaches   129
    Deanna Edwards, Kate Parkinson and People with Lived Experience
        Introduction   129
        Why involve people with lived experience?   129

People with lived experiences of 'traditional social work' practice 130
Involving people with lived experience in generic strengths-based 134
social work
Family Group Conferences 136
Solution-focused practice 140
Conclusion 142

11 Conclusion 145
Deanna Edwards and Kate Parkinson

References 147
Index 171

List of tables

5.1	Signs of Safety questions	61
5.2	Signs of Safety mapping	62
5.3	Signs of Safety scaling	64
5.4	Signs of Safety Three Houses	65
6.1	The MST nine treatment principles	74

Notes on contributors

Lauren Bailey qualified as a social worker in 2010, and worked briefly for the NSPCC before moving in 2011 to Gibraltar, where she practised social work and social work leadership in a variety of roles. Lauren returned to practise social work in her home county of Cheshire in 2022 and is currently completing an MSc in Social Work Leadership and Management at the University of Salford, where she is also a guest lecturer.

Jennifer Cooper is a PhD student at the University of Lancaster. Jennifer has worked as a social worker in both children and adult services and as a teacher at the University of Sheffield.

Anne Edmondson (MSW) is a Multisystemic Child Abuse and Neglect (MST-CAN) Consultant with MST-UK & Ireland, South London and Maudsley NHS Foundation Trust. She is a social worker and has worked in Multisystemic Therapy (MST) for over 20 years.

Deanna Edwards teaches social work at the University of Salford. She is a qualified social worker with an interest and background in Family Group Conferences (FGCs) and Restorative Practice. Her previous roles have included managing FGC services and policy adviser for Family Rights Group. She is an experienced FGC trainer and current programme lead for an academic qualification in FGCs. Deanna is also a social work practice educator.

Mhairi Fleming PGC, MA, BSc is an MST Consultant and Head of Programme for Scotland. She is a social work postgraduate of Stirling University and master's graduate of Edinburgh University who has worked in social work and evidenced-based psychological therapies for over 16 years. She is a passionate advocate of utilising evidenced-based and evidence-informed practice and preventing family breakdown.

Simone Fox is a consultant clinical and forensic psychologist and an MST consultant. She is employed by South London and Maudsley NHS Foundation Trust. Previously she was Deputy Clinical Director and a Senior Lecturer on the Doctorate in Clinical Psychology Programme, Royal Holloway, University of London. She has worked with adult mentally disordered offenders in medium-secure units and prisons, as well as with young offenders within a Young Offenders' Institution. She has significant experience in undertaking psycho-legal assessments for adults and young people in the criminal justice system.

Will Golden is a Family Group Conference coordinator with Just Psychology, where he has been working for the past six years. Before this he was a social worker on front-line child protection, having studied for a master's degree in social work at Salford University. Will also supports students through placements in social work as a practice educator for Manchester University.

Steve Myers is a registered social worker with substantial experience of working in statutory and third sector children's services. As an academic he was an early exponent of teaching strengths-based approaches to social work students. Since retirement he volunteers as the Vice-Chair of the Association of Child Protection Professionals.

Kate Parkinson is Subject Leader for Health and Social Care at the University of Huddersfield. Kate is a qualified social worker, with a practice background in safeguarding children, in a range of front-line and managerial positions. Kate has worked within in an academic environment since 2013, first as a lecturer in Social Work at the University of Salford, before moving on to the University of Huddersfield. Kate has a research interest in strengths-based approaches generally and more specifically in Family Group Conferences and other family-led approaches to decision-making. Kate has several publications in this field of practice.

Sarah Pollock is a Senior Lecturer in social work at Manchester Metropolitan University. She is a qualified and registered social worker, and her practice experience includes working with adults in both community and hospital settings in north-west England. Sarah's research interests include social justice, interpreter-mediated social work and adult safeguarding, with a recent publication considering the legal context of interpreter-mediated social work. Sarah is currently working on funded projects for the Department for Education and the British Academy.

Michaela Rogers PhD is a Senior Lecturer in Social Work at the University of Sheffield. Her research examines interpersonal violence with a focus on marginalised groups, impacts, access to services and service responses. This includes research on elder abuse, trans and non-binary people's experiences, intimate partner violence and children.

Guy Shennan was first trained in solution-focused practice while working in a children and families social work team in Derby in the 1990s. He now specialises in the approach as a therapist, consultant and trainer, and the second edition of his book *Solution-Focused Practice: Effective Communication to Facilitate Change* was published in 2019. Guy remains connected to social work in a variety of ways, including as an Honorary Lecturer at Salford University, and he was the Chair of the British Association of Social Workers from 2014 to 2018.

Emily Weygang is a Senior Lecturer at the University of Chester. She is a qualified and registered social worker and has worked in a variety of areas, including adult mental health, the criminal justice system and children's services.

Alex Withers has worked in social care since 2002, and qualified as a social worker in 2006. They spent 13 years working with adults with substance misuse issues before spending three years teaching social work within the university system. They are currently working as a mental health practitioner within the NHS.

Acknowledgements

We would like to thank the following people: our friends and colleagues at the University of Salford and the University of Huddersfield; the people with lived experience who we have worked with and those who have contributed to this book; contributing authors; our students past and present.

Finally, thanks to our fabulous family and friends who help us to find our strengths.

1

An introduction to strengths-based approaches: inclusive and respectful practice

Deanna Edwards and Kate Parkinson

The aims of this book

The aim of this text is to bring together a body of theory and practice in strengths-based traditions in social work practice. While a good deal has been written about the strengths perspective in health settings, there is less about how the approach is used in a social care arena and yet it is used worldwide in this sector. In the UK adult social care context, strengths-based approaches are acknowledged in the Care Act of 2014, and in Children and Families Services they are recognised as widespread and important (Kemp, Marcenkko, Lyons and Kruzich, 2014).

This book will draw upon theoretical perspectives, academic research and practical applications of strengths-based practice in social work. It includes contributions from people with lived experience of such approaches, academics and practitioners. It will cover many of the models and methods of practice which fall under the umbrella of strengths perspectives, exploring both theoretical underpinnings and practical applications to enable the reader to develop their understanding. It will also locate the strengths-based approach in the current context of social work policy, legislation and guidance and provide a critical understanding of the efficacy of such approaches based upon the international research evidence base.

The organisation of the book

Following this introduction is a chapter on the theoretical underpinnings of strength-based practice, after which there are five chapters which focus upon some of the important applications of the strengths approach. These are:

- solution-focused practice
- Family Group Conferencing
- Signs of Safety

- multisystemic therapy
- narrative approaches

This is clearly not an exhaustive list but it includes some of the most commonly used approaches.

Many of these chapters have a focus on children and family social work, as this is where practice has developed and focused. Chapters 8 and 9 will therefore look at generic strengths-based approaches from the perspective of those working in the adult and mental health sectors.

Finally, Chapter 10 will consider the voices of those with lived experience of social care and strengths-based work.

Most practice-based chapters include an introduction, a case study and key learning points for readers. The reader will also be able to learn more from the suggested further reading at the end of each chapter.

An introduction to strengths-based approaches to social work practice

The strengths-based perspective has a long tradition in social work and was popularised in the 1980s and 1990s by writers such as Rapp and Chamberlain (1985), Weick et al (1989) and Saleebey (2002).

Weick et al have argued that social work has its origins in 'moral conversion' (Weick et al, 1989, p 350) and has retained its focus upon deficits and personal and social problems. In contrast to this, the strengths approach places emphasis upon empowerment, capacity and capability as a countermovement to the problem-focused approach to practice (Konradt, in Teater, 2014).

Glicken (2004, p 3) defines strengths-based practice as a

> way of viewing the positive behaviour of all clients by helping them see that the problem areas are secondary to areas of strengths and that out of what they do well can come helping solutions based upon the successful strategies they use daily in their lives to cope with a variety of important life issues, problems and concerns.

Key learning points

A strengths approach focuses upon hope, empowerment and resilience rather than deficits, problems and pathologies.

Saleebey's (2002) seminal text on the strengths approach similarly argues that social work is constructed largely on the premise that people who use services have deficits, problems, pathologies and diseases (p 4) and uses the 'language of pessimism', which emphasises problems. This, it argues, was much influenced by a biomedical model and results in inequality and power imbalances between the helper and the helped. He thus describes a strengths approach as an attempt to reduce this imbalance and instead focus upon hope, empowerment and resilience. The approach aims to be holistic and multi-disciplinary. An alternative definition proposed by Morgan and Ziglio (2007) states that the approach is about working in a collaborative way which promotes the opportunity for individuals to be the co-producers of services and support rather than solely consumers of those services.

A simplistic way of framing the essentials of the strengths approach is to use what Saleebey (2002) calls CPR, which stands for:

C – competence, capacities, courage
P – promise, positive expectations
R – resilience, reserves, resources

He argues that some of the principles of the approach are as follows:

1. Every individual and group has strengths.
2. Trauma, abuse, illness and struggle may be challenging and difficult but may also be sources of strength and opportunity.
3. One doesn't know the upper limits of capacity to grow and change. Aspirations should therefore be taken seriously.
4. We serve people best by collaborating with them.
5. Every environment has resources.

We can see here the influence of person-centred practice, the roots of which lie in Rogers' (1951) client-centred therapy which emphasise the human capacity to change and grow and the role of the helper as being a facilitator to this this growth. Indeed, the British Association of Social Workers (BASW, 2014) cites one of the principles of person-centred work as: 'supporting people to recognise and develop their own strengths and abilities to enable them to live an independent and fulfilling life' (The Health Foundation, 2014, p 6).

So, in terms of the practical application of this approach to social work, according to De Jong and Berg (2008) it involves helping the person to see the positive attributes they have as well as the problems which they are (usually) only too aware of.

The four elements of a strengths-based approach

1. The harbingers of hints and strengths. Whilst listening to the person's narrative look out for strengths and reflect these back.
2. Stimulate narratives of resilience and strengths. Helping people we work with move from talking in terms of problems to talking in terms of capacity and strength.

3. Using the language of strengths. Helping people to identify their hopes and goals and their strengths in achieving these goals.
4. Capitalising on strengths. Applying what they have learnt to other areas of their lives. (Saleebey, 2009)

According to Douglas, McCarthy and Serino (2014), the strengths-based approach is 'one of the primary modalities of social work practice' (p 219) and a 'cornerstone of social work practice and education' (p 220). Consequently, we need an insight into just how practitioners might practice as strengths-based social workers. Cowger and Shively attempt to address this by suggesting 12 guidelines for a strengths-based assessment:

Key learning points

Strengths-based assessment aims to be person-centred, collaborative, offers meaningful choices and is open and honest with effective communication. It has a focus upon strengths rather than deficits.

Twelve guidelines for a strengths-based assessment

1. Give prominence to the person with lived experiences' understanding of the story.
2. Believe the story of the person with lived experience.
3. Develop an understanding of what the person with lived experience wants from the assessment.
4. Move towards person and system strengths and away from obstacles and deficits in the assessment.
5. Assess on a personal, interpersonal, and structural level.
6. Look for uniqueness.
7. Use the language and wording of the person with lived experience.
8. Work in partnership.
9. Share the content of the assessment.
10. Avoid blame.
11. Avoid cause-and-effect thinking.
12. Assessment is not diagnosis. (Cowger and Snively, 2002, pp 221–225)

Understanding the power of language

Saleebey (2009) reminds us that the way we ask questions in an assessment can lend itself to searching for strengths. These can include survival questions ('How have you managed to survive thus far?'), exception questions ('When were things going better?'), support questions ('Who have you been able to rely upon?') and aspiration questions ('Where do you want to be in five years' time?).

Individual strengths-based approaches will use different tools and techniques, and these will be explored in the appropriate chapters, but it is worth noting here some generic tools that practitioners who wish to adopt a strengths-based approach to practice can utilise. In terms of helping people to move forward Saleebey (2006) utilises the work of both Brown and Levitt (1979) and Hepworth and Larsen (1990) to develop a five-step process to *define the issues*:

1. Elicit a story.
2. Seek to understand what is wanted and expected from the helper.
3. Seek to understand the meaning that the person ascribes to the problem situation.
4. Seek to understand what life would be like if the problem situation were resolved.
5. Discover who is involved with the problem situation.

Once this is elicited, the next step is to step *beyond*, which involves telling the story and identifying strengths by asking open questions about what has helped, what relationships are helpful, what advice you would give to people in similar situations, what spiritual activities helped, what services have helped and what coping mechanisms do you have? The assessment can be framed into one of four quadrants as follows:

Quadrant 1: Social and political strengths
Quadrant 2: Physical and physiological strengths
Quadrant 3: Social and political obstacles
Quadrant 4: Psychological obstacles. (Saleebey, 2006, figure 6.2, p 109)

This has a similar focus to Egan's skilled helper model, which was originally published in 1975. Egan's model outlines three stages of helping:

1. current scenario
2. preferred scenario
3. getting there

These allow people to tell their story, work out what their goals are and develop strategies for achieving them. The 'helper' utilises a strengths approach in helping the person to move through these stages (Egan 2018).

Poulin (2000, p 104) reminds us that there have been a number of instruments developed to 'measure' the 'problems' of people with lived experience, and a number of these, such as biopsychosocial assessment forms which incorporate an ecosystems perspective (Jordan and Franklin, 1995), can be considered strengths-based. Poulin also argues that ecomaps (Hartman 1995) and genograms (McGoldrick and Gerson, 1985) can be considered as strengths-based approaches.

Since these all 'measure' the systems that can offer support to an individual they are helping to identify for strengths. Poulin goes on to suggest several useful worksheets that can be used for a strengths-based assessment. These worksheets include details of culture, values, norms and traditions, which are all widely recognised as a valuable support for individuals in times of difficulties.

On a similar note, Canda (2006) writes that spirituality in people with serious life challenges is of growing interest to social workers and is a source of strength. One might argue here that most people that social workers work with could be defined as having 'serious life challenges' (Canda, 2006, p 61). His findings when working with people with cystic fibrosis were that many of his research participants perceived faith as both a strength and a comfort; it gave significance to life and helped them to manage the anticipation of death. Strength-based practitioners should therefore not underestimate the power of spirituality in helping people to develop and maintain resilience in the face of adversity.

Types of strengths-based approaches

There is a recognition in the strengths-based tradition that any practitioner in the helping professions can utilise the approach in their day-to-day work with people. As already noted, this can be done in a variety of ways and with a variety of tools but can be easily incorporated into everyday practice simply by being mindful of how we work with people. However, there are a number of specific approaches that are considered to be rooted in a strengths tradition, including the following:

Solution-focused practice was first developed by de Shazer and Berg in the 1980s (for example, de Shazer, 1982; Berg, 1994). This approach is a future-orientated, goal-directed therapeutic intervention which emphasises exceptions to the problem, a focus upon the present and future and an acknowledgement of what is going well, with an aim of building upon this.

Family Group Conferences (FGCs) were first established in New Zealand in the 1980s in response to Māori concerns about children and family social work practice with indigenous populations (Edwards and Parkinson, 2018). This is an approach that builds upon the strengths of the wider family and friends network to address a central question regarding the welfare of a child or adult.

Signs of Safety was introduced in 1999 by Turnell and Edwards, who developed it in response to working with native Australian populations in child protection. The approach uses a strengths perspective in child protection conferences and has been adapted for use in adult social work services.

Multisystemic therapy was developed by Hengeller in the 1970s (see Hengeller, 2017). It is an intense, home-based, family-focused therapeutic intervention for young people used predominantly with the 11–17 age group who are offending or at risk of offending. It is strengths-based in that it builds upon existing, positive systems of support.

Narrative approaches. Roscoe and Madoc (2009) describe the stages of a narrative approach as including rapport building, storytelling, exploring the dominant plots and listening for themes and reauthoring alternative 'plots'. It allows the storyteller to lead the process and identify their own coping strategies.

Other strengths-based approaches. Of course, this text will not provide an exhaustive list of strengths-based approaches and there are a number that have not been included here, such as motivational interviewing (see Rollnick and Miller, 1995). It also recognised that the perspective is much wider than social work and is used in health, mental health, psychology and psychotherapy too.

What does the research tell us?

Individual chapters will consider the research context of the approaches they cover, but it is worth here outlining in brief some of the generalist research on the strengths perspective as a whole. For brevity this is a consideration of some of the social work research only, though we recognise that the research into the strengths approach in health services is much broader.

Early research into the strengths-based approach indicated some positive outcomes and satisfaction in terms of goal achievement (for example, Rapp and Chamberlain, 1985; Siegal, Rapp, Kelliher and Fisher, 1995), although Douglas, McCarthy and Serino (2014) argue that this early research has lacked standardisation tools with which to measure outcomes and therefore potentially lacks validity. Green, McAllister and Tate (2004) sought to address this by developing an assessment tool, the *strengths-based practices inventory*, which was designed to assess on four scales:

1. empowerment
2. cultural competency
3. interpersonal sensitivity
4. relationship support

This inventory can be used to assess the efficacy of the strengths approach when used in social care settings. Douglas et al (2014) also argue that this tool can be adapted to measure how well strengths-based practice is utilised by practitioners.

In terms of using a strengths-based approach in a school social work setting, Boulden (2009) found that a behaviour intervention programme that combined Cognitive Behaviour Therapy with strengths-based practice and resilience was effective in reducing disruptive behaviour in the classroom. Similarly, Pulla and Kay (2016) found a positive perception of using strengths-based practice, counselling and social work approach in classrooms. This included asking students to consider the strengths of students previously labelled as 'class troublemakers' (Pulla and Kay, 2016, p 13).

Williams (2019) researched the use of restorative approaches in promoting strengths in the delivery of family services, finding that most families studied saw the service as a positive help, which was likely to engage them rather than alienate. She also found that using a restorative approach as a practice framework can lead to wider change methods, such as solution-focused therapy and motivational interviewing. She goes on to argue that the widening adoption of other strengths approaches such as Signs of Safety (Turnell and Edwards, 1999) indicates increased support for strengths-based practice but calls for work to identify the efficacy of such models.

Finally, in terms of the earlier point about the role of spirituality in a strengths approach, Abdullah (2015) compares the strengths perspective with the Islamic concept of 'fitra' in the sense that both 'presuppose a positive view of humankind: people are viewed as resilient and capable of growth and development' (Abdullah, 2015, p 163). Abdullah hence argues that a strengths-based approach is a good fit for working with Muslim clients (Hodge and Nadir, 2008) and is congruent with Muslim values, making it more compatible with Muslim culture than many other social work paradigms.

Critical perspectives

While some of the evidence above attests to the efficacy of the strengths perspective, it is under-researched and not of course, without criticism. Again, specific critiques will be addressed in individual chapters, but some of the generic criticisms of the approach will be addressed here. One of the potential shortcomings of the generic strengths-based perspective is that it has largely existed as a theoretical and practice concept and philosophy and lacks a large body of empirical validation (Staudt et al, 2001). One might also find a 'mixed picture in terms of implementation' (Kemp et al, 2014, p 27), although we would argue that in terms of child welfare this is hardly surprising given the complex nature of the work. Slasberg and Beresford (2017, p 269), in discussing adult social care, argue that the current focus on a strengths approach is a tipping point and wonder if the approach is an 'elixir or the next false dawn'. In analysing a number of practices that are using the strengths perspective in the UK they have argued that the claims of their success are often somewhat exaggerated and while the move to person-centred practice is to be welcomed and is indeed good practice, this practice cannot exist in a vacuum. Hence, the system must also change, and this change must occur first before we can embed a strengths approach. This is supported by Cowger (1998), who argues that the approach is weak in social services structures that are powered by social control values. Cowger agrees that in order for the approach to be effective policy must first change. Indeed Gray (2011, p 8) argues that, despite using 'the language of empowerment and social justice, strengths-based solutions are grounded in neoliberal notions of individual responsibility' and as such rely on people with lived experience to find solutions to their own issues. While this indeed can be seen as empowering and strengths-based, it may also be perceived as liberating state-led responsibility. Gray (2011) also argues that the approach aims to equalise power between worker and client but that this is unrealistic and fails to account for structural inequalities such as mental health, poverty and racism and is as a result too optimistic and naïve.

The UK practice picture

Despite the above critiques in 2017 the Social Care Institute for Excellence (SCIE) in the UK hosted an event to promote strengths-based social work practice in adult social care. This has resulted in several initiatives, including training programmes and a strengths-based practice framework published by the Department of Health and Social Care in 2019. Incorporated into this is a practice handbook for social workers (Department of Health and Social Care, 2019). This framework and handbook are supported by Lyn Romeo, the current (at time of writing) Chief Social Worker for Adults.

Adult social care in the UK was arguably transformed by the introduction of the 2014 Care Act, which places duties on local authorities to 'maximise the individual involvement in the process'. While the Act does not go as far as directing a strengths-based approach, it did establish a 'wellbeing principle', which emphasises working in a holistic way. It also emphasises the importance of the individual's views, wishes and feelings, their opinions about their life and care and their participation in the assessment processes as well as the involvement and wellbeing of those caring for them. Choice and control are central, and a holistic assessment needs to be inclusive of the role of support from family, friends and others of significance. Accordingly, the SCIE practice framework states that 'the Care Act sets the perfect framework and foundation to enable all social care and support functions to be strengths based' (Department of Health and Social Care, 2019, p 50). It goes on to recommend that social care services embed strengths-based practice throughout their work, including using the approach in staff supervision and using meaningful performance outcomes that reflect strengths-based approaches rather than traditional 'how many' and 'how long' approaches (Department of Health and Social Care, 2019, p 54).

According to Pattoni (2012), there is 'emerging' evidence in terms of the use of the approach with children and families, including the use of the approach to sustain hope and a sense of purpose and helping to identify resources for coping. In the UK context, since the 1989 Children Act, social workers have been encouraged to work in partnership with families and the widespread use of both FGCs and restorative approaches in children and family services has facilitated an emphasis upon the strengths approach. SCIE (2018) also argued that there is a rapid adoption of the approach in children and families work, encouraged by the Munro review of 2011, which highlighted the bureaucratic nature of child protection work. This is also supported by the 2017 evaluation of the Department for Education innovation programme (Rees Centre, 2017). This evaluation concluded that strengths-based approaches were key factors that contributed to improvement in outcomes.

While arguably less well embedded in children's services, the approach is clearly having an impact in both sectors. Examples of practice will be explored in Chapters 3–9.

Characteristics of strengths-led practitioners

The final part of this chapter explores some of the required characteristics of practitioners working with a strengths-based approach. Unsurprisingly, Stuck, Rocco and Albmoz (2011) found that supervisory support is essential in terms of worker engagement alongside job satisfaction (Kemp et al, 2014). Kemp et al (2014) also found that workers' use of strengths approaches also predicted 'buy-in to services' (p 32) or 'willingness to engage with workers or services' (p 33). The SCIE practice framework includes the following in its essential skills for strengths-based practitioners:

- ability to advocate
- effective communication
- ability to ask open questions, to listen and to empathise
- creative and lateral thinking
- collaborative working
- professional curiosity (Department of Health and Social Care, 2019, pp 58–59)

While it might be argued that these skills are essential for all social work practice, it could also be argued that a recognition of the strengths and assets of the people social workers work with, support and advocate on behalf of is also essential. This book aims to explore the strengths-based tradition in relation to both the skills of the practitioner and the perspectives of the people with lived experience of strengths approaches. It provides a critical overview of some of the major strengths-based approaches used by social workers, to enable the reader to develop their understanding of an important growth area in social work practice.

2

Theoretical context for the strengths-based approach

Kate Parkinson and Deanna Edwards

This chapter focuses on the theoretical context of the strengths-based approach. It first explores the origins of the approach and presents its underlying principles and philosophy. It then moves on to locate it within core sociological theories relevant to social work practice: those of social constructionism, agency, social capital and the psychological theory of resilience. This will be followed by a discussion of how the approach aligns with key social work theories and principles for practice. The chapter is aimed at providing an overview of how key theoretical approaches relate to the strengths-based approach, and so it does not explore each approach in any great depth. It is an introductory chapter and, for those who wish to explore the different theoretical approaches in greater depth, a further reading section is provided at the end of the chapter.

As stated in the introduction to this text, 'strengths-based approach' is an umbrella term, which encompasses several practice-based approaches and models. Hence this chapter will focus on the strengths-based approach in its broadest sense, and the theoretical basis to individual approaches will be discussed in separate chapters later.

Origins of the strengths-based approach

Social work throughout history has been defined as a 'problem-solving profession', and much of the theory and practice of social work is based upon deficits, problems, pathologies and disease (Kelly and Gates, 2010; Caiels, Milne and Beadle-Brown, 2020). This problem-defining paradigm, where the professional is the 'expert' who develops the solution to an individual or family problem, has dominated social work practice for much of the 20th century (Berg and Kelly, 2000; Kelly and Gates, 2010; Min, 2011; Caiels, Milne and Beadle-Brown, 2020). For decades there has been tension between core social work values and applying a deficits approach. In response to this, a discourse on a strengths perspective as an approach to social work practice began to emerge in the early 1980s from the University of Kansas's School of Social Welfare, popularised by the academic Dennis Saleebey (Saleebey, 2009). In 1989 Weick, Rapp, Sullivan and Kisthard coined the term 'strengths perspective', with a focus on practitioners recognising the autonomy and strengths of users of social work services. Initially it was used within mental health services and the strengths-based case management approach was developed as an alternative to traditional models of practice with their overemphasis on diagnosis, labelling and problems (Saleebey, 1996). Since then, it has been applied in a range of social work settings across the globe, and in the UK it is widely acknowledged to be best social work practice, enshrined in legislation and subsequent policy (Munro, 2011; The Care Act, 2014; Department for Health and Social Care, 2019).

What is a strengths-based approach?

As highlighted in the introductory chapter, the fundamental basis to the approach is a commitment to focusing on an individual or family's competences and the resources that they have available to draw upon to address the difficulties that they are facing (Caiels, Milne and Beadle-Brown, 2020). Hence, an individual's characteristics and the environmental factors that shape their lives are central to the approach.

Users of services are considered to be the experts on their own situations, with practitioners regarded as partners with expertise, who can use this expertise to support individuals and facilitate a process of change (Foot, 2012; Caiels, Milne and Beadle-Brown, 2020). A belief that situations can change and improve is central to the approach. Indeed Saleebey (2013) argues that hope that things will get better is fundamental to achieve change, stating that the 'fire of hope' can 'start the engine of positive change' (p 8).

The SCIE definition of the strengths-based approach emphasises the importance of a collaborative relationship between person with lived experience and professional which is fundamental to the process. Advocates of the strengths-based approach argue that the professional/user relationship should be one of collaboration rather than one of authority (Itzhaky and Bustin, 2002; Saleebey, 2009) and that a positive collaborative relationship is necessary to facilitate change (Duncan and Hubble, 2000; Manthey et al, 2011). Hence the quality of the relationship between those providing support and those being supported is crucial to the process (Duncan and Hubble, 2000; Manthey et al, 2011). From a strengths perspective a *quality* relationship is one which is hope-inducing (Rapp, Saleebey and Sullivan, 2005), accepting and empathic (Saleebey, 2006). Furthermore, Rapp and Goscha (2006) argue that the strengths-based relationship is also empowering in that it increases individuals' perceptions of their abilities, increases choices and options and increases confidence to choose. Rapp, Saleebey and Sullivan (2008) state that meaningful choice is a key feature of a strengths perspective and that a practitioner's role is to increase and explain choices and encourage individuals to make informed choices and decisions (Pattoni, 2012).

Social constructionism

Social constructionism has become one of the main strands of the postmodernism movement, which challenged the traditional rational and scientific understandings of the world that emerged out of the Enlightenment period of the late 18th century. Modernity seeks to establish truth and absolute knowledge and believes that underlying structures in the physical world, such as the law of physics can explain how things work and how people behave. This reliance on scientific and rational explanations contributed to the development of the medical model and the deficits approach to social work, mentioned above (Pardeck, Murphy and Meinert, 1998). Postmodernists and social constructionists, on the other hand, believe that there is no 'objective truth', that reality is subjective and that individuals and their experiences are shaped by their social and interpersonal influences (Gergen, 1985). According to the social constructionist view, the generation of knowledge and ideas of reality are sparked not by individuals but through social processes (Gergen, 1994). If all reality is socially constructed, 'knowledge is not something people possess somewhere in their heads, but rather, something people do together' (Gergen, 1985, p 270). Berger and Luckmann (1966) proposed that all knowledge is socially constructed, including our knowledge of what 'reality' is. Because people are born into a society and culture with existing norms and predefined patterns of behaviour, definitions of 'reality' are socially transmitted from one generation to the next and are further reinforced by social sanctions. These existing group definitions are learned and internalised through the process of socialisation. This knowledge gradually becomes a part of a person's own worldview and ideology. Because such knowledge is socially constructed, it can vary historically over time and differ across cultural groups, which hold diverse beliefs about human development and nature (Sahin, 2006). The construction of this knowledge involves a dialectical process between individuals interacting with each other and with their social world (Parton and O'Byrne, 2000; Gergen, 2001). People make meanings as they interact with others and try to figure out the meaning of their experiences (de Jong and Berg, 2002). Therefore, the role of language is profoundly important (Parton and O'Byrne, 2000) as the conversations that people have construct knowledge and the understanding of 'reality'.

The strengths-based approach can be argued to be a constructionist perspective in the following ways:

1. The strengths-based approach understands that individuals' experiences and social interactions shape their experiences, understanding and meaning of the world. The focus is on supporting the individual to identify their own strengths and resources within the context of their particular culture and environment.
2. A key feature of the strengths-based approach is the language that supporters use to communicate with those they are supporting. Supporters need to realise that the language they use can influence the hope for change (Pulla, 2017). Therefore, language needs to focus on strengths, resilience, competence and the individual as a valued member of society. The conversations between the two parties can enable an individual to co-construct an alternative

understanding of their reality (their issues and difficulties) and generate the environment, motivation and possibility of change (Myers, 2008).

3. Saleebey (1996) argues that the strengths-based approach can enable individuals from minority groups to have their stories and narratives heard by institutions that have oppressed or marginalised them. This opens up the possibility of a reconstructed relationship, experience and understanding between services and minority members of the community. It also raises the possibility of reconstructing the 'generative themes' (Freire and Ramos, 1970) of the culture, community, neighbourhood or family (Saleebey, 1996).

Agency

Agency can be described as

> The idea that individuals are equipped with the ability to understand and control their own actions, regardless of the circumstances of their lives. ... We exercise agency, for example when we indicate our intention to vote one way or the other, or make choices about what to eat from a restaurant menu. (Webb, Schirato and Danaher, 2002, p ix)

Bourdieu (1977) theorised that an individual's agency is determined by objective social structures, such as those relating to class, ethnicity and gender. In other words, the higher the social class, the more agency an individual has. Parkinson (2018) argues that it is widely acknowledged that the bulk of users of social care services are people who are poor, marginalised and disenfranchised: that is, using a Bourdieusian analysis, they have little agency. Research has emphasised the disempowering nature of social care processes and how individuals can feel powerless and disenfranchised within these processes, feeling that their voice gets lost within the bureaucracy (Adams, 2008; Fook, 2012; Eassom et al, 2014; Featherstone, White and Morris, 2014; Muench, Diaz and Wright, 2016).

The strengths-based approach can be conceptualised as a model which encourages the agency users of social work services, as the focus is on the user's own lived experience, perspective and strengths. It is an attempt to redress the balance of power between a social care professional and a user of services (Saleebey, 1996).

Social capital

Relating to agency is the concept of social capital, and it could be argued that you cannot have agency without social capital and vice versa. Indeed, Ling and Dale (2014) argue that agency is required to mobilise social capital and that social capital facilitates agency. Thus a symbiotic relationship exists between the two concepts.

The definition of social capital is a contested one and there are many different interpretations, which can lead to some confusion in understanding the meaning of the concept (Robinson, Schmid and Siles, 2002). However, within the social science field there appears to be a general consensus that it relates to the role of networks and civic norms and that the key indicators of social capital include social relations, formal and informal social networks, group membership, trust, reciprocity and civic engagement (Office for National Statistics, 2001).

To put it simply, social capital is a resource that arises from social networks and relationships and which generates positive benefits for members of a group, through shared trust, norms and values (Yeung et al, 2020). Social capital enables individual and collective interests to be met (Edwards, Franklin and Holland, 2006) and has been described as the 'glue that holds a community together' (Durlauf and Fafchamps, 2005; Freuchte, 2011).

Social capital is at the heart of the strengths-based approach in the following ways:

- The approach is focused on the quality of the relationship between the supporter and the person being supported. This relationship is aimed at facilitating a change discourse and process.
- The approach recognises the family and the community as a resource that can support a process of change and enable individual and group interests to be met. Indeed Coleman (1990) argues that the relationships between parents and their children and among siblings are a source of social capital which has the potential to enable individuals within the family to realise their interests and potential. He also identifies that extra-familial relationships are a source of social capital and that social support networks can provide families with practical and emotional support to enable positive family functioning. FGCs (discussed in Chapter 4) are very much based upon this assumption.

Resilience

There is a broad consensus that resilience is the ability to respond positively and adapt to adversity. It is commonly referred to as the ability to 'bounce back' (Rose, 2021). It is underpinned by the concept of vulnerability and protective factors, which shape an individual's experience of adversity (Rutter, 1987). Both protective and vulnerability factors include individual characteristics as well as family, environmental and structural factors (Newman, 2005; Walsh, 2015; Dias, and Cadime 2017). Protective factors include strong family relationships, the availability of social support, autonomy, positivity, self-esteem, economic, cultural and social capital. Conversely vulnerability factors include an abusive family environment, social isolation, poverty, inequality, structural racism and oppression.

Saleebey (1996) argues that resilience is one of the key concepts relating to the strengths perspective. The approach can be related to resilience in the following ways:

- Fundamental to the approach is the notion that individuals all have strengths and resilience that can be drawn upon to lead to positive change. Hammond and Zimmerman (2012) argue that the strengths perspective seeks to understand the crucial factors which contribute to individual resilience and 'well-functioning' families/communities (p 7) and support is focused on enabling individuals to draw upon and strengthen these factors (Kam, 2021).
- Rutter (1987) identified that one of the key factors necessary to develop resilience was having a strong social network. The strengths-based approach is focused upon drawing on an individual's social support network and community-based resources to address difficulties and challenges and facilitate change. This is a key feature of FGCs, for example.
- A fundamental principle of the approach is to encourage an individual's sense of autonomy and power over decision-making. Furthermore, autonomy is related to enhanced self-esteem (Marmott, 2003), both of which are recognised as protective factors for developing resilience.

Over the last two decades, the concept of resilience has gained greater prominence within the social work field, and critical perspectives have begun to emerge (Garrett, 2016; van Breda, 2018). Criticism has tended to be centred on the following areas: the emphasis on individuals rather than social structures and wider environmental factors; the discourse of resilience as potentially laden with value judgements and assumptions; and the congruence between the language of resilience and neo-liberalism (Garrett, 2016; van Breda, 2018). For example, focusing on an individual's capacity to 'bounce back' and be resilient ignores social and environmental factors that require an individual to be resilient in the first place: for example, poverty, inequality, structural discrimination and oppression. Walsh (1998, in Seccombe, 2002) states that

> We must be cautious that the concept of resilience is not used in public policy to withhold social supports or maintain inequities, based on the rationale that success or failure is determined by strengths or deficits within individuals and their families. It is not enough to bolster the resilience of at-risk children and families so that they can 'beat the odds'; we must also strive to change the odds against them. (Walsh, 1998 in Seccombe, 2002, p 389)

Furthermore, Mohaupt (2009) argues that the concept of resilience is based upon western values and culture and that concepts that have been created by 'white, middle-class, male academics in the Western World, have their limits in their applicability to other countries – especially developing countries' (Garrett, 2016, p 66).

Finally, it can be argued that resilience can be related to neo-liberalism, because of 'the shared emphasis on an individual responsibility for coping, competence and success' (Bottrell, 2009, p 334) and the failure to acknowledge the role of the welfare state in addressing structural inequalities.

These critical perspectives are also attributable to the criticisms of the strengths-based approach and will be addressed throughout this text.

Social work theory

This section will discuss the strengths-based approach in relation to key theories for social work assessment and intervention:

- empowerment theory
- ecological systems theory
- culturally appropriate social work practice

The approach is neatly aligned to all of the above, and key elements of each theoretical approach demonstrate congruence with a strengths perspective.

Empowerment theory

Empowerment is a central feature of social work practice and is embedded in the language of legislation and policy (Pease, 2002; Braye and Preston-Shoot, 2011). It is also a key underlying principle of the international definition of social work created by the International Federation of Social Work in 2014.

Empowerment theory is focused upon enabling individuals, families and communities to recognise barriers and dynamics that allow oppression to persist, and it promotes actions that create change and allow individuals to take control over their lives (Pulla, 2017). Greene, Yee Lee and Hoffpauir (2005) argue that the goal of empowerment is to increase an individual's social or political power so they can take action to improve their situation.

Much has been written about the relationship between the strengths-based approach and empowerment (see Itzhaky and Bustin, 2002; Rapp and Goscha, 2006; Robbins, Chatterjee and Canda, 2006; Saleebey, 2009; Pulla, 2017). Saleebey (1996) states that empowerment is key to the strengths perspective. He cites Kaplan and Girard (1994), who posit that empowerment means assisting individuals, families and communities to discover and use the tools and resources around them, which is essentially the aim of the strengths-based approach. Pulla (2017) adds to the discussion and argues that the strengths perspective is committed to promoting social and economic justice, which is at the heart of empowerment.

A key principle of the strengths-based approach is that the individual or family, not the professionals tasked with supporting them, is the expert on their situation, issues and difficulties. This clearly relates to the principle of empowerment. Indeed, Tengland (2008) states that for empowerment to be apparent, the professional needs to 'retreat as much as possible from her paternalistic position, and that there is a reduction of the power, control, influence, or decision-making, of the professional and at the same time an increase in power in the individual or group supported' (quoted in Metze, Abma and Kwekkeboom, 2013, p 91). This is congruent with the strengths position that a professional is a facilitator of the process of change, rather than an expert who has all the answers.

Guo and Tsui (2010) state that the strengths-based approach develops the empowerment approach, which is associated with traditional problem-focused models of social work practice. They argue that the empowerment model is still focused on the professional as the expert, with the power to enable people to take back or gain power. However, the strengths-based approach attempts to redress this balance of power and shifts the professional/user relationship on to a more equal footing, with the person with lived experience having the power over decision-making and shaping their own future.

Ecological systems theory

Ecological systems theory is concerned with the interaction between an individual and their social environment. It is based on the principle that an individual can be understood within the context of these interactions. Indeed, the profession of social work was built upon this acknowledgement that individuals and families are shaped by their interactions with their environment (Teater, 2020). The role of the social worker is to understand the 'transaction' between a person and their environment and to promote and enable change in these 'transactions' (Healy, 2014, p 118). Bronfenbrenner's (1979) concentric model based upon the microsystem, mesosystem and macrosystem enables social workers to understand environmental factors and the different types of systems that impact on the lives of people with lived experience (Edwards and Parkinson, 2018).

The microsystem refers to informal systems such as home, family and community; the mesosystem refers to formal systems that have a direct impact on an individual's life, such as schools and social services; the macrosystem refers to society as a whole and the large social institutions of government and business (Healy, 2014, from Edwards and Parkinson, 2018).

Teater (2020) argues that, when individuals feel that the environment is not providing them with the necessary resources at each of these levels, as they are unavailable, inaccessible or non-existent, or they feel that they do not have the strengths and capabilities to access these resources, this leads to a misalignment between an individual and their environment and they may experience stress as a result. This can manifest itself in many of the issues and difficulties that require social work support and intervention. The role of the social worker then is to support an individual to recognise their strengths and capabilities and to support them to access resources within their community which can improve the quality of exchange between the individual and their environment (Gitterman, 2009). This is the very essence of the strengths-based approach.

Systemic social work practice is an example of a strengths-based model which embeds an ecological systems approach. Systemic practice is based upon the belief that most families have the capacity to change and develop. The model focuses on family dynamics and locates psycho-social problems within relationships between family members rather than the individual themselves. It is also concerned with the relationships between the family and other systems, such as school, healthcare and community-based organisations (Laird et al, 2018). This will be explored in detail in Chapter 6.

Culturally appropriate social work practice

It could be argued that the strengths-based approach embodies culturally appropriate social work practice, a concept that has gained ground in recent years. This concept builds upon social work's long tradition of being concerned with the provision of anti-discriminatory practice and anti-oppressive practice, in order to recognise and challenge the structural oppression and discrimination of minority groups (Thompson, 2016: Laird and Tedam, 2019). Gray and Allegritti (2003) suggest that features of what is described in the literature as culturally appropriate practice pertain to what good social work practice should be about anyway, as they include the need to be knowledgeable about the cultural group in question, being self-reflective, being aware of one's own values and potential biases and integrating this knowledge into practice – all key elements of social work practice.

They have identified a number of key features for culturally appropriate practice including the need to listen to the story of the person with lived experience, to learn from them and regard them as experts in their own culture. There is a clear link to the strengths perspective here. In regarding people with lived experience as experts on their own lives and circumstances and being focused on enabling individuals to build upon the strengths and resources available to them in their community, as well as challenging oppressive systems and structural barriers, the strengths-based approach can be applied across a diverse range of cultures (Grothaus, McAuliffe and Craigen, 2012; Pattoni, 2012; Tedam, 2013; Verney et al 2016; Edwards and Parkinson, 2018).

One example of a strengths-based model that can be described as a culturally appropriate approach to practice is that of the narrative approach, in that the focus is on an individual's or family's 'story' and their own experiences. Keddell (2009) argues that as narrative practice approaches focus on deconstructing oppressive discourses, they are ideally placed to understand people's identity expressions and promote individuals' power and control over their own lives. The narrative approach will be explored further in Chapter 7.

FGCs are also argued to be a culturally sensitive approach. Introduced in New Zealand in the late 1980s, they are said to originate in the culture of the Māori people, in response to the disproportionate number of Māori children in care or involved with the child protection system at that time (Edwards and Parkinson,

2018). FGCs are currently used in over 20 countries across the globe and can be applied cross-culturally (Edwards and Parkinson, 2018). This issue will be explored further in Chapter 4.

However, there are many criticisms of the concept of culturally appropriate practice and it is a complex and nuanced concept. There are some who argue that it is based upon a White, eurocentric view of the world and that it ignores the pervasive influence of colonialism on society and societal institutions (Pon, 2009; Carey, 2015). Others argue that a narrow definition of culture tends to conflate culture with ethnicity and race and fails to acknowledge the diversity that exists within groups (Thackrah and Thompson, 2013). Furthermore, Tedam (2013) argues that cultural competence suggests that social workers can understand the culture of those with lived experience by asking questions or reading about different cultures, assuming that the person with lived experience is knowledgeable about their cultural heritage and able to educate the social worker about it. In reality, this may not be the case. Johnson and Munch (2009) state that social workers need to understand and recognise the existence of subcultures within families, groups and communities.

Applying the strengths-based approach can help to overcome some of these shortcomings in that it has a personalised and individualised focus. In allowing individuals and families to define their own meaning around their difficulties and identify their own responses to these challenges, this allows for the diversity within groups to be acknowledged and understood.

Key principles for social work practice

The International Federation of Social Work's (IFSW) (2014) global definition of social work states that

> Social work is a practice-based profession and an academic discipline that promotes social change and development, social cohesion, and the empowerment and liberation of people. Principles of social justice, human rights, collective responsibility and respect for diversities are central to social work. Underpinned by theories of social work, social sciences, humanities and indigenous knowledges, social work engages people and structures to address life challenges and enhance wellbeing. The above definition may be amplified at national and/or regional levels.

This definition is underpinned by internationally adopted ethical standards (IFSW, 2014), which states that social workers should:

- recognise the inherent dignity of humanity;
- promote human rights;
- promote social justice.

The strengths-based approach is clearly aligned to these ethical standards. Primarily, in recognising the person with lived experience as the expert in their own life, this inevitably fosters an environment which respects the dignity of the person being supported. Furthermore, Pulla (2017) argues that a strengths perspective supports engaging actions that pursue social justice and wellbeing and that the approach is committed to promoting social and economic justice. In pursuing social and economic justice, the strengths-based approach is essentially aligned to a human rights approach to practice. Indeed, Mapp et al (2019) argue that rights-based social work is about social workers seeking to build the skills of users of services to enable them to take part in successful personal and political action. The approach is focused on enabling people to change and improve their circumstances to address the difficulties, issues and barriers they face, which is the very essence of a rights-based perspective. As previously stated, it is also a culturally sensitive model of social work practice and one which recognises and respects diversity and indigenous knowledge.

From a UK perspective, the strengths-based approach also fits well with core social work values, such as promoting the rights to participation and self-determination. The British Association of Social Workers' (BASW) Code of Ethics states: 'Social workers should focus on the strengths of all individuals, groups and communities and thus promote their empowerment' (BASW, 2014). This statement is congruent with a key principle that underlines social work legislation, policy and practice in the UK, that of working in partnership with users of social work services. Seminal pieces of legislation in both adult and children's services emphasise the importance of social workers working in partnership with users of services. The Children Act 1989 (amended 2014) places a responsibility on local authorities to work in partnership with parents to promote the wellbeing of children and young people. Furthermore, the Care Act 2014 represents a significant cultural shift towards working alongside users of services, with the emphasis on person-centred planning and users identifying their own needs and priorities. This partnership approach also underpins the application of mental health legislation, with NICE guidance (2011) stating that professionals applying the legislation should: 'Work in partnership with people using mental health services and their families or carers.' (https://www.nice.org.uk/guidance/cg136/chapter/1-guidance).

The strengths-based approach is ideally situated to uphold this principle of partnership, as partnership is at the very core of the approach. Indeed, the approach is widely acknowledged in both adult and children's services to be 'best' social work practice (SCIE, Leeds City Council and Shared Lives Plus, 2018; Parkinson and Edwards, 2018; Department of Health and Social Care, 2019). The Department of Health and Social Care published practice guidance on how to apply the strengths-based approach in adult services in 2019, and over the last decade there has been an increasing move in children's services to adopt strength-based models, such as Signs of Safety, systemic practice and FGCs (Forrester et al, 2013; Munro, 2011; Edwards and Parkinson, 2018).

Related to the principle of partnership is the development of family-led models of decision-making, which fall under the umbrella of the strengths-based approach. Family-led decision-making models do what they say on the tin. The voice of the family is privileged over that of the supporting professionals involved. FGCs were the original version of these models and are used in a number of countries across the globe (Edwards and Parkinson, 2018). As their use has spread, so the model has been changed and adapted to meet the needs of different countries, regions and jurisdictions, to respond to differing policy and practice landscapes. Some of the processes are very similar to the original New Zealand model, while others are very different and are hybrids of the original, having been adapted to reflect the context of a particular country or region (Browne Olson, 2009). Often the name of FGCs has been changed. Alternative names for FGCs or hybrid approaches include Family Group Meetings, Family Unity Meetings, Family Care Meetings, Care Circles, Family Welfare Conferences and Family Group Decision-Making (Barnsdale and Walker, 2007; Crampton, 2007; Harris, 2008). There has been some criticism of the adaptation of the FGC, and it has been referred to by some as 'model drift' (Pennell, 2003). Others suggest that adaptation is necessary to ensure that FGCs meet the needs of their population (Browne Olson, 2009). A detailed exploration of the FGC approach is provided in Chapter 4.

Conclusion

This chapter has introduced the reader to the main theoretical perspectives which underpin the strengths-based approach. For a more in-depth exploration of each of the theoretical perspectives discussed, please see the list of further reading below. The chapter has focused on the strengths-based approach in the broadest sense and as an umbrella term, which encompasses a range of methods for supporting users of social work services. Subsequent chapters will focus on each of these individual methods and will provide a detailed exploration of the applicable theoretical foundations.

Key learning points

Key sociological theory can support an understanding of the strengths-based approach.

Strengths-based approaches are congruent with core social work theories.

Strengths-based approaches are aligned to the values of social work and are congruent with the IFSW definition of social work.

Strengths-based approaches underpin contemporary social work legislation and policy.

Strengths-based approaches can be applied cross-culturally and can be described as a culturally appropriate way of working.

Further reading

Adams, R. (2008) (4th edn) *Empowerment, Participation and Social Work*, London: Red Globe Press.

Burr, V. (2015) (3rd edn) *Social Constructionism*, Abingdon: Routledge.

Field, J. (2016) (3rd edn) *Social Capital*, Abingdon: Routledge.

Garrett, P.M. (2007) 'The relevance of Bourdieu for social work: a reflection on obstacles and omissions', *Journal of Social Work*, 7(3): 355–379, doi:10.1177/1468017307084076.

Guo, W. and Tsui, M. (2010) 'From resilience to resistance: a reconstruction of the strengths perspective in social work practice', *International Social Work*, 53(2): 233–245, doi:10.1177/0020872809355391.

Harper-Dorton, K.V. and Lantz, J. (2007) (2nd edn) *Cross-Cultural Practice: Social Work with Diverse Populations*, Chicago: Lyceum Books.

Teater, B. (2020) 'Social work practice from an ecological perspective', in C.W. LeCroy (ed) *Case Studies in Social Work Practice* (3rd edn), Hoboken, NJ: Wiley.

van Breda, Adrian D. (2018) 'A critical review of resilience theory and its relevance for social work', *Social Work*, 54(1): 1–18. https://dx.doi.org/10.15270/54-1-611.

3

Solution-focused practice

Guy Shennan

Introduction – a usable approach?

It was reading a book chapter about solution-focused practice that got me started on my solution-focused journey. I was a social worker in a social services department in the English Midlands, and on the lookout for ideas that would support me in helping families make changes in their lives. I came across *A Brief Guide to Brief Therapy* (Cade and O'Hanlon, 1993), a title that attracted me, as I had seen the value of 'brief therapy' (Fisch, Weakland and Segal, 1982) when used by social workers doing family therapy at the young people's psychiatric unit where I worked prior to my social work training.

The chapter, 'Exceptions, solutions and the future focus', described a development of this, solution-focused brief therapy, and part of its appeal was the simplicity of the ideas it contained, and a sense that I could actually use them in my social work practice. I learned that an *exception* was what happened when a problem might have been expected to happen but didn't, and that solution-focused practitioners assumed that, whatever the problem, there would always be exceptions to it. Moreover, asking about exceptions might be more useful than focusing on the problem.

As all the people I was working with had problems, I reckoned I could try this out straight away. The day after reading the chapter, I was visiting a family where a parent complained that her two teenage sons were constantly fighting. Or perhaps it just seemed like it was constant. Seeing an opportunity, I asked them: 'Can you think of a recent time when you might have fallen out, but didn't? When you managed to get on OK?' And – with a little help from their mum – they could. I wonder if my solution-focused career would have come to an abrupt end if they had answered 'No'. I was to learn later that it is usually better to ask an open question that assumes there are exceptions – 'Tell me about a time when this problem didn't happen' – rather than a closed one that invites the possibility of a negative response.

In this case, the boys told me about a recent incident when the younger one had borrowed something from his older brother without asking, and yet the older boy had somehow not lost his temper and had allowed his brother to play with it a little longer. I was unsure how to follow up this exception (I wished I had the chapter with me, to swiftly consult), but muddled through a conversation with them about it, which did indeed seem more productive than our usual problem-focused ones.

This experience encouraged me to continue my solution-focused explorations and to learn how to facilitate talk about exceptions and the other aspects of solution-focused conversations you will come across in what follows. The experience was triggered by reading just one chapter, which reflects the solution-focused principle that a small change might be all that is necessary (de Shazer et al, 1986, p 209). I hope that your reading of this chapter will have a useful impact for you in turn.

A good fit?

I have previously noted the claim that there is a good fit between solution-focused practice and social work (Wheeler, 2003; Greene and Lee, 2011), though I also introduced a caveat to this (Shennan, 2019b, p 224). Let me explain this here in the form of a warning about this chapter. Take heed! There is not and never has been a consensus about what social work is or should be, going right back to its beginnings in the late 19th century. Before he was prime minister of the UK, Clement Attlee was a social worker and social work lecturer, and, writing about different visions of social work, he contrasted 'the tone of suspicion' running through the work of the influential Charity Organisation Society with his belief in the need for social workers to place trust in the people they serve (Attlee, 1920, p 65). The present chapter takes the perhaps quaint view that social work is about helping people (Jordan, 1979). Social workers are seen as change agents rather than gatekeepers to services (Perry, 2021) and the people they work with as having resources that will help them make desired changes in their lives.

A little history, including some more usable ideas

It is perhaps unsurprising that there is seen to be a fit between solution-focused practice and social work, given that a significant number of the team who developed the approach from the early 1980s onwards, at the Brief Family Therapy Center (BFTC) in Milwaukee in the USA, trained originally as social workers. They were influenced by the brief therapy referred to above, which originated at the Mental Research Institute in Palo Alto, California (Weakland et al, 1974). This saw problems as arising from attempted solutions to ordinary life difficulties, which made them worse, and the therapist's job was to elicit detail about what was not working, in order to intervene to help the individual or family do something different. The BFTC shifted gradually from a problem focus to a solution focus, with some practice developments being particularly significant, involving end-of-session interventions, exceptions, pre-session change and the miracle question, each of which can influence contemporary social work. I shall introduce these in turn.

Formula first session task

The practitioners at BFTC often saw clients as a team, with one member conducting the session with the person or family and their colleagues observing through a one-way screen. The team would develop an intervention for the family, one example being to ask them to list, between sessions, all the things they wished to change. One day a team member suggested they ask a family to list all the things they did *not* wish to change instead. When the family returned for their next session, as well as reporting what they did not want to change, they reported positive changes (Lipchik et al, 2012). Intrigued, the team asked other clients to do the same thing, with frequently similar results. They codified this into the *formula first session task*, so called because they would routinely give this at the end of a first meeting, whatever problems had been presented: 'Between now and next time we meet, we would like you to observe, so that you can describe to us next time, what happens in your (family, life, marriage, relationship) that you want to continue to have happen' (de Shazer, 1985, p 137).

This wording contains what were to become the two main areas of solution-focused inquiry: what is wanted and what is working in relation to this. So this both laid the foundation of the solution-focused approach and is something that is doable and can be worth doing in many situations social workers find themselves in today. Information gleaned from asking people to list or observe instances of what they want actually happening can both inform assessments and also, as the BFTC team discovered, lead to positive changes.

Exceptions and pre-session change

The shift in focus resulting from this new end-of-session intervention influenced the content of the sessions themselves and the questions the workers asked during them. As the work still began by ascertaining the problems that led people to seek help, one way to focus on what was happening that people wanted to continue to happen was to ask about exceptions to these problems (de Shazer, 1985), which we introduced above. A further development, which led to positive change being asked about even earlier, was the discovery of *pre-session change*.

A 12-year-old boy having problems at school was attending a first meeting with his mother, who mentioned casually, as the worker was about to consult with the team, that for the last three days he 'had been trying in school'. The worker delayed the break and instead asked the boy how he had done this. He said he was 'tired of always getting into trouble', and the worker spent the rest of the session helping the boy work out what he had done and how he might continue to make improvements. The goals of the work were accomplished in three sessions (Weiner-Davis, de Shazer and Gingerich, 1987, p 359).

The team began to routinely ask people in first sessions if they had noticed any positive changes since the appointment had been made, and more often than not they had. This impacted on the team's thinking and practice in two main ways. First, as these changes had happened before their involvement, they had to revise their ideas about their role. From seeing themselves as the initiators of change, they began to see their role as supporting change already under way. Correspondingly, they began to view their clients as playing a more active role in the change progress. Second, they began to elicit what they called 'change talk', as opposed to 'problem talk', increasingly early in the work, by bringing forward questions about positive change from subsequent meetings into the first meeting, often in its beginning stages (Gingerich, de Shazer and Weiner-Davis, 1988).

As an excellent overview of these developments at the BFTC puts it, 'the simplest way to ... promote change became building on when things were already better, that is, finding out how clients made exceptions and pre-session change happen' (Korman et al, 2020, p 56). *How did you do that?* is the most classic solution-focused question of all, and following up with *What differences has that made?* is likely to elicit further positive changes that can be amplified and supported. Once again, these are simple and usable ideas, especially if social workers are vigilant in noticing positive changes and ready to ask such questions when opportunities arise.

The future focus and the miracle question

What of 'the future focus' in Cade and O'Hanlon's chapter title? Brief therapy had always paid attention to goals, on the basis that if it was not established how it would be known that the problem had been solved, the work 'could reasonably go on forever' (de Shazer, 1988, p 93). Another famous solution-focused question, or series of questions, was developed to this end. It owes its origins to one of the main developers of solution-focused practice paying close attention to the words of one of her clients.

Insoo Kim Berg was working with someone who was struggling to answer a question about change happening, saying 'It would take a miracle'. In an inspired moment, Berg began her next question, 'Well, suppose a miracle happened ...', and her client became able to answer (Shennan, 2019a, p 52). Once again, the team noticed the potential of what might have been a one-off event, developed *the miracle question* along the following lines, and started using it in most first meetings:

> Just suppose, that when you go to bed tonight and go to sleep, a miracle happens, and the problems that brought you here today have gone, just like that. But you're asleep, so you don't know that the miracle has happened. So, when you wake up in the morning, what will you notice, that will tell you that this miracle has happened?

With the addition of a series of follow-up questions, to elicit more detail – *What else will you notice?, Who else might notice, and what would they notice?, How might they respond? What difference would that make?*, to name just a few – it became apparent that this could do more than set goals. Describing hypothetical days where the problems that led people to seek help had been resolved appeared to impart a sense of hope and possibility, leading people to feel more able to make desired changes. The miracle question, or a simplified means of helping people describe 'preferred futures' that was developed later and which I shall introduce shortly, is an integral part of the solution-focused process. It can also be used as a stand-alone activity. Such uses by social workers include community engagement and planning (Hollingsworth et al, 2009), as a group supervision tool in child protection (Blundo, 2014) and promoting open communication between themselves and their clients (Toros, 2019).

Two ways

There are two ways one can approach using solution-focused practice (Shennan, 2019a, 7). One is to use it as a whole, in a planned fashion, on a session-by-session basis. The other way is to use aspects of the approach, often in a more informal or unplanned way, as and when opportunities arise. Whereas, for example, a therapist will use it in the first of these two ways, and a detached youth worker, working with young people in their natural community settings, the second, social workers are likely to be able to use it in both, at different times.

Even if you are in a role where it is unlikely that you will follow the whole process, it is useful to have a clear understanding of it, as this will enable you to use parts of the approach in an informed way. Slightly different versions have developed since the pioneering work in Milwaukee. The one I shall summarise here is the one predominantly followed today in the UK, and forms the basis of the accreditation criteria of the UK Association for Solution Focused Practice (UKASFP, 2021).

The BRIEF version

The Milwaukee team wrote about the developments they were making, in a series of books by Steve de Shazer (1985, 1988, 1991, 1994) and in numerous articles, mainly in family therapy journals, and a group of social workers and family therapists working in an NHS service in London (George, Iveson and Ratner, 1990) were among those who became interested. Having learned to use the approach, they began to teach it, as the Brief Therapy Practice, later shortening this to BRIEF.

The shortening was significant, as was the discarding of the word 'therapy' from their name. It was clear that the usefulness of the approach was not confined to therapy and therapists. This was supported by accounts of its various applications by Insoo Kim Berg and her co-writers, in substance misuse (Berg and Miller, 1992; Berg and Reuss, 1997) and children's services (Berg, 1994; Berg and Kelly, 2000; Berg and Steiner, 2003). BRIEF also helped to make the approach relevant and accessible to a wide range of professionals, including social workers.

Taking a developmental role alongside their clinical application and teaching of the approach, BRIEF applied the philosophical principle of Ockham's razor, which was a strong influence on de Shazer's work. This holds that 'what can be done with fewer means is done in vain with many' (de Shazer, 1985, p 58), or 'less is more' in more modern parlance. The resulting 'BRIEF version' (Shennan, 2019a) is a three-part process, the simplicity of which makes it teachable and learnable in a short space of time, as well as being adaptable and hence usable across different helping contexts. The simplicity can be deceptive, as simple is not the same as easy to use. It is, however, a great advantage of the approach that, once they have assimilated the basics, workers are able to put it into practice, which is when learning starts in earnest.

The three parts are: establishing a positive direction for the work; eliciting descriptions of 'preferred futures', when people are moving in the directions they hope for; and eliciting accounts of progress being made towards these futures.

Setting a direction

At the beginning of a piece of helping work, it seems reasonable to assume there is a problem that someone wants help with. This is in fact the assumption that guides the beginning of such work most of the time, with the helper asking about the problem at the outset. However, it also seems reasonable to assume, at the beginning of a piece of work, that someone is hoping something will result from this. This more future-oriented assumption, which looks to what might happen *after* the work to be done, is what guides the initial questions of the solution-focused practitioner. Some ways of wording these can be seen in this illustrative sequence.

Worker: What are your best hopes from our work together?
Client: I just need some help right now.
Worker: So if this was helpful, how would you know? What would be different?
Client: I wouldn't be feeling so low.
Worker: How would you like to be feeling instead?
Client: More motivated, more able to get on with things.

This looks straightforward on paper, though a lot is happening here that we might usefully unpack. The authors of the original strengths perspective paper wrote that 'the question is not what kind of life one has had, but what kind of life one wants' (Weick et al, 1989, p 353), and these questions clearly fit with this. There is, however, a slight but important difference, in that the hopes being asked about in the sequence above are those *from the work to be done*. Solution-focused practice is based on hope, though not generalised life hopes or ambitions. More circumscribed, it is the hope that attaches to a particular helping encounter.

Second, the worker is inquiring about the person's hoped-for *outcome* from the work, rather than what they hope will happen *during* the work. This distinction between means – 'I just need some help right now' – and ends – 'So if this was helpful, how would you know?' – is a crucial one. Third, it is useful to be heading towards a positively framed outcome, rather than away from a problem – feeling low, for example. After the sequence above, the solution-focused practitioner will invite a description of the client's hopes being realised, an invitation that will be more enticing by being focused on a greater ability to get on with things rather than on not feeling so low.

The means and ends distinction is helpful to bear in mind when a service is suggested or requested and is liable to be seen as an end in itself. Take as an example that difficult situation facing social workers in children's services, when parents request that a child is taken into care. A flat refusal can hinder the development of a collaborative relationship with the parents and lead to a raising of the stakes. A solution-focused approach offers an alternative response.

Social worker:	What are your best hopes from contacting us?
Parents:	We would like you to take Alex into care, we've had enough.
SW:	I'm sorry to hear that, things must have become really tough. If we were to do that, what difference are you hoping it would make?
Parents:	Perhaps someone could talk some sense into him; he won't listen to us any more.
SW:	How would you know that had happened?
Parents:	Where do we start? He wouldn't wreck his bedroom … (*List other things that Alex would no longer be doing*).
SW:	What difference would that make?
Parents:	We just want a normal family life, which we haven't had in a long time.

The social worker is assuming the parents have a good reason for asking for their child to be placed into care, and that further hopes must lie beyond the hope expressed for this particular service. Placing the child into care is viewed as a means rather than an end, and now that the desired end of a 'normal family life' has been articulated, a door has been opened for conversations with the family that have the potential to avert the need for care. Let us follow this scenario to help illustrate the next part of the solution-focused process.

Describing preferred futures

The miracle question is one means of inviting people into hoped-for futures, though in the BRIEF version this has been simplified and more closely aligned with the person's hopes from the work. The miracle in the question above was that 'the problems that brought you here today have gone'. Beginning by asking about hopes rather than problems means that the description can be about their realisation rather than the results of the problem disappearing. And does there need to be a miracle? Let's assume that Alex's parents have agreed to family meetings with the social worker, to help work towards the normal family life they are hoping for. After engaging with each family member, the social worker might then ask:

> Suppose, when you wake up tomorrow morning, you find that your family is getting on in ways that are OK for each of you, and you have the normal sort of family life you're hoping for. What's the first thing you'd notice, that would begin to tell you this?

In a conversation with a family group, the social worker can either ask each person a series of questions in turn, to elicit individual descriptions of desired life within the family, or assist the family to create a picture together of the sort of family life they want. The more details people are enabled to include in their descriptions, the greater the chance they will notice that some of this is already happening, or that it begins to.

Describing progress and what's working

As we saw, the shift from a problem focus to a solution focus was made by switching people's attention from what they wanted to change to what they wanted to continue, and from problems to exceptions, and by realising that people were already making changes before professional help began. This focus on what is working continues to be a major part of solution-focused practice, though the increased emphasis on hopes and preferred futures has led to alternative ways of approaching it.

Instances

The developing use of the miracle question led to a shift from thinking about 'exceptions to the problem' to 'times when the miracle is already happening' (Malinen, 2002). One advantage of the term 'exceptions' is that it encapsulated an idea in one word, which helped in its promulgation. 'Instances', as in 'instances of the preferred future', has been put forward as its equivalent (Shennan, 2020). As with exceptions, we can bring instances into conversations simply by asking about them. Imagine that the family have managed to describe between them some details of their hoped-for normal family life. The social worker might then ask, 'What bits of this have you noticed happening, most recently?' Notice that this is an open question, which assumes that someone will have noticed something.

Description and agency

Follow-up questions about instances, or exceptions, can be placed into two general groups: those inviting description, and questions about agency. On hearing, for example, that two family members get on well together at times, description questions aim to elicit concrete detail about this.

> When was the most recent time you got on well?
> What was happening?
> What did you do?
> What did you notice about yourself?
> What did you notice about your brother/sister/mother/father?
> Who else noticed and what did they notice?
> What difference did that make/is that making?

The idea of agency relates to the observation above that clients play an active role in change, and are not just waiting for expert workers to initiate it. Assuming that people are agents in the positive changes they describe suggests questions such as:

> How did you do that?
> What else did you do that helped?
> What did that take?
> What does it say about you, that you did that?

All questions contain assumptions, and it is worth reflecting on what we are conveying by the questions we ask. These examples make the useful assumption of agency on the part of the family members, that it was actions or qualities of theirs that led to the desired behaviours taking place. The belief here is that, if they can make this happen, then they can make other changes in their lives, especially if they become more aware of their helpful actions and abilities, through talking about them.

Scaling questions

A reliable means of eliciting instances is to use scaling questions. With Alex's family, once the direction had been set towards their hoped-for normal family life, and its future occurrence had been described in detail, the worker could ask:

> On a scale from 0 to 10, where 10 is you have the normal family life you are hoping for, as you have just described it, and 0 is the furthest from that it has been, where are you now?

With a family, each person should be asked for their number, after their 10 has been adjusted to include any of their specific individual hopes. Each answer above 0 can be followed up with a mixture of description questions – *What tells you it is at that point and not 0? What is different?* – and agency questions: *How have you managed to get to that point?* with follow-up questions to elicit detail.

Asking about a point further up the scale returns to the preferred future, though via small signs of progress: *What would you notice if you were a point higher?* An alternative might be to ask: *What could you do to move a point up the scale?* However, it would seem reasonable for the person to reply that if they knew that, they would already be doing it, followed by: *You tell me!* It is usually better to ask for signs that would be noticed rather than steps to be taken.

In a first solution-focused meeting, a scale usually punctuates a shift from the future to progress being made towards it. Subsequent meetings also contain descriptions of preferred futures, instances and progress, with one major difference. The order is changed around. The worker begins with progress – *What has been better since the last meeting?* – before later punctuating a shift, this time from progress to future, again using the scale.

Listening with a constructive ear

As well as asking about instances and progress, we can also listen for them. The more details of a preferred future elicited, the more chance that comments like this will be heard:

Parent: He wouldn't spend so long in the shower, and he'd put his dirty laundry in the basket. I'm not saying he never does, but it's rare.

Rare or not, only one instance is needed to develop a conversation about it. In another example, a young woman describes her future self being more assertive with her husband, asking him not to call her in the early hours, as 'When I was depressed I couldn't sleep, and it's only recently I've started to sleep well, and I want to continue sleeping well' (Shennan, 2019a, p 80).

This has been called listening with a constructive ear (Lipchik, 1988). When someone is talking about a problem, this helps us to hear exceptions: 'I've had a terrible week, I've hardly been out at all.' The word 'hardly' suggests the person has been out at least once. 'It's been tough, especially at the weekends.' The constructive ear, also listening for differences, hears that something was, if not better, then not quite as tough during the weekdays. It also involves listening for coping actions and abilities and for people's hopes and desires. What we hear with our constructive ears we can then ask about.

A similar type of listening is advocated in another strengths-based approach, narrative practice, which talks about 'double listening' (Meyer, 2015). When you are hearing a problem story, if you listen for it you can also hear a story of a person surviving or overcoming that problem. 'Both-and' thinking (Shennan, 2019a) is useful: people have problems *and* they get through them. This leads us to respond to people's problem talk in at least two ways. It is important to show we have heard someone's difficulties, and we can follow an acknowledgement with what are known as coping questions: *That sounds tough … how have you been keeping going?*

Further practice examples and tips

For more extended examples of solution-focused social work with families, to add to the brief ones interspersed above, I recommend picking up a copy of a collection of blog posts by practitioners in the Essex Divisional Based Intervention Team. Details of how to do this are in my suggested further reading below, which also includes the excellent NSPCC toolkit. This contains lots of useful ideas for adapting the approach for children and is freely available online. Solution-focused practice is adaptable for use in adult as well as children's social care, so let me share now an example of how it was used in an adult social care team.

Mrs Anderson,[1] in her 50s and with mobility issues, was on the brink of eviction because of the impact her hoarding behaviours were having on her property. She had been assessed as being eligible for a bathroom refit with a walk-in shower, but her bathroom was not accessible so the work could not be done. The workers involved with Mrs Anderson felt frustrated by her inaction, when it had been made clear to her that if she did not clean up her flat, she would be evicted. The social worker decided to try a solution-focused approach, to see if it might lead to a different type of conversation.

Mrs Anderson's best hopes from working with the social worker were to be able to wash independently. On a 0–10 scale, where 10 was that she was able to wash independently and 0 'at rock bottom', Mrs Anderson put herself at a 1. Such a low number surprised the social worker, as it had seemed that Mrs Anderson had not appreciated the extent of the problem, and it had a useful impact in that the social worker sensed they were then working more collaboratively, from a place of mutual concern. She asked about what moving up the scale would look like, and a vivid picture gradually emerged, which included Mrs Anderson being able to have a shower and put on her make-up in a nice bathroom. With the help of questions about what others would notice, Mrs Anderson went on to identify that moving up the scale would involve working with the housing officer.

She did go on to engage with the housing officer, and cleared up some of the debris, making possible the new bathroom with walk-in shower. The shift from the focus on the problem of hoarding to a focus on Mrs Anderson's hopes did lead to a different conversation, a crucial part of which appeared to be Mrs Anderson being able to voice and thereby to experience her specific desire for a shower and to be able to put on her make-up in a nice bathroom.

Does it work?

It would seem reasonable for Mrs Anderson's social worker to say that the solution-focused approach worked with her, given the progress that followed using it, when the situation had felt stuck previously. Solution-focused practitioners have many such experiences, which tell them that the approach 'works', or at least is *useful*. As Berg and Steiner (2003, p 230) suggest, the problems of living that social workers deal with are usually too complex to be able to divide outcomes neatly into 'success' or 'failure', with approaches 'working' or 'not working'. However, it is important to establish that an approach is useful, and by objective means that add to practice wisdom.

Fortunately, there is a growing body of research that supports the usefulness of the solution-focused approach. The European Brief Therapy Association (EBTA) maintains a comprehensive list of publications that report on research. Their latest update (EBTA, 2022) refers to 325 outcome studies, including 143 randomised controlled trials showing benefit from solution-focused approaches and 100 comparison studies, of which 71 favour solution-focused therapy.

EBTA also list a number of meta-analyses and systematic reviews. Of particular note are two reviews carried out by American social work academics. Reviewing 43 controlled studies, where the outcomes were indicated by observed changes in the client, Gingerich and Peterson (2013) concluded that the solution-focused approach: 'is an effective treatment for a wide variety of behavioral and psychological outcomes and ... appears to be briefer and less costly than alternative approaches'. Since then, Kim et al (2019) have found a growth of experimental design studies with diverse populations, showing favourable results.

Solution-focused practice began in the USA, and my focus in this chapter has been mainly on the UK, which might give rise to the question of its applicability elsewhere. Mark Beyebach and his colleagues (2021) examined solution-focused outcome research to determine whether it is predominantly carried out in Western, Educated, Industrialised, Rich and Democratic (WEIRD) countries, and found that the number of such publications generated in non-WEIRD countries is now higher. This suggests that solution-focused approaches are not a WEIRD practice but a global one.

Conclusion

I found that reading a book chapter was enough to get me started on my solution-focused journey, though something more was needed to keep me going. It is a skills-based approach, and we learn skills by doing and by practice. I hope that this chapter contains sufficient information about what solution-focused practitioners do to enable you – if you wish to – to try some of this out for yourself. You might find another aspect of the research useful in this respect. While solution-focused practice is frequently useful, this is not always the case – nothing could work for everyone all the time – but where it is ineffective, it does not seem to do any harm (Macdonald, 2011, p 35).

You will recall that there are two ways of using solution-focused practice. As well as using it as a whole, in a planned way, you can draw on individual elements when opportunities arise, especially if you are listening 'with a constructive ear' to catch such moments. Just one question can make a difference, such as 'How did you do that?' to a person who resisted the temptation to have another drink, or 'What's the first sign you would notice that would let you know you were feeling a little better' to a person who is feeling low.

As you have read this chapter, in this particular book, I assume you would like to be working in a solution-focused and strengths-based way, so let me finish with two questions for you. How are you already doing so? And, if your practice was to continue to develop in a solution-focused and strengths-based direction, what difference would this make to your work?

Key learning points

1. Solution-focused practice was developed by a group of social workers and therapists in Milwaukee, USA, from the early 1980s onwards.

2. A number of practice developments led to this new therapeutic approach, including:

   - inviting people to notice what was happening that they wanted to continue happening;
   - focusing on exceptions to problems and on pre-session change;
   - the miracle question.

3. A simplified and adaptable version has been developed by BRIEF in London from the 1990s onwards, in which the solution-focused practitioner:

   - establishes the person's hopes from the work, which create a direction for the work;
   - elicits descriptions of the realisation of those hopes – the person's 'preferred future';
   - elicits accounts of 'instances' of this preferred future, and progress towards it.

4. Social workers can make use of the solution-focused approach by following this whole framework, or by using parts of it at different times.

5. Research and practice experience indicate that the solution-focused approach is frequently useful, and it is now used in most parts of the world.

Note

[1] This isn't the person's real name, and other details have been changed to ensure confidentiality.

Further reading

D-BIT (2019) *The Reflections of Solution Focused Practitioners in an Edge of Care Service*, Chelmsford: Essex County Council, Available from: essex-self.achieveservice. com/service/The_Reflections_of_Solution_Focused_Practitioners_in_an_ Edge_of_Care_Service

Journal of Solution Focused Practices – all issues of this journal are now freely available online, at https://digitalscholarship.unlv.edu/journalsfp/

Milner, Judith and Myers, Steve (2017) *Using Solution Focused Practice with Adults in Health and Social Care*, London: Jessica Kingsley.

NSPCC (2015) *Solution-Focused Practice: An NSPCC Toolkit for Working with Children and Young People*, London: NSPCC. https://www.nspcc.org.uk/servi ces-and-resources/research-and-resources/2015/solution-focused-practice- toolkit/

Shennan, Guy (2019) (2nd edn) *Solution-Focused Practice: Effective Communication to Facilitate Change*, London: Bloomsbury.

4

Family Group Conferences

Kate Parkinson, Deanna Edwards and Will Golden

Family Group Conferences (FGCs) are a well-established strengths-based approach to social work decision-making across the globe. This chapter provides an overview of the origins of the FGC model and its underpinning theoretical framework. It draws together and presents research findings from the current application of FGCs in social work practice, in the UK and around the world. The chapter concludes with a case study of a FGC in practice, provided by an experienced FGC co-ordinator. Further reading for those who are interested in developing their knowledge on FGCs is provided at the end of the chapter.

What are FGCs?

FGCs originated in New Zealand in the late 1980s in response to the disproportionate number of Māori children and young people who were looked after by the state or involved with the child protection system at that time (Edwards and Parkinson, 2018). They are said to originate in the culture of the Māori people (Ashley et al, 2006), although there is some disagreement about this, which will be discussed later in the chapter.

FGCs are enshrined in legislation in New Zealand, in their equivalent to the Children Act 1989, the Children, Young People and their Families Act, (1989). This has ensured that FGCs are a statutory part of the child protection process and FGCs are the established decision-making process where there are concerns about the welfare of a child or young person (Edwards and Parkinson, 2018).

Since their implementation in New Zealand, FGCs have spread and are now used in 21 countries worldwide (Edwards and Parkinson, 2018). They were introduced into the UK in the early 1990s by the Family Rights Group, the leading organisation promoting the use of FGCs in the UK (https://frg.org.uk/). Approximately 76 per cent of local authorities in England and Wales now have an FGC service (Family Rights Group, 2015).

Although FGCs originated in the child protection field, they are now applied in a broad range of areas, including education, youth justice and more recently in adult social care contexts (Edwards and Parkinson, 2018; Manthorpe and Rappaport, 2020).

At an FGC it is the family who lead the decision-making process, not the professionals involved with the family. The family are asked to develop a plan for the care or protection of a child/young person or vulnerable adult in the family, drawing on the family's own strengths and resources. The family are given a clear framework in which to develop their plan and it is made clear to them:

1. what issues and concerns the plan should address;
2. what services and support are available to meet the family plan;
3. what the local authority's 'bottom line' is: that is, what won't be agreed to. In a child protection context, this is often focused on who the child is not safe to live with or have contact with.

The family are allocated an independent co-ordinator, whose role is to prepare the family for the FGC and support them through the process (Family Rights Group, n.d. available at https://frg.org.uk/family-group-conferences/what-is-a-family-group-conference/). Although in many cases the independent co-ordinator is employed by the local authority, which raises questions about how independent they are, they are independent from decision-making processes relating to the individual family (Edwards and Parkinson, 2018).

There are a number of stages to the FGC process:

1. The preparation stage

At this stage the independent co-ordinator works with the child/ren and their parents/carers of the adult who is the focus of the FGC, to determine who, in their family, friendship group, support network and community, they wish to attend their FGC. It is for the family to decide who they wish to attend. The referring professional (in most cases a social worker) is expected to attend, but the attendance of other professionals is at the discretion of the family, as it is their meeting. Once this has been decided, the role of the independent co-ordinator is to prepare all of those invited and ensure that they understand their role at the meeting and expectations of them. This includes any professionals who are invited. A key part of the preparation stage is to identify a venue for the FGC, as FGCs are held on 'neutral ground': that is to say, not in a family home or in a social care building. This is to redress the balance of power between the professionals involved and family members (Edwards and Parkinson, 2018). Generally, FGCs take place in community-based venues, such as community centres or faith-based buildings. Other practical arrangements are considered during this stage, such as transport arrangements to enable people to attend the FGC and whether an interpreter is needed for the FGC if a family's first language is not English. FGC standards for practice are clear that a FGC should take place in a family's first language, hence the interpreter will be for professionals, independent co-ordinators and family friends who cannot speak the first language.

On average, a FGC lasts between two and six hours (Edwards and Parkinson, 2018), so refreshments are a key feature in providing a comfortable and welcoming environment for a family to develop their plan. In many cultures 'breaking bread' together is a way of demonstrating friendship and respect, and the fact of professionals sharing food with family members at a FGC is a powerful message and potentially starts to redress some of the power dynamics inevitably present when families have social care involvement.

The independent co-ordinator will work with the family to identify a date for the FGC that meets the needs of the family, and which fits in with any statutory timescales.

As the FGC is a family-led decision-making model, it is of crucial importance that children/young people and adults who are the focus of the FGC as well as other family members are enabled to have their say at the FGC. Children and young people are at the heart of the FGC process, and if the FGC is focused on their needs or protection, they have a right to express their wishes and feelings. Hence advocacy is a key element of the FGC process. An advocate can support a child/young person to have their say at the FGC, or if the child/young person does not want to attend or it is deemed to be inappropriate for them to attend, then an advocate can represent them at the meeting. Some FGC services have a professional advocacy service, but many do not. In these cases, children and young people are asked to identify someone outside of the family but who is in their support network to be their advocate at the FGC (Fox, 2015). It is important to note that the default position for FGCs is that children/young people should attend their FGC and contribute to it, unless they choose not to or it is deemed that attending could reinforce the abuse/trauma that they have experienced (Edwards and Parkinson, 2018).

Advocacy can also be provided for adults who may need support in expressing their views at a FGC (Gorska et al, 2016; Parkinson, Pollock and Edwards, 2018).

2. The information-giving stage

The FGC co-ordinator will informally chair the meeting and start with a welcome and introductions. The co-ordinator will also remind everyone in attendance of the purpose of the meeting. Once this is established, the co-ordinator will invite the referrer to present their report to the family. This will have already been shared with the family, so there should be no surprises. The family can then ask questions to ensure that they have sufficient information to enable them to develop a plan. If there are other professionals present, they are also asked to present their information to the family.

3. Private family time

This is unlimited time in which the family are together to develop their plan which they agree and record. No service providers should be in the room during this time unless they are invited back in by the family. This ensures that the plan made at the FGC is a family one and not influenced by professionals. Private family time is fundamental to the FGC process. It is what makes it distinct and ensures that the decisions made and led by the family (Ashley, 2006).

4. Agreeing a family plan

This is the final stage of the FGC process, in which the family plan is discussed and agreed if it meets the following conditions:
- It fully addresses the issues and concerns identified.
- It is safe.
- It is legal.

If a family are not able to agree a safe plan, the referrer will be clear about what the next steps are. There will also be circumstances where referrers cannot agree a plan, such as when a family are in court proceedings. In these cases, the court has the responsibility of agreeing a plan, and this should be made clear at the FGC.

5. Reviewing the plan

An important part of the FGC process is the reviewing of a family plan. A family is usually offered at least one review FGC, to review the progress of the family plan, about four to six weeks after the initial FGC. With the family's agreement, further reviews can be held to ensure that family members and professionals are satisfied with the progress of the plan (Edwards and Parkinson, 2018).

FGCs as a strengths-based approach

Much has been written about FGCs as a strengths-based approach to practice (see Ashley and Nixon, 2007; Barnsdale and Walker, 2007; Metze et al, 2013). If one refers to Rapp, Saleebey and Sullivan's (2008) six principles of strengths-based practice (below) it is clear that FGCs are the embodiment of a strengths-based approach to practice (Parkinson, 2018):

1. Goal orientation. Strengths-based practice is goal-oriented. The central and most crucial element of any approach is the extent to which people themselves set goals they would like to achieve in their lives.
2. Strengths assessment. The primary focus is not on problems or deficits, and the individual is supported to recognise the inherent resources they have at their disposal which they can use to counteract any difficulty or condition.
3. Resources from the environment. Strengths proponents believe that in every environment there are individuals, associations, groups and institutions, all of whom have something to give, that others may find useful, and that it may be the practitioner's role to enable links to these resources.

4. Explicit methods are used for identifying client and environmental strengths for goal attainment. These methods will be different for each of the strengths-based approaches. For example, in solution-focused therapy clients will be assisted to set goals before the identification of strengths, while in strengths-based case management individuals will go through a specific 'strengths assessment'.

5. The relationship is hope-inducing. A strengths-based approach aims to increase the hopefulness of the client. Further, hope can be realised through strengthened relationships with people, communities and culture.

6. Meaningful choice. Strengths proponents highlight a collaborative stance where people are experts in their own lives and the practitioner's role is to increase and explain choices and encourage people to make their own decisions and informed choices. (Rapp, Saleebey and Sullivan, 2008, p 81)

Parkinson (2018) identifies how FGCs meet these six standards for a strength-based approach. She states that FGCs are goal-oriented, in that a family are asked to develop a plan to meet identified needs, issues and concerns and to set goals for their family to meet in addressing these issues. Their philosophy is based upon the fundamental belief that there are strengths in all families, individuals and communities that can be mobilised to meet identified needs. The basis of an FGC is one of hope – that a family will be able to develop a safe plan. Furthermore, the process is a collaborative one in the sense that an FGC is a family-led rather than a professionally led meeting. Finally, families have a choice as to whether to engage with the FGC process or not (Ashley and Nixon, 2007; Barnsdale and Walker, 2007; Fox, 2008 in Parkinson, 2018).

Chapter 2 discussed strengths-based approaches in relation to other theories for social work practice: empowerment theory, ecological systems theory and culturally appropriate social work practice. Parkinson (2018) has contextualised FGCs in relation to these core social work theories, arguing that as the FGC model is a social work process and is used in the majority of local authorities within England and Wales as well as in several countries across the globe to address issues that social workers are facing (Family Rights Group, 2015), it is therefore important that social workers understand the model in relation to the theoretical framework of the profession.

Empowerment theory

Metze, Abma and Kwekkeboom (2013) state that FGCs have long been associated with empowerment, as this is a fundamental and specific goal of the FGC process. Indeed, the idea that FGCs empower families, as a family-led approach to decision making has long been central to the discourse about FGCs. Much is made of the FGC as an attempt to redress the balance of power between the supporting professionals and family members, in shifting decision-making powers to the family (see Adams and Chandler, 2004; Holland et al, 2005; Hayes and Houston, 2007).

While it is acknowledged that FGCs are an attempt to empower families, some argue that there are tensions in applying an empowering approach into fundamentally bureaucratic, risk-averse and professionally led social care processes and structures (Adams and Chandler; 2004; Merkel-Holguin, 2004; Holland et al, 2005). Holland et al (2005, p 65) introduced the concept of 'imposed empowerment' to the use of FGCs in the field of child protection. They raise a question about whether an FGC can truly be an empowering process when families are expected to engage and comply with child protection process and that the local authority and/or the courts make the ultimate decision about the welfare of children (Parkinson, 2018). It is widely acknowledged and accepted that families have the choice whether to participate in an FGC and this is a key principle in standards for FGC practice in England and Wales (Barnardos, NCH and Family Rights Group, 2020). However, Parkinson (2018) argues that the notion of choice becomes questionable, when families are faced with the prospect of 'losing' their children and may feel pressured to engage in the FGC approach. Despite these concerns, she cites Holland et al (2005), who conclude that, even within the 'punitive' world of child protection, FGCs offer the potential for a more balanced relationship between family members and the state, and that an FGC ensures more 'democracy' for family members.

Metze, Abma and Kwekkeboom (2013) argue that FGCs are related to the idea of relational empowerment, which links empowerment to human relationships. Parkinson (2018) states that, given that the process of the FGC is that of a social network working together to develop a plan for the care and/ or protection of a vulnerable member of their group, relational empowerment becomes an appropriate lens through which to understand the empowering nature of the FGC process. Although there is no concrete definition of relational empowerment, the concept is centred on individuals becoming empowered through their relationships with others and the support that they receive from them (Metze, Abma and Kwekkeboom, 2013). Indeed Barringer et al (2016) argue that availability of social support is a key component of individuals feeling empowered (Parkinson, 2018). Related to this is the concept of relational autonomy (Metze, Abma and Kwekkeboom, 2013). It has long been understood that, for individuals to feel empowered, they need to feel that they have autonomy and a sense of individual freedom and self-determination in decision-making (Braye and Preston Shoot, 2011, in Parkinson, 2018). However, individuals often need the support of others when making decisions, and this is referred to as relational autonomy: that is, being able to make decisions independently but being able to draw on the support of others if needed (Christman, 2004, in Parkinson, 2018). Metze, Abma and Kwekkeboom (2013) argue that at an FGC the shared decision-making undertaken by a social group is underpinned by relational autonomy. Everyone participating in an FGC has the opportunity to express their autonomy and have their say (being supported to do so, if necessary, by an advocate) while at the same time drawing on the support of the rest of the group and engaging in a collaborative process to agree a plan and share the responsibility for it (Parkinson, 2018).

Related to empowerment is the concept of 'resilience', which is defined as, 'a dynamic process wherein individuals display positive adaptation despite experiences of significant adversity or trauma' (Luthar, Cicchetti and Becker, 2000, p 858). In other words, resilience is about the capacity of individuals to cope and manage with difficult situations in their lives and to 'bounce back' from these circumstances, thus potentially growing stronger (Parkinson, 2018). Brodsky and Cattaneo (2013) argue that in this sense resilience has been related to empowerment and the feeling of being in control over one's own life. Rutter (1987) identified several factors that contribute to the development of resilience. One of these is that an individual has a positive support network (Ozbay et al, 2008). Parkinson (2018) cites Metze, Abma and Kwekkeboom (2013), who argue that the FGC, in mobilising an individual's support network to develop a package of care and support, can enhance an individual's resilience and their feeling of being in control. They argue that the FGC has the potential to increase an individual's self-esteem, in recognising that others value them enough to contribute to supporting them at the FGC. This, coupled with emotional support that others may provide at the FGC when discussing potentially difficult issues and circumstances, can ensure that an individual feels valued and worthy of support. The sense of control that an individual might feel can thus lead to a feeling of being empowered.

Ecological systems theory

Ecological systems theory tends to have been located in the process of social work assessment and understanding an individual's situation to inform subsequent service interventions. However, Parkinson (2018) argues that it can also be applied to social welfare decision-making processes and provide a framework for understanding FGCs and other approaches to family-led decision-making.

Indeed, Harawitz (2006) argues that FGCs are rooted in ecological systems approaches. The underlying principle of FGCs, that a family or community can understand and assume responsibility for the care or protection of its members, is aligned to the core premise of the ecological approach, that an individual can be understood within the context of their interactions with their social environment (Parkinson, 2018). Healy (2014, p 118) states that the role of the social worker is to understand the 'transaction' between a person and their environment and to promote change in these 'transactions'.

Referring to Bronfenbrenner's (1979) concentric model for understanding the social environment of the individual (outlined in Chapter 2), the FGC is fundamentally concerned with an individual's microsystem, which refers to informal systems such as home, family and community and the mesosystem, which includes formal systems that impact directly on an individual's life, such as schools and social care services (Parkinson, 2018).

With regard to the microsystem of the family, research has suggested that FGCs can lead to improved communication and relationships within the family (see Pennell and Burford, 2000; Litchfield, Gatowski and Dobbin, 2003; Holland et al, 2005; Frost and Elmer, 2008).

Furthermore, Parkinson (2018) argues that placing responsibility on the family to pool their resources to care for or support a child or an adult in their family inevitably has an impact on the individual's transactions with their family, as support for them is potentially increased or provided by another family member. For example, if another family member agrees to care for a child who cannot return to the care of their immediate family, due to levels of risk, the transaction between the child and this family member changes. The child's transaction with their family system is thus improved, as they are now, it is hoped, safely cared for within the family system.

With regard to the mesosystem, Parkinson (2018) highlights research which suggests that FGCs can lead to improved relationships between families and their mesosystems, citing evaluations of FGC services which reflect that family members have reported improved relationships with social workers and other professionals as a result of being involved in an FGC and of feeling listened to and heard (Pennell and Burford, 2000; Litchfield, Gatowski and Dobbin, 2003). Parkinson (2018) also highlights that the outcomes of FGCs often result in a changed and improved transaction between family members and mesosystems. She cites research which suggests that FGCs have the potential to lead to more children being cared for within their families and not entering state care (Titcomb and LeCroy, 2003; Laws and Kirby, 2008; Sawyer and Lohrbach, 2008); FGCs in educational settings lead to improved attendance of young people, when the purpose of the FGC is to address school non-attendance (Crow, Marsh and Holton, 2004; Hayden, 2009; McMorris et al, 2013); and outcomes from youth justice FGCs have shown the potential for a reduction in offending among young people and a decrease in custodial sentences (Barnsdale and Walker, 2007; Fox, 2008; MacFarlane and Anglem, 2014). All these examples represent significant change and improvement with an individual's interaction with the mesosystem (Parkinson, 2018).

The above research is from the children and families' field as research on the use of FGCs with adults is still limited and tends to be based upon small-scale, localised studies, which use different research methods and approaches (Manthorpe and Rapaport, 2020).

Culturally sensitive social work practice

Parkinson (2018) argues that FGCs are congruent with the concept of culturally sensitive social work practice, introduced in Chapter 2. It could be argued that FGCs are the very embodiment of culturally appropriate practice. As previously stated, they are said to be based upon Māori cultural practices and traditions, and are used in 21 countries across the globe, which demonstrates that the model can be applied cross-culturally (Edwards and Parkinson, 2018), and appear to be particularly embedded in countries which have a significant indigenous population, such as New Zealand, Australia, Canada and the US.

Barn and Das (2016) have written about FGCs as a culturally sensitive approach to social work decision-making, identifying five key areas for consideration when planning and organising an FGC: the importance of a culturally appropriate location for the FGC; recognition of cultural traditions; identification with the community, including language considerations; the role of family elders in hosting and convening the FGC; community education and awareness (pp 947–949).

However, Nygård and Saus (2019) argue that the cultural sensitivity of FGCs has been taken for granted, as it is sold on the basis that it is based upon Māori culture. Indeed, some have questioned this assumption and argue that FGCs have been shoehorned into existing social work systems and structures that are based on White colonial perspectives (see Love, 2000; Waites et al, 2004; Ban, 2005) and that as a result FGCs can only really be a token nod towards minority communities, while Love (2000) argues that that there is a danger in adding FGCs to such oppressive and racist structures and institutions as this could potentially lead to FGCs continuing to oppress minority groups, under the guise of 'caring and altruism' (p 30).

Critical perspectives of culturally sensitive practice have been discussed in Chapter 2 alongside a recognition of the complexity of applying this approach in practice.

Therefore, a critical perspective needs to be applied when considering FGCs as an exemplar of culturally sensitive practice, as the concept itself is problematic. Furthermore, while research suggests that FGCs can meet the needs of diverse communities, there is work to be done in ensuring that the model is applied in a way which recognises and challenges the oppressive structural foundations of social work practice in the UK and which reflects the diversity of British society.

Research findings

There is a substantial body of national and international research which has focused on the application of FGCs and their efficacy in social work practice. Indeed, Morris and Connolly (2012) argue that FGCs are one of the most widely researched areas of social work practice. However, despite this, there have been difficulties in developing an international evidence base. Some of this is down to the fact that that research has tended to be focused on localised, small-scale studies (Crampton, 2007; Fox, 2008), which is further compounded by the difficulties in comparing a model that has been adapted to meet the needs of individual countries and regions (Connolly and Morris, 2011). Furthermore, there are few comparative research studies, and some have emphasised that the lack of randomised control trials (RCTs) in the field has ensured that the research evidence is not sufficiently robust (What Works, n.d.). Despite this, a clear evidence base is starting to develop, and several themes can be identified from the literature (Connolly and Morris, 2011).

Edwards and Parkinson (2018) argue that the international literature on FGCs demonstrates that as a result of FGCs:

- significantly fewer children enter state care and remain in the care of their families (see Titcomb and LeCroy, 2003; Laws and Kirby, 2008; Sawyer and Lohrbach, 2008; Rapaport et al, 2019);
- contact arrangements between children in care and their families are improved (see Kemp, 2007; Brady and Millar, 2009; O'Brien and Alohen, 2015);
- families develop safe plans for children (see Pakura, 2003; Walker, 2005; Harder, 2013);
- children and families feel more engaged in the process (see Dalrymple, 2002; Horan and Dalrymple, 2003; Holland et al, 2005); and
- more fathers are engaged than in traditional child protection processes (see Dalrymple, 2002; Horan and Dalrymple, 2003; Holland et al, 2005; Ashley and Nixon, 2007; Ashley, 2011).

Much of the research on FGCs to date has been focused on the child protection and youth justice fields; however, in recent years, as FGCs have begun to be applied in the field of adult social care, the focus of research on FGCs has reflected this and a clear evidence base for the use of FGCs in adult services is starting to emerge. Comparable with the situation with FGCs in children's services, Manthorpe and Rapaport (2020) have identified that while the research studies demonstrate the potential for FGCs to address the needs of adults who come to the attention of adult social care services, studies tend to be small in scale and localised, focusing largely on service evaluations. They make the conclusion that a larger, more robust evidence base needs to be developed for the use of FGCs in adult social care in the UK. However, in drawing together the limited existing international evidence base for FGCs, the authors have identified some benefits of applying FGCs in adult services. These are largely centred around family and user satisfaction with FGCs, professionals gaining a greater understanding of family difficulties as a result of an FGC and an increased mobilisation of family-based support, following the FGC. However, the evidence for the outcomes of FGCs is limited and while some studies have focused on immediate outcomes, there is little evidence for the benefits of FGCs in the medium and longer term, at present.

One of the barriers in developing an evidence base in adult services is the diverse and complex nature of the adult social care setting. Those requiring the support of adult services have a diverse range of needs and adult social care includes a range of services, such as mental health support, dementia support services, safeguarding adults, learning and physical disability services and homelessness support. Therefore, it becomes very difficult to create generalised outcome measures for FGCs in this area. Mitchell (2020) has highlighted the complexity in developing outcome measures for FGCs in children's services, arguing that the definition of what constitutes a positive outcome is complex and nuanced and will be different things to different stakeholders. This can also be applied in the adult social care context. For example, a positive outcome for family members may simply be feeling that they are able to contribute to decision-making about an individual in their family while a local authority is potentially more likely to focus on cost-saving and case closure. Furthermore, Parkinson et al (2018) highlight the complexities involved when applying a model designed to meet the needs of children and families to the adult social care environment. They argue that the model cannot be applied in an adult safeguarding context in the same way as in a safeguarding children's context. For example, a 'bottom line' cannot be given when an adult has the mental capacity and the right to make unwise decisions about their lives. Nor can restrictions be applied about who an adult with capacity can choose to invite to their FGC. Therefore, Parkinson (2020) states that a practice toolkit should be developed to support FGC practitioners to overcome some of the practice issues and tensions that can arise in adult services. Despite these difficulties, though, the early research evidence is promising and there are several areas which have well-established adult FGC services evidencing positive outcomes for users of services.

Critical perspectives

As with any model of intervention, there are those that do not advocate for the use of FGCs or indeed question the efficacy of the model in addressing the needs of users of social work services. Some have expressed doubts about the ability of families to develop safe plans, particularly where abuse and neglect has taken place (Pennell and Burford, 2000; Pakura, 2003; Anderson and Parkinson, 2018). However, there is a significant body of evidence that suggests that families are able to develop safe plans when they are adequately supported to do so, mentioned above. For example, Pakura (2003), in her research on the implementation of FGCs in New Zealand, found that most families developed safe plans, contrary to professional expectation. Further research by Walker (2005) on the use of FGCs in Hawaii found that families developed safe plans in 97 per cent of cases. More recently, a 2013 evaluation of FGCs in British Columbia (Harder, 2013) found that 86 per cent of respondents, including family members and professionals, felt that the family plan was adequately protecting children three months later. Another criticism of FGCs is that there is little research that examines outcomes beyond those that are measured immediately after the FGC. However, this study demonstrates that FGC plans have the potential to remain effective a few months later (Parkinson, 2020).

Others have questioned the evidence base for FGCs and challenge the claims made by advocates of FGCs, that the model achieves better outcomes than traditional social work decision-making processes. For example, What Works (n.d.) undertook a systematic review on the effectiveness of FGCs in the child protection context and concluded that there was little evidence that FGCs improve outcomes in child protection or reduce the numbers of children entering local authority care. However, this review focused largely on RCTs and other comparative studies with quantified outcomes, excluding a wealth of qualitative pieces of research, on the basis that they were not sufficiently robust. A number of social work academics have expressed concern about the ethics of measuring the success of FGCs using RCTs, as using the approach ensures that families who might benefit from a FGC are denied a service, if they are part of a control group (Mezey et al, 2015). Furthermore, in dismissing other qualitative pieces of research, the review has chosen to ignore the voices of professionals delivering FGCs and those with lived experience who have shared their experiences of FGCs as part of research (Parkinson, 2020).

Despite this focus on outcomes of FGCs, Parkinson (2020) states that there is an argument that, whatever the possible outcomes from an FGC, they *should* be offered to families, as it is 'the right thing to do', in line with social work values and ethics.

Case study: Family Group Conference case study (provided by Will Golden, FGC co-ordinator)

Names and identifying features have been changed to preserve the anonymity of the family.

Family members
Harry – 13 months
Charlie – newborn baby
Jane – mum of Harry and Charlie
Tom – dad of Harry and Charlie
Maureen – Jane's mum
Clare – Tom's mum

Introduction
A family referral was received from the social worker with the presenting needs of adult mental health. However, this case soon escalated and became an urgent referral with child neglect and contact issues, due to an escalation of the concerns that the social worker had.

Jane had experienced a long history of social care involvement due to her mental health and she had experienced several hospital admissions due to self-harm, suicidal ideation and suicide attempts.

Social care professionals were becoming increasingly concerned about the impact of Jane's mental health on Harry. Jane stated that she was not receiving the correct support for her needs. At this point the FGC was requested to look at wider family support for Jane and to reduce the risk associated with her mental health and the impact of this on Harry.

Prior to the referral for a FGC, Jane had been sectioned under the Mental Health Act 1983 for a few weeks. Before Jane was able to return home, and while under the care of Tom, Harry was found in just his nappy in the car park of a local shop. Tom stated that he had collapsed in the house and was unsure what had happened and how Harry had got out of the house.

It was recommended at this point that Jane have supported contact with Harry and remain in the family home and that Tom should be the primary carer of Harry and live with Jane's mum in her home and receive support from family.

Jane stated that she was being intimidated in their family home and so moved to her sister's home in a nearby town. Jane also stated that she was pregnant again. The social worker made an application to court for an interim care order (Children Act 1989) for Harry, which, if agreed, would mean that Harry would become looked after by the local authority.

The questions for the FGC then focused on:

- who could offer support to grandparents and Tom to care for Harry safely;
- who would consider themselves as potential alterative carers should Tom not be able to care for Harry;
- how could contact be promoted and supported between Jane and Harry;
- what plans need to be put in place to support Jane with her pregnancy and to plan for baby's arrival safely.

Family preparation

This involved initially signposting the family to what an interim care order meant as the social worker had not been out to see the family to explain this appropriately, so they did not understand what was going on. The FGC co-ordinator signposted them all to the information on the Family Rights Group website (https://frg.org. uk/family-group-conferences/), which they all read and used to inform them about the next steps. The family were very upset and anxious about what was happening and struggling to be able to contact the social worker.

The preparation involved helping the family understand what a care order would mean for them, so it was important that the co-ordinator had this specialist knowledge.

The FGC co-ordinator worked with the family to consider what they could do to support Jane and Tom to allow Harry to remain in the family home and also to allow the family to stay together when the new baby was born. Jane was worried that she would need to have a pre-birth assessment and that the baby could be removed, but the FGC co-ordinator explained that a robust plan and a contingency plan that safely addressed the presenting risks could be presented in court to show evidence that all options have been considered and that the family have been given the opportunity to discuss the concerns and supported to make their own decisions and plans around current strengths and the local authority's worries.

The FGC

This was held virtually, due to the COVID-19 pandemic. The family were supported to access the virtual platform and it was confirmed that they were all comfortable using the technology.

The referring social worker shared their concerns and the issues to be addressed in the FGC at the *information-sharing stage*. The family was supported and empowered to ask questions and to challenge the social worker on things that they did not agree on, and this was all recorded to be included as part of the plan. The family challenged the social worker quite a lot as the family felt that they had not maintained respectful and open communication with the family prior to the FGC. The role of the FGC co-ordinator was one of mediation at this stage, as they aimed to rebuild the relationship that the family had with the local authority.

This was successful in that the social worker promised to keep the family informed of what was happening from then on and it was also made clear to the family that their own solicitor should keep them informed before and during the court proceedings.

The family had *private family time* once they felt confident that they could answer the questions posed by the social worker. The family developed a plan that was both robust and realistic, with the support of the FGC co-ordinator.

The plan considered the safety of Harry and Charlie and included contingency plans: in other words, alternative plans in the event of the first plan not working. It was agreed that Harry should live with Maureen, his maternal gran, and that paternal grandparents would also provide some of Harry's care. All agreed to supervise any contact between Harry and his mum and dad. A clear plan of support was offered by extended family, such as babysitting and help with practical things such as transport to nursery and medical appointments.

The local authority then had to make assessments of the suitability of Maureen and paternal grandparents to care for Harry and Charlie, to present to the court, alongside the family plan. In cases where care proceedings are ongoing, it is the responsibility of the court to ultimately agree a family plan.

Review

A review was held three months later. At this time, Harry was living with Maureen, under an interim care order. Both the family and the social worker were satisfied with how the family plan was progressing. Harry and Charlie were seeing a lot of extended family and developing strong family bonds. Jane, who was receiving appropriate mental health support, was having regular contact with Harry; she and Charlie lived with Tom's mum, Clare, while psychological assessments of her mental health were being completed. The interim care order was in place for another nine months following the review, after which Harry and Charlie returned to the care of Jane and Tom, following psychological and parenting assessments.

Feedback

The family felt that it was a positive experience and they felt that the social worker and themselves worked better together following the initial conference. The family were glad that both families had come together and built up lines of communication. The social worker felt that this had been a positive way to plan while the court process was ongoing and to allow the family to address concerns themselves. She stated that she would use the service again.

Conclusion

This chapter has introduced FGCs as a strengths-based approach to practice and contextualised the model within core social work theory. Key research findings on the outcomes of FGCs have been presented alongside a discussion of the critical perspectives of the model. The case study has demonstrated how FGCs can work in practice. It is important to note that this chapter is only introductory and has provided only a 'whistle-stop tour' of FGCs. For a greater knowledge and understanding of the application of the model and the core research findings, please refer to the further reading at the end of the chapter.

Key learning points

- FGCs are a family-led decision-making process.

- Family members, not professionals, make plans about the care/protection of a child or an adult in need of support.

- Private family time is a core part of the FGC process and what makes it distinct.

- FGCs draw upon existing strengths and resources within a family network.

- Research on FGCs demonstrates positive outcomes for families.

- FGCs can be applied cross-culturally.

- FGCs are congruent with values of social work practice.

Further reading

Ashley, C. and Nixon, P. (2007) *Family Group Conferences: Where Next? Policies and Practices for the Future*, London: Family Rights Group.

Edwards, D. and Parkinson, K. (2018) *Family Group Conferences in Social Work and Social Care: Involving Families in Decision Making*, Bristol: Policy Press.

Fox, D. (2018) *Family Group Conferencing with Children and Young People: Advocacy Approaches, Variations and Impacts*, London: Palgrave Macmillan.

Frost, N., Abram, F. and Burgess, H. (2014a) 'Family group conferences: Context, process and ways forward', *Child and Family Social Work*, 19(4): 480–490.

Frost, N., Abram, F. and Burgess, H. (2014b) 'Family group conferences: Evidence, outcomes and future research', *Child and Family Social Work*, 19(4): 501–507.

Manforth, J. and Rapaport, J. (2020) *Researching Family Group Conferences in Adult Services: Methods Review*, London: King's College National Institute of Health Research, School for Social Care Research.

Skaale Havnen, K.J., and Christiansen, O. (2014). *Knowledge Review on Family Group Conferences: Experiences and Outcomes*, Bergen, Norway: Regional Centre for Child and Youth Mental Health and Child Welfare (RKBU West) Uni Research Health.

Tapper, L. (2010) 'Using family group conferences in safeguarding adults', *Journal of Adult Protection*, 12(1): 27–31.

5

Signs of Safety

Lauren Bailey and Steve Myers

Introduction

This chapter outlines the development, principles and research basis of Signs of Safety (SoS), using the example of a real safety plan to demonstrate how the model works in practice. SoS is a safety- and strengths-oriented approach based on child protection practitioner experience of what works in developing safety in families where there are concerns about the welfare of children. It is also being used in broader social care contexts where there are concerns about vulnerability and the need to develop safety. SoS provides a framework for practitioners to bring together their practice experience, wisdom, skills, theory and expertise to co-construct safety and reduce dangers in situations where risk has been identified. The approach uses the existing and potential strengths of the person and their family to ensure that safety plans are meaningful to them and therefore are more likely to be successful and sustainable. It is underpinned by good working relationships, critical thinking skills and a focus on local and individual solutions to problems. The approach is popular with practitioners, who find it gives them hope and creativity in working with often difficult situations of high risk and professional anxiety.

Development

This chapter will explore the development of the approach, its theoretical and research underpinnings, how it works in practice and some of the challenges it has met.

The SoS approach to child protection casework was developed in the 1990s in the state of Western Australia. It was created by Steve Edwards and Andrew Turnell in collaboration with child protection workers and was stimulated by the experience Steve Edwards had as a statutory child protection social worker. In his front-line practice he had been dissatisfied with the existing theories and models that had informed his training and the way that child welfare organisations delivered services, particularly to disadvantaged communities. He felt that there was a disconnect between the policies and guidance that he and his colleagues had to work to and the real, lived experience of undertaking child protection investigations that were complex, fraught with emotion and anxiety and frequently adversarial (Turnell and Edwards 1999; Turnell and Murphy, 2017).

Andrew Turnell was a solution-focused brief therapist who was working with families referred from child welfare services. Solution-focused approaches are explored in greater depth in Chapter 3. Edwards and Turnell worked together and began to see opportunities to work differently in child protection based on their experiences of what practices were helpful to people with lived experience and practitioners. These solution-focused brief therapy (SFBT) influenced approaches were introduced into mainstream child protection services during the 1990s in collaboration with 150 front-line practitioners in Western Australia, where they were based. The experience of these practitioners heavily influenced the development of what became the SoS through training events that built on the applied learning through practice. The training programme took an action learning approach that enabled practitioners to reflect on what worked most effectively, and when and how this happened.

Edwards and Turnell were able to facilitate these sessions and help identify themes and practical approaches that seemed to be most effective at creating positive change. The reflection focused on where practitioners were making a positive difference in people's lives using SoS and so learning from this direct practice experience. This developed a culture of appreciative inquiry about practice (Turnell and Essex, 2006) that could be used to inform the organisational change required to deliver effective practice, recognising that the organisational context is crucial to achieving this. SoS theory and practice were first outlined in an article 'Aspiring to partnership: The Signs of Safety approach to child protection' (Turnell and Edwards, 1997) and developed in the book *Signs of Safety: A Safety and Solution Oriented Approach to Child Protection Casework* (Turnell and Edwards, 1999).

The approach has proved popular with many practitioners and was taken up by individual services in the UK, USA, Australia, New Zealand, Japan and Europe. Turnell and Murphy (2017) identify 200 child protection organisations globally that have implemented SoS, and SoS being used as a practice framework in 45 local authorities in England and in parts of practice in a further 49 (Baginsky, Ixer and Manthorpe, 2021). In England, the approach was successful in gaining funding through the Children's Social Care Innovation Programme, which included redesigning organisational procedures and processes to implement SoS fully in ten local authorities. This followed the Munro Report (Munro 2011), which had raised concerns about the development of overly defensive and bureaucratic practices in child protection, and the need to move to a more risk management approach that was focused on the needs of the child.

Signs of Safety can be defined as a practice framework, integrating practitioner expertise, skills and theory to act as a practice guide (Baginsky et al, 2020). This is a useful way of thinking about SoS as providing a helpful structure within which to work with children and their families, although there is an emphasis here on safety being absolutely central to practice. SoS may utilise family and systems strengths, but these are only helpful in the context of developing and sustaining safety.

Principles

Three key principles inform the SoS model: working relationships, thinking critically and landing grand aspirations.

Working relationships

Good, purposeful, productive working relationships between child protection professionals and families, and between the different professionals themselves, are key to effective practice in safeguarding children. There is evidence that developing and sustaining such relationships help to create good outcomes for children and are valued by the families and the workers (Salveron et al, 2015; Turnell and Murphy, 2017). However, there have been concerns raised in the past about colluding with abusive families and failing to see the dangers that some children are facing by being too optimistic about family capacity and capability to change, leading to dangerous and naïve practices. This has led to professional anxieties about being seen to be 'too close' to families and to a more distant 'objective' approach to them that gives an image of a certain style of professionalism. Of course, people frequently respond to how they are treated, and such an approach mars the quality of the relationship between the worker and the family by creating and maintaining barriers that compromise working together to develop safety. It also makes it difficult to see any strengths that the family may have by seeing only dangers.

SoS understands that working relationships between the worker and families should be transparent, honest and respectful to achieve a shared understanding of what needs to change and how this will happen. Communication needs to be clear, accessible and as free from professional jargon as possible (Bunn, 2013; Baginsky, Hickman, Moriarty et al, 2020). It is possible to be collaborative with but also critical of the abusive family in open ways so that everyone understands each other and what needs to change. These relationships are not formulaic or straightforward but messy, always developing and sometimes contradictory, because that is the reality of life.

Investigations into child deaths have often found that the relationships between professionals have contributed to the tragedy through a lack of understanding of different perspectives and of how power and authority are used within these relationships. SoS recognises that the same principles of respect, openness and transparency need to be applied by professionals in their working relationships with each other. Professionals need to have healthy, constructive and critical conversations to ensure that they have the best possible understanding of the abusive family and the risks and opportunities of change.

Thinking critically

People often make initial judgements about situations and then find or interpret new information to support this first understanding (Milner, Myers and

O'Byrne, 2020). This *confirmation bias* has been seen in child protection where a preferred story about the abuse and the family can be constructed that does not make space for any questioning and cannot respond to information that may go against this way of thinking. This can produce a very 'thin' story that the family does not recognise, and it narrows options for change. Taking a stance of critical inquiry not only reduces the chance of getting it wrong but also helps to create a culture of reflective practice and appreciative inquiry (Bushe, 2013), where it is possible for professionals to admit that they are uncertain, that mistakes can be made and that they need to be open to changing their minds as new information emerges. Appreciative inquiry enables constant review of the balance of strengths and dangers in an abusive family situation. It helps to avoid drift by providing renewed focus on change, and guards against either an overly optimistic or pessimistic view of the family by providing the space to challenge and be challenged.

Landing grand aspirations

SoS aspires to be a bottom-up approach that recognises and values the lived experience of practitioners undertaking complex interventions in often messy situations. This is contrasted with approaches that are top-down, prescribed by organisational systems, academics and senior managers in ways that marginalise the wisdom and experience of front-line practitioners. These centralised approaches can be too rigid to respond safely to the uniqueness of each family by imposing external models that minimise the skills and knowledge of local practitioners and of the families themselves.

SoS values the experience of practitioners through working with them to help identify what are the most effective ways to intervene and incorporating these into the approach. Practitioners in Australasia, North America, Europe and Japan have been consulted to hear what they have found useful, and this has been used to inform SoS. This means that SoS should reflect the most relevant, appropriate and successful practice based on a wide range of sources and take into account how the approach can be effective in different national and cultural contexts.

Risk

The use of strengths-based approaches in contexts where there is a high level of risk or danger is often met with some incredulity, in that it is assumed that if you are focusing on strengths then you are minimising the dangers, which could have catastrophic consequences in child protection. No one would deny that the risks and dangers need to be understood, reduced and managed; however, focusing solely on the problems in a situation provides a narrow framework that does not easily allow for change, as every case has both strengths and dangers that are often intertwined, and by focusing on one we lose potential opportunities to co-create a safe future. Seeking to understand strengths can provide valuable understanding of what might work for that particular family in developing safety (Skrypek, Idzelis and Pecora, 2012).

The focus on strengths, as well as concerns, recognises parents as being caring (even though this may at times be compromised) and capable of change, which helps to motivate them and also the workers around them (Keddell, 2014). When risks and dangers outweigh the SoS, practitioners are able to communicate more clearly to parents why subsequent actions are taken, such as removal of the children or conditions placed on access. Indeed, there is evidence that parents felt more empowered using SoS, which strengthens safety (Reekers et al, 2018). Recognising and building on family strengths contrasts with much child protection practice, which has been criticised as preoccupied with risk and danger (see, for example, Featherstone et al, 2018).

Using scaling helps workers to benchmark concerns and quantify change, recognising that risk/danger is fluid and often relative. This avoids a simplistic 'safe–not safe' binary and allows for consideration of 'how safe?' and 'what would make it safer?', while the formulation of 'danger statements' enables practitioners to articulate clearly the potential impact of adverse parenting behaviours. Such approaches establish shared understandings of the need for change, facilitating the creation of clear goals which reduce the need for social work intervention and increase parents' ability to care safely.

Case study: Lucy

The next part of this chapter will focus on a piece of work undertaken in 2018 in a small community which had a population of around 33,000 people.

The SoS approach believes that 'it takes a village to raise a child', meaning that a whole community of people should play a part in each child's life to develop, thrive and grow in a safe environment.

The example will focus on the transition of a young woman named Lucy, who had been in the care of a children's residential home since she was 15. Prior to moving into residential care Lucy had been in foster care since the age of four. Lucy was placed in foster care due to a traumatic brain injury which was the direct result of physical abuse, neglect and trauma experienced in her young childhood at the hands of her caregivers. When Lucy reached the age of 16, questions were asked about where Lucy would live when she turned 18. The options were for Lucy to live within a disability residential service or an adult social care semi-supported living service, or for Lucy to live independently without the input of formal services. This led to an array of complex debates and lines of inquiry being opened between professionals with Lucy in the middle, confused and unsettled about where her journey into young adulthood would take her.

What was clear during these discussions was that assessment frameworks between services were different; with differing aims and goals came contradictory solutions. It was an Alice in Wonderland scenario of 'if you do not know where you are going, any road will get you there' (Carroll, 1865), but the professionals all agreed that they wanted clarity, focus and direction for Lucy to ensure that she did not feel trapped in her version of Wonderland.

What followed were professional discussions using the idea that it takes a village to raise a child. Debates were held, wondering if that same village could act as a safety net for adults at risk of harm and who need protection. The local children's services had been applying the framework and principles of SoS since 2016, and although SoS had not been used in adult protection, discussions began to be held about applying this framework across all social care services within the authority.

SoS is a relationship-based model that looks at how we grow safety, with a balanced approach between risk and safety. The approach has clear focus, purpose and sense of direction. It is a way of building partnerships and honouring and respecting a person's connections and culture. It was agreed that social care services would adapt the SoS framework so that active work could begin to consider Lucy's transition from the children's residential home.

The SoS framework is a paradigm shift from paternalism to partnership, teaching to facilitating. Professionals had now decided on a universal framework to support Lucy. In applying this framework, they heard the most important person, Lucy, voice her opinion, express her concerns and explore her aspirations.

Words and pictures

Words and pictures help to explain to children and young people what is happening in their lives and why. This tool can also be applied when working with adults who have learning disabilities. In Lucy's case, the impact of having an acquired brain injury resulted in her having learning disabilities that included loss of organisation and reasoning skills, memory loss and difficulties processing and recalling complex information. Lucy had always been very vocal that, when she became 18, she was an adult and that she wanted to live on her own, in her own home, without support staff.

Words and pictures are created around the following four questions: Who is worried? What are we worried about? What happened because of the worries? What is happening now? The following words-and-pictures explanation was devised by Lucy's social worker, Sandra. This was to aid in helping to explain to Lucy about an initial mapping meeting that would be held to explore Lucy's transition out of children's services.

This is the words-and-pictures exercise that was used to explain to Lucy the reasons and the purpose behind the support network meeting with her to explore what life could look like for her once she became 18.

Table 5.1: Signs of Safety questions

Who is worried?	Sandra is worried that if Lucy leaves her home at Wilton Children's Home and lives on her own, bad things could happen to her.

What are we worried about?	Sandra is worried about bad things happening to Lucy such as people taking her money, taking her to places she does not know, being in her house when Lucy does not want them there or touching her private parts when she does not want them to, like when this happened before Lucy came to live here.

What is happening because of the worries?	Because of these worries, all the people who support Lucy are thinking about what life will look like for Lucy when she leaves Wilton Children's Home.

What is happening now?	All of the people who support Lucy want to work with her to think about how she can be safe and happy and feel supported when she leaves Wilton Children's Home. This will mean that Lucy will be invited to attend a meeting, to think about this.

Adult safeguarding and SoS – mapping out Lucy's case

In its simplest form, the SoS framework can be understood using the four domains: What are we worried about? What is working well? What needs to happen? Where are we on a scale of 0 to 10, with 0 being the highest risk and 10 being maximum safety? The SoS tool has seven categories that are used within the assessment framework. These are as follows: harm, danger statements, complicating factors, existing strengths, existing safety, safety goals and next steps. Scaling is then used to ascertain each person's point of view. The assessment framework below depicts the discussions held with Lucy and her support network in figuring out the next steps.

Initial mapping meeting

Table 5.2: Signs of Safety mapping

What are we worried about?	What is working well?	What needs to happen?
Harm Lucy's support team are worried that if Lucy were to leave the children's home to live on her own, without her support team, she would struggle to maintain her home, money, health and could not always keep herself safe. **Danger Statements** 1. Lucy's support team all agree that Lucy is a kind, caring and trusting young woman. We are worried that if Lucy lives on her own without her support team, she will make friends with amber and red people who want to be her friend for the wrong reasons. Like the time when Lucy gave all her money and was touched on her private parts when she did not want to be by people that she thought were her friends. We agree that Lucy should be proud of herself for all the learning that she has done, like keeping safe work and managing money. We know that Lucy would like to live on her own, and we are worried that if this happened too quickly, she could go missing with strangers, and never return home. 2. Lucy's team agree that she tries her hardest to be as independent as possible, but she does still need to be reminded and supported to take her medication, shower, shop and cook. We are worried that without her support team Lucy will forget to pick up, take or mix up her medication, which could mean that she may end up in hospital very unwell or die.	**Existing Strengths** Lucy will tell her worries to her social worker, Sandra, and her key worker, Kristina. Lucy knows most of the bus routes around the area, and how to get home. Lucy and her team have a 'traffic light' communication tool, for people, places and things. Lucy has said that she likes this way of learning. On the days that Lucy is having a good memory day, she does not need as much support from her team. Lucy visits the youth club three times a week and is going to go on a trip abroad with them. Lucy is completing an apprenticeship in youth support work and working towards getting a job at the youth club once she turns 18. **Existing Safety** When Lucy feels unhappy or unsafe, she will call her support team and ask for help. Lucy knows that staying overnight at her dad's house is not a good idea, and even if he asks her to, Lucy will say no. Lucy has a check list on her door to make sure that she remembers her mobile phone, bus pass and purse. Lucy rarely forgets these items when she goes out.	**Safety Goals** 1. For Lucy to live on her own without a support team we would need to see before she leaves the children's home at age 18 that at times when she is at risk from other people, Lucy will recognise the risk and get herself out of danger or, if needed, ask for help. We would need to see that Lucy speaks only to green and amber people on her phone, and only meets up with green people on her own. We know that Lucy is working hard with Kristina to learn more about how she can keep herself safe from other people, and before Lucy lives alone, we would need to be sure that she knows how to do this. 2. For Lucy to live on her own, without a support team, we would need to see that she can take care of herself before she leaves the children's home. This would mean that Lucy would cook, clean, shop and handle her money responsibly on her own. She would also need to pick up and take her medication in the right order at the right time. We would need to be sure that Lucy can look after herself without the help of her support team. **Next Steps** Starting straight after the meeting, Lucy's support team will only prompt Lucy when she asks for help or if they can see that she is in danger.

Table 5.2: Signs of Safety mapping (continued)

What are we worried about?	What is working well?	What needs to happen?
Complicating Factors Lucy's memory can change from day to day. Some days Lucy does not need much support from her team, and other days she does. The only person that Lucy has family time with is her dad. Lucy sometimes sees her dad. When he has been drinking lots of beer, she does not like to see him. Lucy makes friends very quickly and will give people who she thinks are her friends anything that they ask for. Lucy and her team do not have a clear outline about Lucy's capacity and learning journey into young adulthood.	Lucy is close to her previous foster carer, Mary, and to Mary's two children, Rose and Henry, who view Lucy as their sister. Although Lucy does not always agree with having a support team around her, she does understand that her team are there to help keep her safe.	For Sandra to visit Lucy tomorrow to speak to her about how she feels (outside of today's meeting) about seeing a medical person who she has not met before. The medical person will speak with Lucy and her team about things that she can do and things that she would like to do. The medical person will then think about whether Lucy can decide where to live on her own. For Lucy to carry on learning in her weekly keep safe sessions with Kristina and to continue to know more about the traffic light communication tool. Lucy to begin a life skills module next week with Rosie at the youth club each Wednesday. Lucy has said that she is happy to give feedback to Kristina and Sandra on a weekly basis about what she has learned. She has also agreed to cook for her team on a weekly basis.

Step 2 Judgement: scaling questions

Table 5.3: Signs of Safety scaling

On a scale of 1–10, where 10 means that Lucy is safe enough to live on her own and social care services can close this case, and 0 means that things are so bad for Lucy that she needs around-the-clock supervision, where do you rate this situation today?

Lucy 7

Mary (previous foster carer) 4

Kristina (Lucy's key worker) 5

Sandra (Lucy's social worker) 4

Rosie (Lucy's youth worker) 6

Henry (Lucy's foster brother) 6

Rose (Lucy's foster sister) 5

Chris (social worker for disability services) 3

Beth (social worker for adult social services) 6

Rebecca (Lucy's independent advocate) 5

Scaling questions

Scaling questions provide everyone involved with the opportunity to express their own opinion. They also respect people's differing points of view and give an understanding of individual safety thresholds. For example, in the case of Lucy, we could say to her key worker, 'Kristina, you have rated safety as currently being a 5. What would you need to see for this to move to a 6?' Knowing what increased safety looks like to her key worker gives Lucy a small, measurable, achievable, realistic target (SMART). SMART goals are tangible and focus on where people want to get to in building trust, hope and safety.

SoS language

The premise of SoS is building relationships, so the language used within the SoS framework should be clear, concise, simple and, most importantly, without professional jargon. Professionals often use abbreviations and technical terms which some clients do not understand. When people do not understand what is happening within the assessment process this can lead to anxiety, anger, mistrust and feelings of inadequacy.

Social workers using this framework should not make plans about clients and families without them present. When making decisions and carrying out assessments the language used throughout the process needs to be compiled in collaboration and in partnership using methods that clients understand. Building trust and showing respect are two fundamental principles needed in relationship building.

My Three Houses

The Three Houses is a tool to enable the voice of vulnerable people to be expressed, heard and brought to the key people in their life. Using this tool, professionals can explore their clients' worries and aspirations and the positive parts of their lives. Before Lucy visited the psychiatrist, Lucy and her social worker, Sandra, completed this work. Sandra spoke to Lucy about how this was a tool for her voice to be expressed. Lucy agreed for this work to be shared with the psychiatrist.

Lucy's Three Houses

Table 5.4: Signs of Safety Three Houses

Lucy's House of Good Things	Lucy's House of Worries	Lucy's House of Dreams
I like living at Wilton Children's Home. My room is how I planned it and I helped to decorate it. I like going to the youth club, and I like that I can go there and back on my own and do not have support workers with me when I am there. I like the apprenticeship that I am doing in youth support work. I like seeing Sandra once a week and going in her car and having long chats. I like the sessions that I have with Kristina, and I like that Kristina is my key worker. I like good memory days, they make me feel more normal and I like doing things for myself like shopping and cooking and sometimes, but not always, cleaning. I like it when Mary or Henry or Rose take me on holiday with them or when I go to their house for special occasions.	I worry that I will always have support staff around me and I will never live a normal life. I worry that people laugh at me because I am in care and I do not want to always be in care. I worry about when I have bad memory days and I cannot do the things that I can do on good memory days. I have bad dreams about bumping into the people who took me to their house and laughed at me and did bad things to me and took my money. I cry when I think about when I made Mary sad for always running away after the bad things happened. I panic if I see my dad when he has been drinking beer and I worry about my dad drinking lots of beer. I worry that I will never have a girlfriend or a boyfriend and that I will always be lonely. I get sad when I think about people who do not speak to me any more because I do not give them money.	I dream that one day I will be a paid youth worker, like Rosie. I dream that one day I will have a black poodle called Doodle. I dream that one day I will only ever have good memory days. I dream that one day I will live on my own with my boyfriend or girlfriend. We would go on holidays together on our own, and I would have lots of money from my job at the youth club. I dream that one day I will not have support workers around me all the time, especially the ones I have nothing in common with. I dream that one day my dad stops drinking beer and that we can have nice days out having picnics. I dream that my mum comes back to find me and she lives next door to me. I dream that I live on my own and that Kristina is my friend and not my support worker.

Lucy's journey ... so far

By using the SoS framework Lucy and her team had the tools to devise small, measurable, achievable realistic targets with clarity on who was doing what, why, when, where and how. Lucy had clarity, and her team had focus. They knew where they were heading and why.

Each danger statement was linked to a safety goal. In the case of Lucy, the first danger statement and safety goal were about Lucy keeping herself safe from others. The second danger statement and safety goal were about how Lucy could take care of herself.

By involving Lucy in the entire process and using tools such as Words and Pictures and My Three Houses, Lucy knew what was happening in her life and why, thus creating a sense of trust, stability, safety and responsibility. Lucy was at the centre of her safety plan; this helped her understand that the person who decided if this plan did or did not work was herself. It also meant that the safety plan clearly included her wishes and perspectives, which made it more robust and more likely to succeed.

SoS is not a shopping list of requirements that simply give instructions to people, such as 'Lucy to complete a youth support worker apprenticeship course'. A better example would be: 'Lucy is clear that she would like to earn her own money. For this to happen, Lucy can continue to engage in the youth support worker apprenticeship course at the youth club, and once completed, become a paid member of the team.' This statement explains cause and effect and is linked directly to safety planning or aspirations.

Shopping or to-do lists that state someone should do X, Y and Z without any rationale or cause and effect give them little motivation to move forward. The *impact* is the most crucial aspect and how this helps people move forward in their safety plan.

Lucy did visit the psychiatrist and continued to see the same psychiatrist on a yearly basis from the age of 16 through to 18. During each visit it was noted how Lucy's determination to learn and follow her safety plans combined with the robustness from her team was enabling her to edge closer and closer to achieving her safety goals.

The brain injury that Lucy sadly suffered as a young child did affect her learning and development, but it did not stop her from learning and developing. Lucy believed in herself and her team around her believed in her too. At the age of 18 it was discussed as a collective with Lucy present that, while her insight into keeping herself safe and taking care of herself had grown remarkably, she did still require a support team. The good news for Lucy was that this did not mean 24 hours a day. At the age of 18, having achieved clear goals within a SoS framework developed by herself and her team, Lucy moved into semi-supported accommodation provided by adult social care services.

Lucy now has a team around her when she needs them or if she is at risk. However, Lucy also has time to explore the world on her own as a young woman, continuing to live as independent a life as possible, with her house of dreams forever evolving, changing and growing. Lucy has not given up on the hope that one day she will live on her own independently, and neither has her support network.

Research

SoS is one of a number of practice frameworks designed to improve direct practice and outcomes for children and families who are involved with children's social work services. Many UK local authorities and other child welfare organisations adopted practice frameworks following the Munro review of child protection (Munro, 2011) and encouragement from Ofsted (the quality assurance agency) and the chief social worker for children's social work in England (Baginsky, Ixer et al, 2021). Baginsky, Hickman, Moriarty et al (2020) found that about two-thirds of English local authorities use SoS as their overall practice framework or use aspects of it in their child protection practice.

SoS has been taken up enthusiastically by many practitioners, who have found the approach to be relevant, refreshing and energising, and it has been promoted in a bottom-up way by workers who are committed to it. Baginsky et al (2017) identified a range of reasons given for its more systematic uptake by UK local authorities. These included: changing the organisational culture; improving consistency of practice; empowering families; simplifying existing systems; improving understanding of risk and risk management; and supporting practitioner morale, skills development, recruitment and retention. SoS came to the fore at a time when child protection services were open to changing their existing approaches, and it was seen as being able to drive front-line and systemic improvements.

White, Bell and Revell (2022) discuss that, although SoS has been widely introduced, there are two key concerns about the approach. These are about the practice limitations and the robustness of the evidence base to support claims of its efficacy.

Stanley and Mills (2014) found that some social workers were concerned that the approach was too optimistic about parents and diverted attention from the children and others raised concerns that they found using SoS challenging or inappropriate: for example, in families that were described as 'chaotic' or 'high-risk' (Baginsky, Hickman, Moriarty et al, 2020).

Revell (2019) also highlighted that, while SoS clearly enabled workers to have difficult conversations with parents, there was a danger that it could become yet another standardised tool that marginalises professional judgement. The framework in the example used to capture the three main elements of SoS (what are we worried about?, what's going well? and what needs to happen?) may oversimplify the complexity of data collection and analysis and may result in vital information being excluded, particularly by novice practitioners who have not benefited from a grounding in more in-depth, holistic assessment (Baginsky, Manthorpe et al, 2021).

The growing prevalence of SoS in practice may appear out of step with the evidence base for its efficacy. It has been criticised as under-researched, with over-reliance on small-scale evaluations, which have often lacked independence, such that, 'support for SOS has tended to rest heavily on practice wisdom rather than research-based evidence' (Baginsky, Moriarty, and Manthorpe, 2019, p 108). SoS is a complex and relatively new intervention, not rigorously defined, and may be implemented differently in different care systems and areas, all of which make establishing its efficacy difficult (Sheehan et al, 2018). Baginsky et al (2017) undertook a large-scale independent evaluation of practice within ten English pilot sites. This provided multiple perspectives from managers, social workers and parents, but was not able to measure the long-term outcomes or any link between SoS and outcomes. Baginsky, Hickman, Harris et al (2020) subsequently found no strong evidence that SoS improved outcomes for children and families or impacted on staff turnover. While the approach was liked by social workers, they concluded that practitioner skill and competence were more significant than the specific approach used, and that adoption of SoS did not lead to consistent improvements in practice.

Conclusion

The implementation of SoS has been met with enthusiasm by practitioners, who find it an engaging and creative approach to managing difficult conversations and processes about danger and safety. It also seems to be popular with parents, carers, children and other users of services. Longer-term evaluations are necessary to understand the full impact of SoS in developing safety in families and reducing the need for more drastic intervention in their lives.

Key learning points

- SoS is a framework based on the practice of experienced child protection workers.

- It assesses both strengths and risks in developing safety plans.

- The worker co-creates safety with the service user.

- SoS is a clear and transparent approach, with specific and measurable goals.

- Practitioners find the approach helpful and hopeful.

- It can be used in a variety of situations with a range of service users.

- Research evidence for the efficacy of SoS is still developing.

Acknowledgement

The fictional case study part of this chapter, written by Lauren Bailey, was based on her experiences while working for social services in the overseas British territory of Gibraltar. Lauren would like to express her gratitude for the support received from the service during this time, for being given the autonomy to think creatively and for the budget to commission an external SoS consultant to assist in extending this framework to adult and disability services.

Further reading

Turnell, A. and Edwards, S. (1999) *Signs of Safety: A Solution and Safety Oriented Approach to Child Protection*, New York: Norton.

Turnell, A. and Essex S. (2006) *Working with 'Denied' Child Abuse: The Resolutions Approach*, Buckingham: Open University Press.

Turnell, A. and Murphy, T. (2017) (4th edn) *Signs of Safety Comprehensive Briefing Paper*, Perth: Resolutions.

6

Multisystemic therapy

Simone Fox, Mhairi Fleming and Anne Edmondson

Development of multisystemic therapy worldwide

Multisystemic therapy (MST) is a community-based, family intervention for young people with complex social, clinical and educational problems, such as aggression, substance misuse and offending behaviour. The main aim of MST is to reduce further challenging behaviour and to prevent out-of-home placements, either in care or custody. MST was developed in the USA in the late 1970s to address the limitations of traditional services working with young people with antisocial behaviour (Henggeler and Borduin, 1990). MST utilises a strengths-based approach by empowering families to make and sustain change and sees them as the key agents of change. One of the core treatment principles of MST focuses on identifying and leveraging existing positives and utilising systemic strengths to support change.

Since the first efficacy trial (Henggeler et al, 1986) and subsequent implementation of MST, the treatment has been expanded globally. There are now more than 550 MST programmes across 15 countries worldwide. A range of MST adaptations have also been developed to extend beyond working with young people with antisocial behaviour. These include MST-Problem Sexual Behaviour (MST-PSB; for example, Letourneau et al, 2009), MST for Child Abuse and Neglect (MST-CAN; for example, Swenson et al, 2010), MST-Building Stronger Families (Schaeffer et al, 2021, a programme for families experiencing child maltreatment and serious parent substance misuse), MST-Psychiatric (for example, Henggeler et al, 1999), MST-Health (diabetes; for example, Ellis et al, 2012 and obesity; for example, Naar-King et al, 2009) and MST-Family Integrated Transitions, which supports young people to return home of from residential or other out of home placements (MST-FIT; for example, Trupin et al, 2011).

MST has been extensively evaluated both by the model developers and by independent researchers. To date there have been over 85 published outcome, implementation and benchmarking studies conducted on MST with over 58,000 families included across the studies, including 28 randomised trials. In general, the MST research demonstrates a reduction in long-term re-arrest rates in studies with serious juvenile offenders, a reduction in out-of-home placements, improved family functioning, decreased substance misuse, fewer mental health problems and considerable cost savings (MST Services, 2021). MST has also demonstrated sustainable positive results in 22-year and 24.9-year follow-up studies with those who received MST having fewer arrests, fewer days in custody and fewer divorce, paternity or child support suits compared to management as usual (Sawyer and Borduin, 2011; Borduin et al, 2021).

Several meta-analyses and large-scale reviews of MST have been conducted by researchers associated with the treatment developers (for example, Curtis et al, 2004) and independent researchers (for example, Littell et al, 2005; van der Stouwe et al, 2014; Olsson et al, 2021). These meta-analyses have produced mixed results. Those in support of MST have found favourable outcomes for MST compared to usual services in terms of reducing 'out-of-home' placements, antisocial behaviour, substance abuse and improving family relationships (for example, Curtis et al, 2004; Schaeffer and Borduin, 2005; and van der Stouwe et al, 2014). In contrast, Littell et al's (2005 and 2021) meta-analytic reviews were less favourable regarding MST outcomes, suggesting that the evidence for MST was mixed, with inconsistent effects across studies. While the authors acknowledged that MST is widely regarded as a well-established evidence-based programme, they concluded that reductions in out-of-home placements and arrests/convictions observed in the US were not replicated in other high-income countries. The discrepancies between findings in Littell's meta-analyses could be due to a number of factors, including the earlier stage of implementation of MST, model infidelity (Löfholm et al, 2014) and countries outside the US offering strong alternatives to MST that make the comparison groups in trials a higher quality.

Overview of MST

MST is based on a social ecological model (Bronfenbrenner, 1979) and as such follows the assumption that antisocial behaviour is multi-determined and is related not only to the risk factors of the young person but also to the wider ecology around the young person such as the family, peer group, school and community (Henggeler et al, 2009). Thus, interventions need to be able to address these wider systemic risks as well as to identify and build on the strengths if they are going to be effective in reducing antisocial behaviour.

In the UK, an MST team consists of a supervisor and three to four therapists. Supervision is provided weekly on-site by the MST team supervisor and an off-site MST expert consultant. The therapist has a small caseload of four to six families and is in the main responsible for the delivery of the intervention with the family and systems around the young person. The intervention lasts for three to five months. Although the intervention is relatively brief, the process is intensive and involves multiple contacts each week between the therapist and the family. Families have access to an MST therapist 24 hours a day, seven days a week, for several key purposes such as removing barriers to service access, enhancing therapeutic engagement and responding in times of crises.

The majority of the intervention is carried out with the primary caregivers, who are seen as the main agent of change. The interventions are focused on empowering the caregivers through the acquisition of skills to manage their child's behaviour effectively (Henggeler et al, 2009). As such, the MST therapist works with the family to overcome barriers that prevent effective caregiving and management of child behaviour (for example, systematic monitoring, reward and discipline systems, supporting caregivers to improve communication and problem-solve day-to-day conflicts). The theory is that, as the caregivers' effectiveness increases, so will their impact on the other systems around the young person, thus reducing the risk of challenging behaviour.

Theoretical orientation and principles

MST incorporates an MST analytic process and nine treatment principles. These principles are described in Table 6.1 (Henggeler et al, 2009). The reciprocal nature of interactions is embedded within social-ecology theory. Understanding how individuals view their current situation and understanding what they would like to see change are necessary throughout the course of treatment. The MST analytic process starts with understanding the range of behaviours that has brought the young person to be referred. The therapist will begin by collecting desired outcomes from the family and key stakeholders involved, including social care, the school and other professionals. From these, a number of overarching goals are co-created which are the goals that the family will work towards to inform treatment success. During the assessment process the therapist gathers sequences from multiple perspective to inform the 'fit' of the referral behaviour. The 'fit circle' is a conceptualisation of the presenting issue with drivers from multiple systems that might contribute to the behaviour. These drivers will then be prioritised and guide the intervention process, which will be regularly reviewed to identify barriers and advances to progress.

The therapist draws on a number of evidence-based models, including cognitive, behavioural and structural and strategic family therapy. The intervention is idiosyncratic to the needs of each family and is guided by the assessment and the fit.

Multisystemic therapy for child abuse and neglect (MST-CAN)

As mentioned earlier, there are a range of MST adaptations that focus on the needs of different families. One of these adaptations is MST-CAN, which is designed to address the main risk factors associated with physical abuse and/ or neglect of children. In a five-year randomised effectiveness trial, MST-CAN had a 98 per cent recruitment and retention rate compared to 83 per cent with the Enhanced Outpatient Treatment (Swenson et al, 2010). Seventy-eight per cent of the families participating were from diverse backgrounds, primarily

Table 6.1: The MST nine treatment principles

1. Finding the fit
   The assessment process aims to understand the factors (or drivers) that contribute to the problems. This is called 'the fit'.

2. Positive and strength-focused
   Therapeutic contact should emphasise the positive and use systemic strengths as levers for change.

3. Increasing responsibility
   Interventions are designed to increase responsible and decrease irresponsible behaviour among family members.

4. Present-focused, action-oriented and well-defined
   Interventions focus on what is happening in the here and now, with therapists having clear action steps to take immediately with a clear and well-defined target.

5. Targeting sequences
   Interventions target sequences of behaviour within and between multiple systems that maintain identified problems.

6. Developmentally appropriate
   Therapists work hard to ensure interventions are understood and appropriate to the needs of the caregiver and young person.

7. Continuous effort
   Interventions are designed to required daily or weekly effort by family members.

8. Evaluation and accountability
   Intervention effectiveness is evaluated continuously from multiple perspectives, with providers assuming accountability for overcoming barriers to progress.

9. Generalisation
   Interventions are designed to give the caregivers the skills to continue addressing behaviours upon treatment completion.

African American. Follow-up 16 months post-baseline demonstrated, relative to a rigorous comparison group, greater reductions in out-of-home placements and in maltreatment by parent (mild and severe assaults, psychological aggression and neglectful parenting) and greater increases in natural social supports. Both caregivers and young people experienced improvement with mental health difficulties, in particular trauma symptoms.

There are similarities and differences with the standard MST and MST-CAN clinical structure. As with standard MST, the majority of the work with MST-CAN families is conducted in their homes, with sessions typically a minimum of three times per week, reducing towards end of treatment. All families have access to 24/7 on-call support. Caseloads are slightly lower, with up to four families per therapist and treatment length is longer (six to nine months as opposed to three to five months). The treatment team is comprised of three therapists, frequently social work qualified professionals, a full-time supervisor, a family resource specialist worker, and 20 per cent full-time equivalent psychiatrist or psychiatric nurse prescriber.

In MST-CAN referrals are due to caregiver behaviours of child abuse or neglect. As a result, this model includes a great deal of individual caregiver treatment to reduce risk. Therapists assume the lead responsibility for developing interventions alongside families. Strength-based practice is vital in the creation of interventions leveraging the existing skills, interests and ideas of family members and their wider support system. The family resource specialist works across all families to support with practical needs and skill development such as housing, budgeting, gaining employment and technology. Therapists and family resource specialists complete drug-testing protocols when caregiver substance misuse is a referral concern. Psychiatric support contributes to the assessment of underlying mental health concerns, medication oversight and support for life-threatening risks.

Families referred are involved with the social care system, often with many children on a second child protection plan. Some families are at the door of court, and pre-proceedings have been initiated. Social workers refer families to MST-CAN with recommendations for changes needed and the desire for the families to care for their children safely at home. Families are referred when there is a new credible report of physical abuse and/or neglect within the previous 180 days. All family members will be included in the treatment process. At least one child in the family will be within the age range of 0–17 years. While MST-CAN is typically an edge-of-care service, there are times when children may need to be temporarily placed for their immediate safety. MST-CAN may begin working with families prior to a child's return home provided there is a clear short-term plan for reunification.

Within this model, there are four overarching goals central to the work with families. These are: 1) to keep families together safely; 2) to prevent re-abuse and neglect; 3) to reduce mental health difficulties experienced by adults and children; and 4) to increase natural supports (Swenson et al, 2018).

As keeping the children's safety is at the forefront of all work, the MST-CAN team complete safety-related assessments at the start of treatment. An intake safety checklist involves direct observation of the home with the primary caregivers to assess for items and behaviours of family members that may be harmful to children. An initial safety plan with the caregiver, children and extended family members is developed to address immediate risks. Additional assessment measures to consider practical needs and the family's access to resources and activities within the community occur early in treatment.

In addition to the range of treatment options within MST, MST-CAN incorporates evidenced-based treatments to address common risk factors associated with child abuse and neglect. Reinforcement-Based Therapy (Tuten et al, 2012) is a treatment programme designed for adults who misuse substances. After completing a functional analysis with the caregiver, the therapist and caregiver co-create alternative activities and strategies to address their specific triggers for substance misuse. Activities are chosen based on the strengths and interests of the caregiver and include recreational and vocational activities. As relapse is a part of recovery, safety plans are created with caregivers and their social networks, so a sober adult has responsibility for the children when a caregiver is using. A voucher system is in place to recognise caregiver progress as they abstain from substance use.

For several years, trauma-informed practice has influenced a variety of helping professions. Within MST-CAN there are two evidenced-based interventions for adults and children who experience continued symptoms following traumatic events. With children and young people, Trauma-Focused Cognitive Behavioural Therapy (Cohen et al, 2017) can be provided. Young people develop skills to manage recurring symptoms, and caregivers learn strategies to support their children. Prolonged Exposure Therapy (Foa et al, 2019) helps adults learn to manage and resolve trauma symptoms through psycho-education, *in vivo* and imaginal exposure activities and cognitive processing.

If a primary referral concern involves the use of aggression by an adult or young person, an individualised CBT-based anger management programme can be completed. Family communication skills and problem-solving strategies offer the space for all voices in the family to be heard and for positive communication skills to be either enhanced or developed. As children often internalise responsibility for the actions of their caregivers, a clarification and healing process is completed. Within this process, caregivers take responsibility for the abuse and/or neglect. This process makes clear to children that they were not responsible for the actions of the caregivers and gives them the opportunity for questions to be answered. Families often experience this as a vital step in their healing.

Integral to this model is collaboration with both family members and social care. Throughout treatment, therapists collaborate with family members with each of the goals and plans. As noted in 'Working Together to Safeguard Children', regular reviews with multiple professionals are needed to assess if there is developmental progress towards goals or if a child is continuing to be harmed or is at risk of harm (HM Government, 2018). When experiencing adversity, some caregivers may experience difficulty retaining important discussion points or action steps created during core group meetings. Therapists often invite caregivers to reflect on the social work processes and expected changes in order to step down from social care involvement. To prepare for core group meetings, therapists encourage caregivers to consider their questions for social workers and other professionals. Caregivers subsequently can be empowered to share their perspective with increased confidence and gain clarity for points they do not understand in respectful ways.

Development of MST within the UK

The first MST teams in the UK were started in 2000, and by 2008 an additional ten teams were funded (see Fox and Ashmore, 2011). In 2009 the first team was set up in Scotland and the adaptation, MST-CAN, was introduced to the UK. By 2012 there were enough MST teams in the UK to form a network partnership, which meant oversight and leadership of the UK MST teams moved from the US to the UK. In 2017 MST-UK agreed to support teams in the Republic of

Ireland, which then formed the MST UK&I network partnership. In 2020 the first team in Wales was developed. There are now 36 active MST, MST-CAN and MST-FIT teams across the UK and Ireland (http://www.mstuk.org/mst-uk/mst-uk-teams).

Workforce and social work context

The MST workforce in the UK and Ireland is made up of professionals from a multi-disciplinary background, including social work, psychology, family therapy, cognitive behavioural therapy, occupational therapy, education, youth justice and other degree-level applied allied professions.

MST teams are implemented in a number of ways, with many teams embedded in local authority children's services. These teams can either be fully funded and integrated into children and family departments or funded on a fixed-term basis either by local or national funding. Some teams are implemented by third-sector organisations who provide a commissioned service to a specific local authority. In these teams the MST staff are employed by the third-sector organisation but work with children, young people and their families within a specific local authority area in collaboration with local authority staff. In Wales, some staff are employed through the health trusts.

Communication between MST teams and social care is frequent, and safety plans to address significant risk factors created with the families are reviewed between professionals and the families together. Daily to weekly communication between the MST-CAN team and children's social workers facilitates a partnership and collaboration on the goals of intervention (Hebert et al, 2014). This communication of contextual information has been found to increase social workers' understanding of clients and increase positive feedback to the child protection workers (Hebert et al, 2014).

Referrals to MST

Families are referred to MST teams in a variety of ways, often via an allocated social worker. Some MST teams have a direct referral process where professionals (most often the allocated social worker) can directly refer a family to MST. Other teams may be part of a referral panel process, where children, young people and their families are referred (by an allocated lead professional) to a panel where referral information is discussed and then directed to the service that best meets the needs of the family. Following any of the referral processes, the MST supervisor then undertakes an assessment to ensure MST is the best service for the family by ensuring they meet the inclusionary criteria and do not meet exclusionary criteria. This often involves meeting the family and gaining their consent and agreement to begin work with MST. From the earliest point of an MST team learning about a family, a strengths-based approach is implemented to empower the family to make decisions about working with MST, to find out baseline strengths from as many perspectives as possible and to develop a collaborative approach with all key participants (Fox and Ashmore, 2014).

Young people being referred to MST are frequently assessed as being at risk of family breakdown and on the edge of being placed into local authority care or at risk of custody/secure care. There could be a variety of legal and safeguarding measures in place, ranging from young people whose caregivers wish to give voluntary consent to placing the young person in care, on a child protection plan (England) or on the Child Protection Register (Wales and Scotland) or subject to children's court orders. In Scotland young people coming into MST may be referred to the Children's Reporter or be subject to an order from the children's hearing system. Across the UK and Ireland some young people referred to MST may be subject to court orders and have specific bail conditions, such as curfew, restriction of movement orders and residence conditions.

MST's strengths-based approach in the context of UK social work

Social work practice in the UK has always been grounded in policy and legislation and increasingly informed by evidence and research. As frameworks evolve and new evidence emerges, the need for new and creative evidence-based and evidence-informed ways of working grows. Strengths-based approaches are one such result of this shifting and evolving context.

The implementation of the Care Act in 2014 in England, Social Services and Well-Being Act (Wales) (2014) and the Carers Act (Scotland) (2016) was a pivotal driver for change. They all stress that strengths-based approaches in relation to assessments and interventions are one of the key principles, along with collaboration, prevention and personalisation.

The second treatment principle of MST emphasises that all aspects of MST should be strengths-based. Therapists communicate a positive and optimistic perspective to the family and other members of the young person's ecology throughout the assessment and treatment process. Strengths-based approaches are shown to be effective in developing and maintaining hope in individuals, and consequently many studies cite evidence for enhanced wellbeing (Smock et al, 2008). Therapists look for potential strengths across the different systems, the individual young person, the family, peers, school and community. Supporting a family to recognise their own strengths and capabilities has been shown to promote their own sense of wellbeing (Park and Peterson, 2006) and allows the MST therapist to identify specific strengths that can be leveraged in interventions. For example, through work with the therapist, a member of the extended family might be identified as the best person to help monitor the young person at high-risk times when the young person is most likely to associate with negative peers, giving practical support during these times and leveraging an already positive and established relationship between the young person and the extended family member. The MST intervention might go as far as to detail the activities and shared interest the two may have and detail step-by-step plans on how to provide monitoring, schedule activities and assess potential barriers to problem-solve in advance. This intervention is leveraging strengths in the natural ecology while problem-solving a time of high conflict between the young person and their primary caregiver. A strengths-based perspective is anchored in the belief that a problem does not define a person's life, and MST therapists start with the underlying assumption that everyone is doing their best in the specific circumstances they are in. This does not mean challenges or risks are ignored, a common critique of strengths-based approaches (McMillen, Morris and Sherraden, 2004), but that a focus is placed on what a family and young person can do rather than on what they can't, on what they have rather than on what they lack and on successes rather than failures (Henggeler et al, 2009). Strengths-based approaches assume that, when families are given positive support, they have the inherent power to change their own lives (Greene, 1999) and that this is linked to more positive outcomes (Greenberg and Pinsof, 1986). This approach also supports sustainability of change and reduces reliance on professional services for progress to be maintained as the family themselves are empowered and taught independence whenever possible.

Case study 1 – standard MST

Nicole, aged 16, was referred to MST by social care due to concerns around several missing episodes, substance misuse (including at parties in different cities), school non-attendance and aggression in the home. She was deemed at high risk of criminal exploitation, and there were concerns that she was being groomed by older females.

The MST therapist met with the mum and stepdad, Nicole and professionals to gather their goals for treatment. Sessions were initially three times a week with caregivers and occasionally Nicole, as well as other agencies (including school and the police) to understand Nicole's behaviour from a systemic approach. The therapist gathered sequences around each of the referral behaviours to help understand the 'fit' of that behaviour. A number of drivers were identified, including low supervision and monitoring, parents not obtaining information before Nicole went out, unclear expectations of what was expected of Nicole and poor emotional regulation. These also linked to school-related drivers of poor morning routine, inconsistent and unclear expectations around school and low supervision and monitoring in the morning. To target the aggression at home, sequences were reviewed to support caregivers to recognise how their role might contribute to an increase in Nicole's aggression and support with de-escalating behaviours. A safety plan was collaboratively developed with the family which aimed to de-escalate situations quickly, safely and calmly through communication and recognition of the triggers of aggression. The plan included supporting caregivers with alternative scripts of how they could respond to

Nicole differently, drawing on the principles of authoritative caregiving – being firm but warm and identifying when to use the MST on-call service. The therapist also worked with Nicole to develop alternative strategies to help her manage her emotions such as practising relaxation techniques, identifying her triggers and supporting Nicole by advocating to caregivers the support she needed from them. This plan was reviewed regularly with all family members. Family sessions became a safe place for everyone to express how they were feeling and to perspective take and explore ways they would all work together to resolve conflict and increase the warmth between them, including building their communication and coping skills.

Another safety plan was developed with the family and multiple agencies to minimise Nicole's associations with certain peers in the community, targeting the behaviours around going out. This contained retrieval steps for caregivers to bring Nicole home if she did not return on time or left home without permission. Caregivers were supported in gathering information of any known addresses of associated peers/caregiver contact details by working closely with the social worker, missing teams worker, school and police. The family were encouraged to close down opportunities leading to Nicole going missing, which included increasing supervision at these risky times. School would update caregivers when Nicole did not arrive at school which would trigger off the retrieval process. Collaborative working with the social worker, support worker, police and missing team helped caregivers identify and assess risk around certain peers, build networks with peers' caregivers and look at contextual factors that were associated with the negative peer group.

To reduce Nicole spending time with peers engaged in negative behaviours, the therapist, mum and school explored ways Nicole could be supported going back into school. Morning observations conducted in the family home showed an inconsistent morning routine and mum not being present at home in the morning. The therapist and mum worked together to adapt mum's working schedule so that she could have more of a presence at home to ensure that Nicole's morning went as smoothly as possible. School made adjustments to Nicole's diary to allow her to start school slightly later to avoid meeting certain peers and supported her to complete her Year 11 work with minimal distractions in school.

Direct work was completed with Nicole to explore characteristics of a positive peer group and explore her relationships with certain peers who were identified not to always have her best interests at heart. Using sequences and situations that occurred with her peers, Nicole's thought process was challenged to help her see how her misplaced loyalty to certain peers would put her in risky and dangerous situations. Nicole was supported to make more informed and safer choices when with certain peers and troubleshoot how she would deal with these situations if they arose through role plays to increase her confidence. Mum was included in sessions to continue supporting Nicole to troubleshoot situations together and guide Nicole to make positive decisions. Nicole changed her mobile number and deleted social media from her phone. In addition to this, alternative positive activities for Nicole were identified to occupy her time. At the weekend, mum took Nicole to work on the allotments to earn extra pocket money.

A behavioural contract was developed with caregivers and Nicole to address her referral behaviours. This was reviewed weekly to ensure its success.

Towards closure, sustainability plans were developed to support Nicole and her family to continue gains made post-MST. These plans covered scenarios and step-by-step plans of solutions the family and Nicole would undertake to overcome difficult situations in the future. By the end of 20 weeks, Nicole had abstained from smoking cannabis and remained at home more with her caregivers. Relationships had improved, they were no longer arguing and Nicole was no longer going missing. Nicole successfully finished Year 11 and was successful in gaining a place at college.

Case study 2 – MST-CAN

A father (Joe) and his two children (Michael, 13, and Mia, seven) were referred to the MST-CAN team when children's social care were considering applying for a court order for Michael and Mia to remove them from their dad's care. Prior to MST-CAN involvement, adult family members had been staying at the home and using substances. The father had already made great strides in ensuring these adult family members were living elsewhere and the children were no longer exposed to substance use prior to MST-CAN involvement. Social care referred this family to MST-CAN, hoping that sufficient changes could be made to prevent these children entering the care system. At the time of the referral, social care was worried about the cleanliness of the home and the impact this had on the children. The home was particularly sparse following the removal of essential furniture after a bed bug infestation. Many of these items were in the back garden awaiting removal. Children were often seen in unclean clothing and often reported being hungry. The children were often significantly late for school and sometimes missed full days. Fit factors for the referral behaviours included Joe's struggles with depression and anxiety. He reported daily sleep difficulties due to worrying thoughts and was often too tired in the morning to ensure the children went to school. Other fit factors were based on this father's childhood and early adult life. He had not learned skills of providing healthy meals, routines, maintaining cleanliness in the home and financial planning.

At the start of treatment, the therapist met with the family, social work and school personnel to clarify referral concerns, discuss everyone's desired outcomes of treatment and develop a comprehensive strengths and needs assessment. A practical needs assessment completed with the father helped identify some of the essential items needed within the home. The therapist and family resource specialist worked with Joe to devise a schedule for clearing out the back garden, acquiring funding for immediate need items and budgeting to ensure healthy food would be provided to the children.

Early in treatment, the therapist met with all family members to discuss their communication patterns. Within this meeting, the children were given the space for their voices to be heard. Joe listened attentively to his children's needs. This open dialogue within the family started to shift the family communication patterns so difficulties could be discussed and problems solved. In time, this problem-solving framework extended to include the mother, who lived elsewhere.

The process of establishing goals early on in treatment, together with the father and family members, was continued as the family worked to address all referral concerns. This theme of collaborative goal generation that emphasised what the father wanted to see change, in addition to what social care needed, began the shift from a father who struggled with constant worries to a father who could evaluate experiences, establish goals and create small steps to achieve these goals. He developed routines for cleaning, food shopping and the family's morning and evening.

In his childhood, the father had lived in unkempt conditions. This had become the life to which he was accustomed. Within six months of starting treatment, this father made significant improvements for the care of his children. The children lived in a safe, clean home, they had healthy food options and they were attending school consistently. Joe was managing his anxiety with CBT anxiety management skills, goal creation, routines, a healthy sleep schedule and consistent medication compliance, with regular monitoring with his GP. The children remained living safely with the father, who loved them.

Conclusion

Over the last 20 years MST has expanded significantly across the UK and Ireland. There are now over 36 MST standard and adaptions delivering interventions to children and families who are at high risk of care. The evidence base for MST is strong, particularly from the USA. More research is needed into the implementation of MST and the adaptations to specific populations in the UK. MST fits very well with a positive, strengths-based approach and draws upon the individual, carer and systems capabilities to inform and develop interventions. As the body of evidence grows to support the effectiveness of strength-based approaches like MST, so policy, legislation and social work frameworks will shift towards commissioning these approaches in their spectrum of services, empowering those in need of support, shifting the balance of care and developing services that focus on prevention, independence and sustainability.

Key learning points

- MST is a community, family intervention for young people on the edge of care or custody.
- It is well evidenced and has delivered in over 15 countries worldwide.
- There are several adaptations, including MST child abuse and neglect.

- MST draws on the systems around the young person, including the family, the peer group, school and community.

- MST leverages the strengths within each of the systems to implement change.

Acknowledgements

We would like to thank the two families, teams and therapists who participated in the writing of this chapter. We have not named anyone in order to protect anonymity. Thank you also to Cynthia Swenson, Joanne Penman and Cathy James for reading drafts of this chapter.

Further reading

Henggeler, S.W., Schoenwald, S.K., Borduin, C.M., Rowland, M.D. and Cunningham, P.B. (2009) (2nd edn) *Multisystemic Therapy for Children and Adolescents*, New York and London: The Guilford Press.

Swenson, C.C. and Schaeffer, C.M. (2018) 'A multisystemic approach to the prevention and treatment of child abuse and neglect', *International Journal on Child Maltreatment: Research, Policy and Practice*, 1(1): https://link.springer.com/article/10.1007/s42448-018-0002-2

www.mstuk.org

www.mstservices.com

7

A narrative approach to social work

Michaela Rogers and Jennifer Cooper

Introduction

Scholarship has long since documented the narrative turn (the use of narrative concepts and methods across an array of disciplines). This chapter will discuss the influence of a narrative turn in strengths-based social work, arguing that social work is intrinsically a 'narrative activity' (Baldwin, 2013). To understand narrative, it is critical to grasp its plurality. Indeed, narrative is found in a range of forms, as literary critic Roland Barthes noted in 1977:

> Narrative is first and foremost a prodigious variety of genres, themselves distributed amongst different substances … narrative is present in myth, legend, fable, tale, novella, epic, history, tragedy, drama, comedy, mime, painting … stained glass windows, cinema, comics, news item, conversation. (Barthes, 1977, p 79)

The point is that narratives are present in various formats and central to life itself, as Barthes also reminded us that 'narrative is present in every age, in every place, in every society'. It is obvious then that narrative should also be integral to social work practice. Indeed, the workings of social work depend on language in both written and spoken forms. Moreover, human beings are natural storytellers, and the everyday use of language, through talk and text, is critical in enabling people to tell the stories of their lives. Reflecting strengths-based practice, taking a narrative approach in social work contrasts with the so-called traditional approach, which positions professionals as experts, by positioning the person with lived experience (the person receiving support) as the expert and storyteller. Social work practitioners then retell that story or work with people to retell, or reauthor, that story. These processes are termed 'narrative practice', which refers to the activity of storytelling, the resources used to tell stories and the conditions under which stories are told (Gubrium and Holstein, 2009).

The ways in which people construct and share stories about themselves is critical in how they detail particular events and periods of time and in describing what these experiences mean; people engage in a process of sense-making. However, there is currently no consensus on what narrative 'is' or how narratives should be analysed (Ahmed, 2015). It is common to find debates about the very meaning of the terms 'story' and 'narrative', and their distinctions. For brevity, in this chapter we will use the terms interchangeably as this type of usage is also reflected in the literature on narrative approaches to social work.

To understand the value of narrative practice in social work, it is important to grasp the basic principles and concepts of narrativity, and we begin the chapter by describing the structural elements of narrative. Second, we provide an overview of master-narratives and counter-narratives to offer a framework for understanding contrasting narratives and interpretation as a process of meaning-making and as a process of understanding. We then move to talk about a narrative approach to social work in general before providing a more detailed account of narrative tools and techniques for practice.

Narrative concepts and methods

There are various concepts associated with narrative, and these are briefly described here. First, and fundamental to storytelling or constructing a narrative, is *plot*. Put simply, plot represents the twists and turns of a story as a dynamic sequencing of events. This sequencing, or arrangement of events, can take many forms. For example, literary scholarship outlines different types of plot as illustrated in Booker's (2004) typology, which describes, in detail, seven common story plots, including:

- overcoming the monster (from the bad guy to the hero);
- rags to riches (detailing crisis and success);
- the quest (on seeking and finding);
- voyage and return (detailing a bold exploration or journey);
- comedy (from confusion to enlightenment);
- tragedy (the price of fatal flaws);
- rebirth (about finding the personal light).

To understand how analysing plot enables deeper insights into a person's experiences, see Ahmed and Rogers's (2017) paper, which examines the narrative of Polly, a male-to-female trans woman, and her gender migration journey using the plot typology 'the quest'. In their analysis, Ahmed and Rogers point out the value of narrative to social work while also noting that narratives are not, and cannot be, separated from the context in which they are told. They argue that the value of analysing stories is in gaining an understanding of an individual's unique biographical account, and in many cases, and certainly for Polly, it is also in giving voice to seldom heard communities.

Second, the importance of *characters* and *characterisation* is self-evident as without believable characters any 'narrative [would] fall flat' (Baldwin, 2013, p 15). There are debates, however, about whether narrative relies on being plot-driven or character-driven. In actuality, both are critical. Here the role of social work is to identify characters, their role, relevance and characteristics, to understand their perspectives and actions within a particular social and cultural context (the setting). It is important to understand characters are *forming*, rather than *formed*. This requires an acknowledgement that an individual is complex and multifaceted, not two-dimensional and fully developed (and thus incapable of change). The capacity for change must be foregrounded in an analysis of character as this is essential to practice.

Third, the term *genre* refers to the style or content of a text. This is easily understood when thinking about films or books, which come in different forms such as comedy, horror or science fiction. In social work it is helpful to think of different formats for narrative as providing frameworks for sense-making and meaning. Moreover, the products of social work (case records, court reports, assessments) can be considered as constitutive of a particular genre. When the people we are working with engage in narrative activity, often they will engage in storytelling, reflecting a particular genre, and often the story is rehearsed; it has been told on several occasions.

Fourth, the notion of *authorship* holds significance in social work as it requires a consideration of the author as the originator or producer of the story as opposed to the *audience* (who are the consumers of the story) (Baldwin, 2013). This is important as the author has the power to affect or persuade the audience in particular ways. It is also important to remember that the author may tell a story in one way to a particular audience (the social worker) and in another way to a different audience (their family). Moreover, the author has the power to construct, deconstruct and reconstruct a story.

Finally, there are two important concepts with regard to voice and authorship that were identified by Bakhtin (1986). These are *polyphony* and *heteroglossia*. Polyphony refers to the expression of multiple voices or perspectives within a narrative. These voices or perspectives are not necessarily those of the author but are those which are privileged by the author and given equal status. Heteroglossia is also an important concept which describes the coexistence of distinct and different social meanings that are embedded within a single text or story. Both are salient in social work practice as the co-presence of different perspectives or voices (polyphony), which may or may not reflect different sociocultural understandings (heteroglossia), and often play an important role in the life of someone who is receiving support or working with a social worker, or play a critical role in the social worker process of assessment and planning.

Master narrative and counter-narrative

It is important to draw attention to two oppositional narrative forms: master narratives and counter-narratives. As narratives offer a framework in which people can make sense of their experiences, it is possible to identify master narratives: those dominant frameworks which embed normative ideology and perspectives. A counter-narrative offers an alternative way of organising and interpreting experience in contrast to the master (or dominant) narrative. The key learning points box overleaf explains two oppositional narrative frameworks in relation to domestic abuse victims/survivors and perpetrators.

Key learning points

Master narratives versus counter-narratives

A master narrative is in operation that details who is a domestic abuse victim/survivor and who is a domestic abuse perpetrator. This master narrative has been called the 'public story' of domestic abuse (Donovan and Hester, 2014). The master narrative embeds a normative assumption that domestic abuse is predominantly physical violence perpetrated by heterosexual men against heterosexual women of child-bearing age. As a result of this public story (or master narrative), the experiences of minoritised victims/survivors have been neglected and marginalised. This includes older adults who have been described as 'hidden' or 'forgotten' victims (Rogers and Taylor, 2019). The story of an older adult who is a victim/survivor of domestic abuse which does not reflect the characterisation and cultural context of the public story can be said to be a counter-narrative. This offers a different version of domestic abuse, albeit one which is less heard and does not reflect the normative, dominant narrative which conveys strong messages about what domestic abuse is (for example, physical violence) and in terms of who is the typical victim/survivors, and who is the typical perpetrator (a younger, heterosexual couple). A significant consequence of the master narrative in this example is the routine absence from domestic abuse and sexual violence research, policy and practice of older victims/survivors, and this has been drawn into sharp focus within academic literature (Rogers and Taylor, 2019).

The ways in which master and counter-narratives operate within social work practice is salient. For example, think about how social workers based in children's social care services have to make professional judgements and everyday decisions about children's wellbeing and parents' capacity to care appropriately and adequately. Reflect on the notion of 'good enough' in relation to parenting practices. There is a narrative framework about 'good enough' parenting which establishes a (subjective) benchmark that social workers employ. In actuality, a social worker might deem another adult's parenting as 'good enough', making sense of it through the master narrative of acceptable parenting that is employed in social work practice (although it might not be good enough for their own child). In a different scenario, a health visitor might deem a mother or father's parenting as not 'good enough', but a social worker might disagree and judge the parenting in such a case to be adequate.

This draws attention to different narrative frameworks found across disciplines. Furthermore, think about a parent who takes their child to live in a commune, and embraces a group approach to parenting (in that all commune members parent their child) with informal everyday learning in the environment of the commune (for example, learning how to live off the land) as more beneficial than formal education (for example, acquiring a traditional school education). Making sense of this 'alternative' lifestyle draws upon a counter-narrative of family living as the more dominant master narrative of family reflects a much more conservative version of family configuration and practices: that is, a typical family is constituted by birth parents, their children (usually 2.4) and a dog/cat, and they all live together in a house with a garden and a white picket fence. Stereotypes are often foregrounded through or underpin master narratives.

The development of narrative approaches in social work

Put simply, the process of narrating can be understood as a mechanism through which people examine their lives and gain understanding of the social and material worlds in which their experiences are set, and it is the process of analysing narratives that gives voice to the complexity and contextuality of people's experiences (Ahmed, 2015). This is important because narrative, as a feature of someone's biography or experience, has complex, intersecting structural, cultural, temporal and spatial contexts. Narratives are subjective accounts, rooted in time and space, and as such they are inevitably perspective-laden and often linked to culture, history or structural influence, such as social norms, politics and privilege. Narratives are understood against a backdrop of different social systems, whether this might be that of a family, community or wider society.

To understand this further in relation to social work, it is useful to acknowledge the influence of narrative therapy. The most widely acknowledged pioneers of narrative therapy are White and Epston (1990), who developed the model drawing on White's interests in family therapy and sociological approaches. The family therapy approach 'looks at problems within the systems of relationships in which they occur and aims to promote change by intervening in the broader system rather than the individual alone' (Burnham, 1984, p 2, cited by Walker, 2012). Such systems reflect structures and culture and are set with spatial and temporal contexts. A narrative approach to social work takes a similar stance in terms of locating problems in social-cultural contexts, and in attempting to look at problems as entities in themselves; the problem is the problem, rather than a failing in the person themselves. Additionally, as accounts of someone's life, such narratives are made sense of in relation to society, culture, time and spatial contexts.

Undoubtedly the family therapy model has influenced more contemporary models for practice. For example, systemic practice, aka the 'Hackney Model' (Goodman and Trowler, 2012), requires the identification of systems within which a person exists and of the influences these systems have on them – either through our interactions with the system or through the influence of another system. The process of narrating reflects how an individual makes sense of these experiences and how systems have impacted on them, as well as their interactions with different systems. However, how we view ourselves may be quite different from how others view us; this can be both helpful and problematic. A narrative approach to social work enables the exploration of a story from multiple perspectives, inviting alternative views (or counter-narratives). It also offers a useful and constructive model for practice that views 'the problem as the problem' – a feature of a story – rather than an intrinsic aspect of the self.

No approach or model should be used uncritically. Walker (2012) asks whether externalising a problem may absolve a person from responsibility for their own actions. Does discussing substance misuse and alcohol dependency as the problem, rather than resulting from the individual's decision-making and actions, assist or support our understanding? Does 'the problem' become the responsibility of others rather than the person taking responsibility for their own behaviour? There is also the issue of other people creating a negative picture, or narrative identity, of another through their storytelling. For example, the carers of Daniel Pelka created a narrative whereby the identity of Daniel was that of a 'naughty boy' who stole food in school whereas an alternative story would depict Daniel as a 'neglected boy' who stole food in school because he was not cared for and fed at home. Narrative identity is another useful concept, but it is important to remember that narrative identity is not fixed, nor does it have an essence (Ahmed, 2015); it is constructed, multiple and dynamic. In social work there is a danger in not questioning narratives constructed by others, and there is a clear need for professional curiosity in narrative practice.

Using a narrative approach in practice

Personal narratives are developed through the process of interpreting and examining experiences. Narratives can require further interpretation externally as well as internally, and that is part of the role of a social worker – to understand and interpret the narrative of the people they are working with. The way a person recalls an event, the way something happened, how it happened and why it happened is unique as it is the person's perspective which is shaped by their individual experience. How you remember a situation may be very different from how someone else remembers the same situation. This is the same for the people social workers work with on a day-to-day basis, so to receive two (or more) conflicting versions of the same event is not unusual (and an example of polyphony within a narrative about an event). Working with people means dealing with the fallibility of memory, or people attempting to protect themselves by trying to manage their story to make them look favourable, and understanding that people's previous experiences impact upon how they perceive and experience situations in the present. It is important therefore to understand that the information received from the person you are working with is their particular story. It is not invalid just because it does not match someone else's, nor does it (necessarily) mean they are not telling the 'truth' – it is their narrative truth.

Assessments

Assessments are an integral aspect of all areas of social work practice. From an initial referral received by the first point of contact in a service to undertaking a mental capacity assessment or parenting assessment, the information received all reflects part of a person's story. Whether it is a new referral that is received which has very little background information or a referral for someone that has had significant previous social work intervention, as a social worker you will probably be required to undertake an assessment with them at some point during your involvement. The way in which social workers record information becomes part of the professional narrative of that person's experiences, their journey and social care involvement with them. How information is recorded is a vital part of this narrative, and ensuring that in your professional role, as much as possible, you use objective language, factual description and, where necessary, the person's own words helps to ensure their perspective and experiences do not get lost within professional interventions. For example, if you attend a property and it smells strongly of cat urine, there are dirty plates on the floor and rubbish strewn around the kitchen, it is better to describe *this*, rather than writing 'the house is smelly, dirty and untidy'. Your definition of 'smelly, dirty and untidy' might be quite different from someone else's. Think back to the example of 'good enough' parenting discussed above. The views you have on what is 'good enough' or what counts as 'dirty' are shaped by your own experiences and are subjective. Using language which describes what was observed, rather than what you thought, helps ensure other professionals have a similar understanding of the situation.

Most assessments are highly structured and have specific headings and areas that require covering. For example, a child and family assessment under the common assessment framework (CAF) requires exploration of parenting capacity, family and environmental factors and a child's developmental needs (Department for Education, 2018), whereas a Care Act assessment will explore areas including personal dignity, physical/mental health and emotional wellbeing, contribution to society and social and economic wellbeing (Care Act, 2014). As a result, when a social worker engages with a person in need of support, they are often working to a specific agenda to find the information to answer the questions and tick the right boxes. As a result, the information deemed important by professionals becomes prioritised over what the person who they are supporting might deem important, and that person's voice and story can become lost in the procedurally driven approach – as Broadhurst and Mason (2014, p 580) note the information gathered and held by professionals 'usurps that gained from direct engagement with families'. It is essential therefore to explore the key issues as the individual sees them, as this might be very different from the referral information that the social worker has received, and understanding their perspective can help build relationships and allows a focus on interventions and service delivery in a more personal way. In line with a strength-based approach, narrative practice recognises the individual as the expert in their own life: they are the ones who bring the knowledge and experience (see case study: Jo). The professional is there to take a supporting role.

> ## Case study: Jo
>
> Jo is 17 and moving out of residential care into semi-independent living (a supported living environment where young people can develop the skills they need to live independently). Jo's gender identity is complex. Jo identifies as non-binary, uses the 'they' pronoun and is clear that they wish to undergo gender reassignment surgery once they are 18. Jo has identified as non-binary gender since they were 14 years old and has been on the waiting list for the gender identity clinic since they were 15 years old but has yet to have an appointment.
>
> To obtain a flat in the local semi-independent provision, Jo needs to provide photo ID and complete a number of forms. The forms Jo has to complete have tick boxes for male/female gender, but neither reflects Jo's gender identity; however, Jo's photo ID is a passport from when they were 13 years old and states their gender as male. Jo has spoken to their leaving care personal adviser (who supports and advises them) about obtaining a new passport but has been advised that they would still only be able to acquire one stating they are male as there is no option for a neutral gender in a UK passport.
>
> Jo does not want to complete the forms and use their passport as ID as this means they would be placed in the male side of the accommodation. Jo has been identifying as non-binary for three years and does not feel they would be able to continue to do so if they were placed in the male accommodation. The accommodation provider states they are unable to place Jo in the female side of the accommodation because their ID states they are male.
>
> This example demonstrates the master narrative that gender is binary – you are either male or female. Jo's identity and experiences demonstrate a counter-narrative – they do not fit neatly into the categories of the gender binary. However, as the master narrative requires them to identify as such, they find themselves facing additional problems trying to navigate day-to-day situations that do not account for their self-identified gender.

Externalising the problem

A key aspect of the narrative approach involves separating the problem from the person; the person is not the problem, the problem is the problem (White and Epston, 1990). This allows for the exploration of the problem as a separate entity, something not inherent in the person, and addressing external issues can often feel more achievable than addressing or confronting ourselves.

Through externalisation, the master-narrative can be challenged and the replaying of this can be interrupted, creating a sense of self-efficacy and personal agency which can allow for change (Burack-Weiss, Lawrence and Mijangos, 2017).

Externalisation can be worked towards through skilled use of questions which separate the presenting issue from the person. Some examples are detailed below:

> *When did you start feeling anxious all the time?*
> Mental health is something that we all have, and at times, it can bring challenges which we might refer to as mental health difficulties. Can you talk to me about some of the situations that can increase the intensity of how you are feeling?
> *Why do you argue with your partner about these things?*
> Are there any patterns you can identify that might lead up to an argument? Are there things that are said or done that make an argument more likely?
> *Why do you feel the need to keep all these things?*
> The way we hold onto memories is different for all of us. Some people keep pictures or items that remind them of past events. What stories do these possessions tell?

Narrative questioning is a skilled activity that can rely upon trust and confidence built though relationship-based practice. Burack-Weiss et al (2017, p 7) suggest that a core element of effective social work lies in 'understanding that the client-worker relationship is an essential ingredient of the helping process, having respect for the individual story, and linking an individual story to larger social concerns'. This relational process resonates with power-sharing approaches to social work with individuals and families.

Narrative and biographical work

Narrative approaches with children and young people

Undertaking direct work is a key aspect of children and family social work, whether working with a young disabled child on a child in need plan or a teenager in residential care. The underlying premise of the work is the same – to help the child or young person to understand and own their story. The narratives that young people hear from those around them in childhood – whether parents, siblings, extended family, teachers or friends, can have a huge impact as they grow up and throughout their adult lives. The experiences may be confusing or frightening and brains can distort them as a way to try to protect the child, which leaves them with a narrative that does not make sense, or fit with what they have been told.

Using narrative within direct work can be done in many different ways: biographical work, for example, when a child is placed for adoption. A number of different tools might be used to convey a child's story.

Life-story books: A life-story book is usually put together by a social worker to explain to a child their story. It will (hopefully) contain pictures of their birth family, age-appropriate information about why they were not able to remain living with their birth family and details and pictures of their foster carers (where relevant) and conclude with information about their adoptive family, along with pictures of them. Some formats may include blank pages at the end for the child to add to their story as they grow.

Parallel stories: Other tools may include parallel stories, which echo the child's story in the form of an age-appropriate storybook: for example, detailing an alien who comes from somewhere else and does not understand the way things work where they are now, but who finds new friends and family who help them and teach them all the things they need to know.

Therapeutic stories: Similar to parallel stories, therapeutic stories identify a theme or issue that is troublesome and explore this in story form. The children's tale 'The Ugly Duckling' is such an example, exploring difference within childhood. There are many such stories available, both in book form and online; however, writing such a story is something that could be undertaken with a child or young person. Many people find it far easier to give advice to other people who may be in a situation they are experiencing than they do to identify solutions and take action on their own situation – which links closely to the concept of externalisation. The process of creating a story where the main character faces an issue the child is dealing with, explores how to deal with this issue and ultimately overcomes this issue both challenges the dominant narrative and creates a space for hope – 'If the character can do it, then so can I.'

Later life letters: These are usually written by the allocated social worker for the child to access when they are 18. Later-life letters are addressed directly to the child and provide more in-depth detail about social work involvement in the child's life. They tell the story from the perspective of the professionals involved with the child, highlighting the worries and risks and explaining why the decisions regarding that child's care were made. It is important to be mindful that the information recorded in these letters is what was seen, heard and experienced from the perspective of the social worker and other professionals. This may become the dominant narrative that the young person has heard throughout their life. Alternatively, it may be that this narrative runs counter to the stories told by the child's birth family and/or significant others. It is important therefore to be clear when writing such letters that it is from the professional's perspective, and that the information the child may have heard from other people may be different. Often these letters are written at the time a child is placed for adoption, and from accessing information in the child's file. A child may not have contact with their birth family until they are over 18 years old, so there are likely to be discrepancies in the narratives told by family members at that time compared with what the social worker wrote 16 years previously.

Pathway planning: Pathway planning is a key aspect of preparing children with care experience for moving on to independence and is a requirement for children leaving care (Children (Leaving Care) Act 2000). A pathway plan both assesses the young person's needs and supports planning of future service provision for them. The plan will be completed in conjunction with the young person and future service provision – and their engagement with that will probably be influenced by the narratives the young person holds about their past experiences. Narratives are constructed by professionals, and these are often the narratives that then form part of a child's story – especially when a child comes into care. Depending on the age at which a child came into care, they may have their own well-developed narrative about their experiences; others will develop their understanding of their circumstances through the information they receive from professionals, carers and family if they continue to have contact. A teenager entering care will have their own narrative of the circumstances that led them to be in care; some may understand and recognise the issues that were occurring in their lives that led them to be in care. For others, their experiences and the information they received growing up may be hugely negative towards social care and this may impact their ability to engage with social workers and placement.

Narrative approaches with adults

Narrative approaches with adults in social work can be similarly diverse. Through use of narrative approaches, people may be supported to explore and interpret their own life experiences and challenge narratives that have restricted them throughout their lives, and they may be supported to reauthor and reframe some of their experiences to regain ownership, invoking a sense of autonomy, self-efficacy and hopefulness. In this sense, narrative practice can be therapeutic. Jirek (2017) studied the impact of narrative reframing and reconstruction in helping people to integrate traumatic experiences, arguing that social workers can help trauma survivors to reconstruct their life stories to promote empowerment and social justice.

A narrative approach can include the use of assessment tools such as genograms and ecomaps (for example, see Rogers and Cooper, 2020), which not only provide the professional with the information required for an assessment but can support a person's own exploration of their relationships and experiences. Narrative approaches can enhance a professional's understanding of a person's cognition, affect, decision-making or actions (see Case study: Cyril).

Case study: Cyril

Eighty-year-old Cyril moved into a care home following a deterioration in his dementia, which had resulted in safeguarding risks when he was living alone. Every morning on waking Cyril seemed agitated; he got fully dressed and tried to leave the property. Support staff could not understand the behaviour and struggled to distract Cyril from his intent to leave. A conversation with Cyril's daughter shed light on the situation as she explained that for most of his life he had lived and worked on a farm and it became evident that on waking Cyril thought he needed to be going outside to milk the cows. This example demonstrates how a narrative approach can advance understanding *and* guide intervention.

Life-story work: For people who have experienced life-changing events, the way they perceive themselves may be very different from the way they present and the way they are seen by other people. An example might be a person in their early 50s who is a successful business owner, married with children, but suffers a stroke and requires significant rehabilitation including re-learning to speak, write and walk. Using a narrative approach in this situation would include gathering information, perhaps pictures or important items from family or friends that can be used to explore the person's understanding and memory of their history. Using stories and examples of people around them (for example, in a brain injury unit) can support the development of their understanding of their current situation, as they may be able to see their experiences reflected in other people. Gathering a history and understanding this work also provide further information for those working them to understand the life they enjoyed prior to their stroke.

One-page profiles: One-page profiles are exactly as described: they are a one-page document with information about the person. These are often used in residential homes and with people with learning disabilities. A one-page profile may contain a picture, their preferred name, likes and dislikes and some background history. The key aspect of one-page profiles is that they highlight what things are important to the person they are about and how they want to be supported by those working with them. They are a simple tool for working in a person–centred way, and allow for communication about important information in a clear, accessible manner.

Reminiscence groups: Reminiscence groups can be used to bring people together, to explore or recall a shared time in history and to provide support, promote wellbeing and a sense of belonging. They can be run in different ways and may utilise stories, pictures, re-enacting memories or music to connect people. They can have a positive impact on a person's wellbeing through developing connections with others and also reconnecting with themselves. Some people with dementia may withdraw from the world around them and stop communicating as they struggle to understand what is going on. This was the case for one such lady who attended a reminiscence group. It was believed she had potentially lost the capacity to communicate verbally as she had not done so for a number of years. However, after attending a number of group sessions, where songs from her childhood and teenage years were routinely sung, she began joining in and singing along. This experience helped her reconnect with the world around her and also to connect with a part of herself.

Narrative approaches to social work with family and social networks

As with many aspects of social work, narrative approaches link well with other social work theories and models and with both individuals and groups (Burack-Weiss et al, 2017). One such example is the overlap between narrative approaches and systemic practice. Both approaches look beyond the presenting problem – with narrative seeking to do so by externalising this and systemic practice seeking to understand the problem as arising from interactions between various parts of the system. The impact of the experiences of a person's family and wider network on how they see the world and interpret their own experiences cannot be overlooked. Using narrative approaches to explore feelings and understanding of the experiences of others can help with the interpretation and comprehension of a person's own experiences and internal narrative.

An example of combining narrative social work with a family systems approach is illuminated in the collection of poems by parents and children affected by imprisonment entitled *Seen and Heard* (Baldwin and Raikes, 2019). In *Seen and Heard* poetry is used to convey the narratives of children and parents about their experiences of parental imprisonment and as a way of making sense of what has happened to them and their families. Interpreting their experiences and documenting them in this way can support people's understanding of their experiences and their emotions, and help them express things they might struggle to voice in other contexts.

Conclusion

This chapter has provided an overview of narrative concepts to equip the reader with an understanding of the components of narrative practice. Thereafter more detailed discussion of how narrative can underpin social work practice, or complement other models such as a family systems approach, is provided. Throughout the chapter there is emphasis on the strengths-based approach that underpins narrative practice in centring the individual as the expert of their life and in ways that value the diversity of experience making sense of people's experience relative to master and counter-narratives. This chapter has illustrated the ways that narrative practice complements the foundations of social work, including relational practice, assessment and direct work. In describing different narrative techniques we have provided the reader with knowledge about various ways to engage children, young people, adults and families in narrative practice to enable them to examine and make sense of their lives and experiences, and to move forward in positive ways.

Key learning points

Narrative approaches enable people to interpret their lives through story-telling, and require social workers to interpret the stories that people tell.

Using a narrative approach means acknowledging that there can be several different stories and voices that describe the same event. All stories have value and importance; they represent different narrative truths.

Taking a narrative approach in social work enables an individual to construct, deconstruct and reconstruct a story, and therefore it is an empowering approach and aligns with strengths-based practice.

Narrative approaches can use creative methods, art or music, for example, to enable people to tell their story, and can provide powerful experiences for people who may have communication impairments.

Further reading

Ahmed, A. and Rogers, M. (2017) 'Polly's story: using structural narrative analysis to understand a trans migration journey', *Qualitative Social Work*, 16(2): 224–239.

Baldwin, C. (2013) *Narrative Social Work*, Bristol: Policy Press.

Burack-Weiss, A., Lawrence, L.S. and Mijangos, L.B. (eds) (2017) *Narrative in Social Work Practice: The Power and Possibility of Story*, New York: Columbia University Press.

Thompson, R. (2011) 'Using life story work to enhance care', *Nursing Older People*, 23(8): 16–21.

Watson, D., Latter, S. and Bellew, R. (2015) 'Adopters' views on their children's life story books', *Adoption and Fostering*, 39(2): 119–134.

8

Strengths-based approaches in adult social care

Sarah Pollock and Alex Withers

Introduction

This chapter will track the emergence and development of strengths-based approaches in the field of adult social work and social care. Initially we will explore the history of the approach in relation to work with adults, including the important influence of political ideology on the development of the approach, from community social work through the move to social work as commissioning, and finally to the introduction of the Care Act and its underpinning principle of 'well-being'.

The Care Act (2014) was described by Lyn Romeo, then Chief Social Worker for Adults, as a 'defining moment' for adult social care. This chapter will examine the policy discussions that informed the Act and its guidance. We will critically explore the introduction of the Act and its reinforcement of strengths and asset-based approaches at a time of government-implemented austerity measures across the sector and British society more widely.

As in other fields of social work, strengths-based approaches in adult social work and social care are diverse in their development and application. In this chapter we will focus on two new iterations of the approach. The first of these is Three Conversations, an assessment and intervention framework developed by the independent organisation Partners4Change, advocated by Lyn Romeo and piloted and evaluated by several English local authorities. The second approach to be considered is 'Making Safeguarding Personal', an initiative that has been subject to large-scale national peer-reviewed research and evaluation and is included in the Care Act (2014) guidance.

Exploring two different ways in which strengths-based approaches can be utilised in practice will demonstrate the flexibility and diversity of methods available, dependent on the social work or care setting. These approaches are not without critique, however, and the final section of this chapter will be a critical appraisal, identifying some of the challenges in practice and introducing some of the key theories engaged in this debate.

Before we start, it is important to clarify the terminology used throughout this chapter. During the development of strengths-based approaches from community social work, a division has developed between individualised and community-based interventions. Although this is contested (NICE, 2020), throughout this chapter the term 'strengths-based approaches' will be used to refer to interventions with an individual or family and the term 'asset-based approaches' to refer to interventions that involve a larger group or community. Adult social work is part of a wider workforce that includes care workers, community workers, charitable organisations, local services and too many more to mention. This means that adult social work and adult social care are often used interchangeably; this was starkly apparent as the COVID-19 pandemic swept across the globe, and there was little mention of social work specifically, but the umbrella term 'social care' was frequently referenced (McGowan, 2020). In this chapter, the term 'adult social care' is used to refer to this wider workforce and service provision, which includes social workers. When the term 'adult social work' is used, this refers to tasks, duties or responsibilities that are specific to qualified and registered social work professionals.

Finally, this chapter makes frequent reference to the Care Act (2014). This legislation underpins adult social work and social care in England and Wales. Scottish practitioners utilise a combination of the Adult Support and Protection (Scotland) Act (2007) and the Social Care (self-directed support) (Scotland) Act (2013) in order to support adults requiring adult social care. In Northern Ireland the Health and Social Care (reform) Act (2013) is the legal basis for intervention, alongside separate regulations for adult care settings. Despite the different legislation and guidance in the devolved nations of the United Kingdom, the advocation of strengths-based practice is a common theme.

The history and development of strengths-based approaches

Focusing on a person, family or community's strengths is not new to adult social care, and many social workers and other care professionals would suggest that this is how they have always practised (Gollins, 2016; Baron et al, 2019). Community social work has a strong history in the UK, with the Seebohm Report of 1963 acknowledging it as one of the most important aspects of support and the Barclay Report of 1982 citing that 'the bulk of social care is provided not by the statutory or voluntary social services agencies but by ordinary people who may be linked into informal caring networks in their communities' (Barclay, 1982, p 199). The report continues by identifying the precarious balance of communities and informal care networks providing support for the most in need, proposing that the focus of social services (now adult social care) should be on scaffolding support around these community networks in order to ensure they are able to continue their roles, concluding that this would reduce referrals and dependence on formal provision.

As we explore the recent developments later in this chapter, we will see the similarities between the picture painted by the Seebohm and Barclay reports and contemporary duties enshrined in the Care Act and interventions such as Three Conversations.

Throughout the latter decades of the 20th century, the political ideology in the UK became increasingly neo-liberal. For social care this meant a move towards individualising people's need for support and repositioning social workers as care co-ordinators, identifying needs through an assessment process and meeting them with commissioned support, such as home carers or day centres, via a care plan. This new care co-ordination role was formalised in the National Health Service and Community Care Act (1990). This Act dictated the eligibility criteria (known as the Fair Access to Care Services (FACS) criteria, Department of Health, 2002) through which an individual's needs were identified and measured, falling into one of four categories: low, moderate, substantial or critical. Local authorities were able to choose at which level they provided support, creating a postcode lottery of care provision. The process was deficit-focused, as it required people to identify what they could not do, with little focus on what they could do, or indeed what they would like to do.

As austerity measures began to escalate throughout the first decade of the 21st century, choice in the 'care market' for people needing support was reduced, as traditional day services closed and smaller, local care agencies folded, leaving larger, generic providers meeting the needs of only those with substantial or critical needs. In 2011 a legal challenge found Birmingham City Council to have acted unlawfully in restricting the provision of care to only those residents with critical care needs, meaning that they would be likely to die without the support (England and Wales High Court 1147). For social workers, practising in this environment was a challenge to the core values of the profession, such as empowerment and advocacy, with a lack of autonomy due to heavily bureaucratic systems implemented to measure 'outcomes'.

The introduction of the 'resource allocation system' (RAS) further limited social workers' autonomy. The RAS is a software program developed to generate a personal budget for an individual by selecting responses to a series of deficit-focused questions about their needs. The system then generates an amount of funding with which the individual should be able to meet these needs, either by taking the funding as an individual budget to manage themselves or by using social work support to purchase a care package. This rational–technical approach further distanced social workers from the core value of empowerment by creating a situation where social workers, conscious of the minimal funding available, were reduced to encouraging individuals to 'think about their worst day' when completing assessments, in order to help secure more funding to meet their needs. Despite the developer of the RAS themselves identifying that the system was unable to accurately provide adequate funding to meet individual needs, it is still used alongside the Care Act (2014) in many authorities (Centre for Welfare Reform, 2012).

The Care Act (2014): introducing the 'new' strengths-based approach

Advocated by Lyn Romeo, former Chief Social Worker for Adults, the introduction of the Care Act in 2014 was an opportunity for adult social care to embrace strengths (Department of Health, 2017). Underpinned by a central theme of 'well-being', the language of the Act indicated a change in direction for adult social care, with strengths interwoven into both the legislation and accompanying guidance. However, introduced at a time of austerity, many social work academics and practitioners questioned whether the impact of the Act in practice would meet its aspirations (Feldon, 2016; Cooper et al, 2018).

The Care and Support Statutory Guidance that accompanies the Care Act (2014) describes the assessment process as 'a critical intervention in its own right', outlining how this can 'help people to understand their strengths and capabilities, and the support available to them in the community and through other networks and services' (Care and Support Statutory Guidance, chapter 6.2). The guidance continues to highlight that assessment of individuals with complex needs must consider individual strengths alongside risk and need, to ensure a coordinated response (chapter 6.7). Essentially the Act requires the participation of individuals throughout their involvement with adult services, from establishing what they would like their life to look like through to creating a plan to get there, utilising existing support and developing new connections throughout the process. The Care Act continues this commitment to partnership working into the new safeguarding duties for local authorities, under Section 42 of the Act, which will be explored later in this chapter.

The contemporary context

In 2017 the Department of Health commissioned a Roundtable Report, issuing a 'call to action' (Department of Health, 2017, p 5) to the social work profession, to embrace the strengths-based way of working advocated by the Care Act (2014). The event was hosted by the Social Care Institute for Excellence (SCIE) and was attended by Lyn Romeo and Tony Hunter (chief executive of SCIE) alongside Ruth Allen from the British Association of Social Workers (BASW) and many academic and practice experts in adult social work. Hunter described the event as 'liberating' and 'positive', acknowledging the connection social workers felt between a strengths-based approach to practice and their professional values. It was recognised, two years on from its implementation in April 2015, that there were still challenges in embedding the approach. These challenges ranged from the entrenched care management culture to the lack of peer-reviewed evidence supporting strengths-based methods. During the event, users of adult social work support identified concerns that strengths-based approaches could be used as a rationale to cut services, and that unrealistic expectations of quick fixes could leave people in vulnerable situations. They expressed a need for structural support to embed the approach in practice.

At the roundtable event, it was recognised that there was a lack of strong, peer-reviewed evidence for the success of strengths-based approaches in adult social care, and although there were excellent examples of good practice identified (in Leeds, Kirklees and Greenwich), these were sporadic and inconsistent across the country. This conclusion was also reached by a National Institute for Health Research commissioned literature review in 2020 (Caiels et al, 2020), which indicated that, of 5,030 published studies about strengths-based approaches, only 15 related to adults, with eight being specific to Making Safeguarding Personal (MSP), an approach discussed later in this chapter. This left just seven studies exploring the approach, and the review concluded that the 'findings are limited by the lack of available evidence in the UK' (Caiels et al, 2020, p 4).

Strengths-based framework for adult social work

One of the next steps from the roundtable event was to build on the enthusiasm for a strength focus in the adult social work field by developing a framework for practice. Research indicates that practice frameworks can promote effective practice (Connolly, 2007) and are described as able to 'integrate empirical research, practice theories, ethical principles and experiential knowledge in a compact and convenient format that helps practitioners to use the knowledge and principles to inform their everyday work' (Connolly and Healy, 2009, p 32). It was thought that such an aid would be useful to practitioners and organisations to support implementation.

The practice framework for strengths-based social work with adults was devised by a team of academics, practitioners, experts by experience and researchers led by Professor Samantha Baron and Dr Tony Stanley. It is based on the five-quadrant mode l developed by Stanley (2016) and consists of 'practice triggers or prompts brought to action' (Baron et al, 2019). The five domains are:

- practice and co-produced knowledge and research
- social work values and ethics
- social work theories and methods
- practice skills
- practitioner experiential learning

These domains are abbreviated to the acronym KcVETS. The framework considers each of the five domains through three separate but interconnected lenses.

- professional practice level – including practitioner reflection
- supervision
- quality assurance

Through these interconnections, continuity in professional practice can be facilitated. Each of the five professional practice domains includes reflective questions for practitioners to consider, which help them to focus their thinking and therefore their practice on promoting strengths. The supervision lens can then be used to enhance this focus in individual social workers' supervision, which not only facilitates the practitioner's learning and development but enables them to experience the approach they are adopting with the adults they work with. Finally, the quality assurance lens ensures that the strengths focus is consistent throughout adult social care institutions and organisational structures, with appropriate consideration given to valuing the input of those with lived experience, ensuring the emphasis is on the quality and appropriateness of services and support.

The practice handbook that accompanies the framework explores the enablers and barriers to embedding a strengths-based approach in adult social work, outlining the importance of factors such as strong leadership, shared commitment and accountability, trust in the workforce and the development of staff strengths, including arming them with the appropriate tools, processes and systems to carry out strengths-based work (Baron et al, 2019). In addition, the skills required to achieve a strengths focus are identified within the framework; these are reflective of the Knowledge and Skills Statement for Adults (KSS) issued by the Department of Health in 2015. Both indicate a commitment to professionalism, professional curiosity, reflection, empathy, listening and critical thinking. Finally, the reinforcement of strengths by the national social work regulator, Social Work England, through the first of its six professional standards, 'promote the rights, strengths and wellbeing of people, families and communities' (Social Work England, 2019), indicates the growing commitment to this approach at practice leadership level.

Strengths-based approaches in practice

'Strengths-based approaches' is an umbrella term for a number of different methods, interventions, assessments and ways of working, which have in common the central theme of supporting individuals, families, groups and communities to identify and develop their strengths. In adult social care, there are many such strengths-based approaches. Three examples are described below, and additional reading about these can be found at the end of the chapter:

- Local Area Co-ordination (LAC): This is where local area co-ordinators are employed and given small budgets to support individuals to connect to their communities and develop networks for those who are struggling to call on the strengths of the community in which they live.
- Shared Lives: Here individuals in the community may be matched with families or individuals who can support them to develop strengths and gain more independence: for example, by supporting someone who is care-experienced to learn activities of daily living in preparation for independence.
- Family Group Conferences: Originally adopted for use with children and families in child protection procedures, this model utilises external facilitators to support families in designing their own safety plans. FGCs have been more recently used in adult safeguarding but not without criticism (see Parkinson, Pollock and Edwards, 2018).

Focus on the Three Conversations approach

In the same year that the Care Act was passed through parliament, Sam Newman, a qualified social worker, established Partners4Change, the organisation that developed the Three Conversations approach. Described specifically as 'not a model' (Partners4Change online), this way of working aspires to change adult social care by implementing a set of Care Act-compliant rules, believing that people are experts in their own lives and that listening to their wishes and identifying their strengths are key to successful support. Application of the approach provides consistency through crises, by avoiding making assumptions or categorising people, not filtering people through a system of different teams or workers, and, through moving away from dehumanising language such as 'care package', 'triage' and 'assessment'.

Alongside the rules, the Three Conversations is, as the name suggests, a set of three different conversations for social workers to use with individuals requiring support:

> Conversation 1: Listen and connect; this initial conversation requires practitioners to listen carefully to what people say about their lives, what their strengths and support systems are, and then use their knowledge of the local area to connect people to existing provisions or support. This conversation meets the Care Act duty to 'prevent, reduce or delay the need for long term support'.
>
> Conversation 2: Work intensively with people in crisis or at risk; here practitioners work with individuals who require immediate support, for example, due to carer breakdown or a new or rapidly advancing illness, and with those at risk. They work with the person to identify the cause of the crisis or risk and implement a short-term 'emergency plan', remaining in contact until the situation stabilises. This conversation meets the Care Act section 42 safeguarding duty.
>
> Conversation 3: Build a good life; this conversation is not always required as conversations 1 and 2 can often provide the preventative or short-term support required. For those that do need more long-term support, practitioners are able to help locate the correct support to enable people to live 'the best life possible' (online). This final conversation has the means to meet the Care Act, Section 8, duty to assess and address the eligibility criteria for support.

Evidence from the 'innovation sites' (Partners4Change speak for services commissioning their approach) indicates that replacing a traditional Care Act assessment model with Three Conversations increases the capacity for social workers to speak to more people needing support at Conversation 1 level, while reducing the number of people requiring long-term care and coming back through services for additional support, meaning fewer people having Conversation 3. All sites reported a reduction in spending on care, with each suggesting that practitioners were happier with working in this way, feeling it was more in line with their view of what social work should be (Partners4Change online).

Although the evidence here is undeniably positive, it is important to note that this evidence comes in the form of evaluations, co-authored by local authorities or 'innovation sites' with Partners4Change, and blog posts published on their website. At the time of writing, there are no peer-reviewed journal articles reporting such outcomes, or indeed reporting on this approach specifically at all. It could be argued that these organisations have a vested interest in providing evidence that supports the success of strengths-based models of working. There is much in the literature that suggests that service users are happy with strength-based input, yet it is questionable whether this constitutes acceptable supporting evidence. An appraisal of your own service delivery runs the risk of bias and demonstrates a lack of transparency. Additionally, the attention paid to cost reductions reinforces the critical position on strengths as a way to reduce spending, rather than improve the lives of individuals with care needs (Slasberg and Beresford, 2017).

Focus on Making Safeguarding Personal

Making Safeguarding Personal (MSP) is an approach to working with adults at risk of abuse and/or neglect that utilises elements of the strengths-based approach in order to facilitate their safety and wellbeing. Initiated in 2009 by the Local Government Association (LGA) and Association of Directors of Adult Social Services (ADASS), the programme of work embraced a person-centred position, centring the perspectives, rights and desired outcomes of the individual at risk. The programme began with a small number of local authorities adopting a range of more inclusive practices and expanded each year following evaluation, until the approach was integrated into the Care Act statutory guidance as part of adult services duties (Gollins et al, 2016).

The language that surrounds adult protection changed with the introduction of the Care Act, with the terms 'victims' and 'perpetrators' being replaced by 'person at risk of harm' and 'source of harm'. This shift aimed to remove blame and the suggestion that being abused or neglected was somehow due to a 'vulnerability' or deficit on the part of the person at risk. The new language repositioned them as a person capable of deciding how to address the risks of their current situation.

The Care and Support Statutory Guidance, chapter 14.5, states that:

> Making safeguarding personal means it should be person-led and outcome-focused. It engages the person in a conversation about how best to respond to their safeguarding situation in a way that enhances involvement, choice and control as well as improving quality of life, wellbeing and safety.

MSP starts from the premise that individuals themselves are experts in their own lives, and that professionals must acknowledge this and work to facilitate those at risk to develop a plan to keep themselves safe, with support where necessary. They must also respect individuals' decisions not to engage with professionals.

The MSP toolkit and handbook were published by the LGA and ADASS in 2019, consolidating the links between strengths-based approaches and the MSP programme and laying out a framework to help individuals to consider their desired outcomes. Following on from the strengths-based framework for social work practice with adults, this framework establishes an outcomes measure to evaluate the success of safeguarding interventions in relation to their person-centred nature. The evaluation includes asking individuals about areas such as how involved they felt in decisions about them, how listened to they felt and how happy they were with the end result. In addition, the evaluation questions are also framed for informal carers, where individuals themselves are unable to respond.

Interventions included under the MSP umbrella include:

- Circles of support: Here individuals are connected to others in their community or existing relationships in order to offer support and empathy. This might include connecting individuals to survivor networks, companions or community groups: for example, to replace exploitative friendships with positive ones.
- Advocacy: There are many types of advocacy work, including formal or informal, issue- or location-based and short- or long-term. This might include referring someone for an Independent Mental Capacity Advocate or Care Act Advocate to ensure the person's perspective is heard or connecting someone to a local self-advocacy group to raise an antisocial behaviour issue that is negatively impacting an individual's mental health. (*Making Safeguarding Personal*, 2019)

MSP can work in conjunction with the Three Conversations approach and is addressed in Conversation 2, where short-term, urgent support and safety planning can be provided, and the Care Act, Section 42, duty is fulfilled. However, unlike Three Conversations, robust, peer-reviewed research has been published to learn from the approach. Research suggests that professionals find the approach more effective because they can have more open and less prescriptive conversations with individuals, leading to increased confidence and awareness (Butler and Manthorpe, 2016). Practitioners in this study saw the approach, and strengths-based practice more generally, as a return to the social work core principles. Supporting this small-scale three-authority study, Cooper et al (2018) surveyed 76 per cent of English local authorities, finding similar benefits but also raising practitioner concerns about lack of resources and increased referrals impeding implementation.

Older adults (85 years plus) constitute the majority of safeguarding adult concerns, making up 20 times more safeguarding concerns than the 65–74-year-old bracket, and so their opinions about MSP and the opinions of those who work with them are crucial to its development as an approach. Cooper et al (2018) identified that social workers working with older adults were 'enthusiastic about MSP', suggesting that it is a 'more efficient use of resources'. The professionals in this study did, however, identify barriers to MSP, including the impact of mental capacity, communication, systemic and individual ageism and dependency. The connection made consistently in research and policy between financial savings and the strengths-based approach is present again here and reinforces the concerns of those ideologically opposed to its current iteration in practice.

Many strengths-based approaches with adults have been adapted from work with children and families: for example, FGCs and Signs of Safety. However, it has been suggested that the opposite could be a possibility for MSP. Research has suggested that as child protection procedures as described under the Children Act (1989) were developed to protect children from abuse or neglect within the home, this legal framework is not always best placed to support older children and young people, particularly where risk comes from outside of their family. Cocker et al (2021) suggest that here MSP could be utilised, so that older children can work in partnership with professionals and their families to develop plans that both keep them safe but achieve their desired outcomes.

The case of Luke Davey: *R (Davey) v. Oxfordshire CC*

So far in this chapter we have explored the national development and adoption of the strengths-based approach into social work practice with adults. We have considered the introduction of a framework for strengths-based practice and two specific approaches identified under this umbrella: Three Conversations and Making Safeguarding Personal. Research suggests that these advancements have been received positively by both practitioners and those requiring their support; however, it is important that the challenges to strengths-based approaches are addressed. The following section presents the case of Luke Davey, and the implications that this case has for the credibility of strengths in practice.

Mr Davey is an individual with care and support needs, whose care was re-assessed, along with all individuals receiving care from their local authority, on introduction of the Care Act in 2015 and the closure of the Independent Living Fund (ILF) in the same year. The outcome of this assessment was a substantial reduction in Mr Davey's allocated budget for care due to a disagreement between his own and the local authority's assessment of his needs. The disagreement centred on the amount of time Mr Davey was able to spend alone – which fundamentally related to different interpretations of 'wellbeing'. The social work assessment suggested that extending periods of time alone would support Mr Davey to develop independence, hence enhancing wellbeing, whereas Mr Davey believed that the presence of his long-standing support workers enabled him to be independent and that increasing time alone would negatively impact his independence and hence his wellbeing. Although the detail of the case at both judicial review and court of appeal challenged many aspects of the assessment, the final judgment to uphold the budget reduction has implications for the legitimacy of the strengths-based approach.

The case was an opportunity to demonstrate the commitment of the Care Act to valuing individuals' assessments of their own wellbeing and centring their position as experts in their own lives, as per Section 1 of the Act. Instead, the case utilised the Act to overrule Mr Davey's own assessment of his needs and the use of his strengths – in this case, his long-standing and close relationship to his care team – in favour of the social work assessment. The justification for this decision was that the assessment had 'due regard' for Mr Davey's assessment of his own needs, but this regard did not legally prevent the social worker, and local authority, from taking a different position. Mr Davey's case includes much learning for practitioners about the quality of their assessments and legal literacy, described at length by Feldon (2017); however, it does pose a challenge to the credibility of the strengths-based approach for those requiring support. Essentially, their 'expert' status and ability to self-define their needs is conditional on agreement from professionals.

Responsibilisation

Luke Davey's failed legal challenge is not the only critique of strengths; theoretical challenge comes from sociologists and critical social work activists. One such criticism is the notion of neo-liberal responsibilisation (Bourdieu, 1998), which lies at the heart of strengths-based practice. Responsibilisation is a process whereby people are held to be responsible for their issues. Ferguson states: 'Under neoliberal capitalism … it is not difficult to see the ways in which individuals are encouraged into seeing themselves responsible for every aspect of their lives including their health' (Ferguson, 2017, p 76).

Gray (2011), discussing these issues as relating to strengths-based practice in social work, notes that while strengths provide people with the right to care for their own family or access support from carers, they also make individuals responsible for care. He continues, setting out how, in asset-based models of practice, individuals, families and communities are required to take responsibility and finding solutions for their own problems (Gray, 2011, p 8). This is particularly difficult given the decimation of community services through the implementation of austerity measures since 2008.

If we consider the Wigan Deal, a strengths-oriented way of delivering adult social care in the borough of Wigan, we can see the process of responsibilisation reflected. In 'The Deal' document each section ends with a sub-section entitled 'Our Part, Your Part', outlining what Wigan as a local authority will do but also, in turn, what residents are responsible for (2019). For example, the documents states that residents should 'Take responsibility for your own health and wellbeing' and 'tell us if you care for a family member or relative and make sure you look after your own health and happiness as well as the person you are caring for'

(Wigan, 2019, p 34). Wigan residents are made (or nudged) to *be responsible*. It is their part of 'the deal'.

This is indicative of 'responsibility in the guise of empowerment' (MacLeod and Emejulu, 2014, p 13). On the surface, strengths make it look like people are being given control over their lives; however, Gray (2011) and Jordan (2004) highlight that strengths-based approaches deflect responsibility from states to provide for populations and in so doing place the emphasis on those populations to provide solutions themselves.

This has further implications. If we accept that there is a neo-liberal hegemony (Hall, 2011; Cowden and Singh, 2017), through the uncritical embodiment of aspects of neo-liberalism, such as responsibilisation (Gray, 2011), strengths-based practice can contribute to the existence and consolidation of this hegemony.

Care

Harris (2002) and Chatzidakis et al (2020) set out how care has been individualised in our neo-liberal world as we have moved from a more collective understanding of what care is. Houston (2016) states that while some aspects of individualisation, such as personalisation, can be welcome in practice, the emphasis on it as a benefit creates issues. Fisher (2014) states that 'each individual member of the subordinate class is encouraged into feeling that their poverty, lack of opportunities, or unemployment, is their fault and their fault alone.' Consequently, people are made to feel responsible for the issues they experience, and structural drivers of inequality, class, gender and race are sidelined. States can abnegate responsibility for their citizens, as the issues that citizens experience – for example, poverty – become the responsibility of citizens to manage and address.

Despite the utility of strengths, critics of the approach suggest that a reconceptualisation of care in social work practice that has real collectivity at its heart is required. Chatzidakis et al state, 'the notion that care is up to the individual derives from the refusal to recognize our shared vulnerabilities and interconnectedness, creating a callous and uncaring climate for everyone' (Chatzidakis et al, 2020, p 9). While it can be argued that strengths-based practice is inherently about interconnectedness, it is asserted that strengths' embodiment of neo-liberal characteristics such as responsibilisation means its commitment to care is tenuous.

There is need for further critique of strengths because of the profoundly gendered nature of care. Garrett (2018), drawing on the work of Skeggs (2014), sets out how care is overwhelmingly provided by females, with an estimated 6 million carers providing unpaid labour. While it is true that strengths allow families and individuals to provide care, it is clear that care will often fall to women as opposed to men, with all the societal assumptions about the capacity for care that women have (Garrett, 2018). This is troubling, given that strengths is an approach to practice that is purported to have empowerment at its heart.

Despite this inherent flaw, it is important to recognise that care has always been gendered – the post-1945 welfare settlements, for example, have always put forth highly gendered conceptions of care (Garrett, 2018) – yet perhaps, the difference is the centrality of empowerment to strengths.

Community

It is asserted that the dominance of strengths is indicative of Bourdieu's notion of the 'fiscally prudent' right hand of the state (Bourdieu, 1998). The organisations using assets (the 'right hand') do so as a way to constrain expenditure (or continue service delivery in a time of government-imposed austerity). The left hand (social work practitioners) use assets as a fiscally prudent way of addressing community issues, accounting for the positive view taken of assets by practitioners, while in turn, inadvertently, helping to cement the inequalities that remain through more structural factors not being addressed. This is apparent in the feedback from social workers in relation to barriers, and evaluations of strengths-based approaches as being financially good value, identified earlier in this chapter (Romeo, 2017; Slasberg and Beresford, 2017)

In strengths-based work, the emphasis on the use of community can be highly problematic. Gollins (2016) indicates the importance of community and notes that community is about relationships as opposed to a place. Yet, for certain populations, communities are not safe places for many to draw support, whether communities are defined as places or networks. The experience of refugees and asylum seekers in the UK's racist 'hostile environment', is an example of this (Pollock et al, 2019). For asylum seekers and refugees, resources or 'assets' such as the healthcare system have become methods of control and exclusion, and agencies can become means by which individuals and families are deported. White (2020) writes of how (UK) communities, under neo-liberalism, have fragmented along class and racial lines, and yet consideration is not given to this within the conversation about strengths. White western positivistic understandings of community need to be recognised and then challenged by a critical view of the experience of community for many in 2023.

Furthermore, the sense of community stressed in many documents produced by local authorities (Wigan Council, 2019) that have strengths-based practice at their heart can be interpreted as being characterised by what Gilbert (2014), describes as meta-individualism. This reflects the neo-liberal culture in which strengths has thrived. If we again look to the Wigan Deal, citizens are the actors in assets coalescing around the asset-based project which is put forth by the local authority. The citizens are charged by the ruling body with aims and objectives to create a sense of community: for example, 'if residents see someone not taking care of our borough, we encourage them to tell us through our Report It app' (Wigan Council, 2019, p 49.) This is a 'top-down' way of creating 'community', as opposed to one that is genuinely horizontal.

Furthermore, other than consultation, citizens do not seem to have been responsible for co-creating the 'Deal' as a model of service delivery. It has been presented to the citizens in a top-down fashion. As Booth states, 'This ensures that power remains outside of the communities as opposed to it being transferred to those who may benefit from holding power' (Booth, 2019, p 277). The vertical relationship posited by Gilbert remains.

Consequently, in strengths-based models of working, a sense is given of people acting in and around a centrally created and propagated *idea of community* provided by those in power. This is opposed to community being something *created by the community itself*. The result is arguably one whereby a false sense of community is created that has the potential to exacerbate feelings of loneliness and isolation that contribute to mental distress (Fisher, 2014), because it is still built around the individualism at the heart of the neo-liberal ideology.

Conclusion

This chapter has followed the development of strengths-based approaches in adult social care and social work, with a focus on the implementation of the Care Act (2014) and the strengths-based framework for social work practice with adults (Baron at al, 2019). Drawing on research, we have considered the implementation of two methods of practice, Three Conversations and MSP, from the perspective of practitioners, researchers and individuals receiving services. Acknowledging the importance of Luke Davey's case in undermining the credibility of the approach for those with lived experience of social work intervention, we have also considered critiques from a theoretical position. The impact of austerity on communities and the neo-liberal position of responsibilisation, the failure to address structural inequality and the intersectional nature of how communities are experienced are important challenges to consider, if those most critical of the approach are to support and accept it in practice as more than a budget reduction strategy.

Key learning points

- Strengths-based approaches are not new to adult practice; they draw on a strong tradition of community work in the UK.

- There are many diverse applications of strengths-based approaches in adult social work, meaning it is a flexible way of working with people, dependent on their needs and the level of risk.

- The implementation of the most recent iteration of strengths-based approaches alongside the Care Act (2014) has been impacted by its introduction coinciding with government-implemented austerity measures and the changing nature of 'community' within a neo-liberal economy.

- There are examples of good, strengths-based practice in local authority adult social work, but there is little peer-reviewed evidence of its success in the practice setting.

Further reading

For more detail about the current policy and practice context in England:

Baron, S., Stanley, T., Colomina, C. and Pereira, T. (2019) *Strengths-Based Approach: Practice Framework and Practice Handbook*, London: Department of Health and Social Care.

Gollins, T., Fox, A., Walker, B., Romeo., Thomas, J. and Woodham, G. (2016). *Developing a Wellbeing and Strengths-Based Approach to Social Work Practice: Changing Culture*, London: Think Local Act Personal.

For a more critical and international perspective on strengths-based work with adults:

Gray, M. (2011) 'Back to basics: a critique of the strengths perspective in social work', *Families in Society: The Journal of Contemporary Human Services*, 91(1): 5–11.

Slasberg, C. and Beresford, P. (2017) 'Strengths-based practice: social care's latest elixir or the next false dawn?', *Disability & Society*, 32(2): 269–273.

9

Strengths-based approaches in mental health services

Emily Weygang

Introduction

This chapter will focus on the application of strengths-based practices within adult mental health provision. Initially the chapter will argue that strengths-based practice has become integrated and subsumed within a neo-liberal culture of individualism which fails to recognise the determinants of mental distress. In such a hostile climate the potential for strengths-based practice to flourish is undermined. Following on from this, the chapter will focus on practice which further undermines the potential of strengths-based practice, namely, the dominance of the medical model, the risk agenda and the state benefits eligibility criteria. The final part of the chapter will consider an alternative type of space which reframes strengths-based practice and suggests that, in the right conditions, it can be more aligned with a humane and collective response to recovery. This final section includes the voices of people with lived experience, David and Lynne, who kindly gave their time to be interviewed and permission for their views to be included in this chapter. Other testimonies are also included, with permission, but these participants have chosen to remain anonymous.

The pathology of mental distress

Promoting recovery and strengths-based practice was championed at least in part by mental health survivors' movements, which by the 1980s had gained momentum as more recipients of mainstream mental health services wrote about their experiences and their recovery (Healy, 2005). As well as advocating and campaigning for change, they demanded more independence and autonomy over their care (Chassot and Mendes, 2014). Perhaps most significantly, survivors were able to describe the culture of gloomy prognoses and accompanying stigma within mainstream provision. While the meaning of recovery is broad and contested, there is one definition which is central to the survivor movement. This definition understands 'recovery as a process of overcoming the multiple invalidations service users have survived: the experiences that caused their impairments, the social invalidation of rejection and stigma, and the invalidation of professional action, such as objectifying diagnoses' (Chassot and Mendes, 2014, p 14). For these survivors, experience of mental distress has been experienced, framed and labelled by professionals as a deviation from the 'norm', which compounds stigma. The possibility that the causes of mental distress may reside elsewhere is not entertained. The pathology of mental distress is critically questioned by survivors whose focus becomes a personal journey that involves 'regaining hope, taking responsible action for one's life, challenging other people's expectations, developing values, relationships and a new meaning for life' (Chassot and Mendes, 2014, p 15). In this sense, recovery becomes aligned with strengths-based practice, which is, at least in principle, focused on individual needs and strengths and moves away from a deficit model. However, there is one crucial difference between the survivors' priorities and the strengths-based model because, for survivors, the environment and social structures in which illness is experienced and in which recovery takes place are paramount. Recovery is dependent on conditions which are conducive to recovery, and this is the central dilemma for proponents of strengths-based practice.

The most-cited definition of recovery is quoted in the document produced by the (Cameron–Clegg) coalition government of 2010–2015, *No Health without Mental Health* (2011). Recovery is '[a] deeply personal unique process of changing one's attitudes, values, feelings, goals skills and/or roles' (Anthony, 1993, quoted in Department of Health, 2011, p 90). Here, recovery is to do with personal resolve, about individual attitude, one's values; in short, recovery becomes about self-management and individual morality. This emphasis overlooks a crucial aspect: it cannot be denied that mental distress in part, at least, is socially constructed and, one could argue, a consequence of social inequalities. If mental distress and social exclusion are exacerbated by social and political determinants, 'can they be addressed by models of recovery which are couched in such individualistic terms' (Backwith, 2015, p 133)? As far back as the 1950s Thomas Szasz went as far to say in *The Myth of Mental Illness* that, if social inequality and social issues were addressed, mental illness would not exist (Szasz, 1961).

Personal is political

As strengths-based practice has become embedded in legislation and policy, attention to the social context has become increasingly sidelined. There is an irreconcilable conflict between the origins of the concept of recovery and strengths-based practice and its translation into policy. Since around 2009, policy development has been dominated by austerity with its attendant emphasis on self-care, personal responsibility and shifting understanding of social inclusion to simply mean inclusion within the labour market (Moth, 2018). While many policies emphasise consultation and participation, responsibility is placed on 'service users to not only be experts on their conditions but on services provided and the ways in which they are delivered' (Baker and Brown, 2012, p 70). The

Care Act (2014) focuses on choice and freedom through its personalisation agenda, which is broadly understood to be an enabler of strengths-based practice. Yet through personalisation the service user becomes subject to market norms and is recast as a consumer who is responsible for the choices they make (Ferguson, 2007). Within this framework strengths-based practice serves and buffets a neo-liberal ideology for, by searching for people's strengths and 'assets', their problems are relocated with them: 'The corollary of self-responsibility is that the causes of failure are seen as being located within the individual. Thus social and political issues can be reformulated as psychological ones' (Baker and Brown, 2012, p 14).

In everyday workplace reality, the social worker/care co-ordinator is in danger of becoming a moralising agent, required to uphold the myth of individual choice and responsibility and encouraging those at their most vulnerable to find personal resolve. In addition, if service users are cast as being responsible for their own recovery, cuts to services and decreased provision appear logical (Ferguson, 2007; Moth, 2018), and the state can justify retraction from traditional roles. Nonetheless, the official advice for those working in social care is to: 'support the person to identify the strengths and assets available in their community' (NICE, 2019). Yet those practitioners tasked with supporting service users to access community 'assets' are face to face with the consequences of austerity and the hollowing out of the very 'assets' presented as the solution: the closure of day centres, public libraries, Sure Start centres and swimming pools, for example. With the additional pressures of unemployment, precarious employment, poverty and homelessness, the search for 'community assets' seems overly optimistic (Cummins, Parkinson and Pollock, 2020). While the government deny that the aim of strengths-based practice is to reduce support, they acknowledge that the 'reduction of packages of support' is 'generally a collateral benefit' (Department of Health and Social Care, 2019). The notion of collective responsibility has been eroded and, with it, many of the community 'assets' which strengths-based practice promotes.

Lost for words

In a culture of austerity and individual responsibility it becomes increasingly difficult to reduce the stigma associated with mental health. Despite a backlash against the medical model, it remains 'potent' because it 'holds sway in public opinion and thereby generates stigma and self-stigma – both of which cause social exclusion' (Backwith, 2015, p 120). In this context a move away from a deficit model to a strengths-based model cannot mitigate stigma and social exclusion, which is partly perpetuated by the dominance of the medical model. While most psychiatrists work within multi-disciplinary teams and acknowledge the part that social context plays in mental distress, the diagnostic criteria, with their treatment pathways and prognoses, nevertheless dictate the response to distress and firmly locate the root cause as biological and the subject as the 'patient'. Secondary mental health provision, such as community mental health teams, may notionally acknowledge the importance of strengths-based approaches, but practitioners have a difficult task. One survivor describes her experiences of secondary mental health services in the following way: 'I started to talk about myself in medical terms ... I started to lose track of what's my story about myself ... I lost my words' (*Word of Mouth*, 2022). In hospital she was told not to listen to intrusive voices, to distract herself, but by not listening she feels she missed the opportunity for healing and felt stuck. She realised that the voices needed listening to so that her experiences could be understood within the context of her life, within the context of trauma. If mental distress is pathologised, it could be assumed that this would 'squeeze the conceptual domain in which responsibility might be exercised' (Baker and Brown, 2012, p 70), but this isn't the case because mental distress becomes reconfigured as failure of the will. The diagnosis and label of having a personality disorder illustrate this point well. To be personality-disordered 'is accompanied by inferences that the person is wasting the time of practitioners, is being manipulative or is attention seeking' (Baker and Brown, 2012, p 77).

The use of medical language, while contested, remains powerful and 'becomes a locus, not only for the construction of reality and meanings, but also for the negotiation of social positions and power. When the experiences of clients are discredited and marginalized ... epistemic injustice inevitably occurs' (Bogo et al, 2019, p 32). While strengths-based practice appears to advocate for a move away from social worker as expert to service user as expert, the service user has already been and continues to be interpellated by medical professionals – silenced, marginalised and objectified. Clinical mental health practice is, as Saleebey says 'suffused with the language of pessimism and doubt' (Saleebey, 2002, p 2). The use of pessimistic and judgemental language extends beyond medical terminology and into the ways in which service users are described and how their behaviour is explained. Those service users who miss appointments are seen as 'hard to reach' or 'difficult to engage' and those who don't take prescribed medication are 'non-compliant'. Adopting this language contributes to the construction of the social identities of both professionals and services users and shapes the networks of social relations in which they emerge. The invalidation, rejection and stigma articulated by survivors is also evidenced in language and, inevitably, strengths-based practice does not sit outside of this. Identifying a service user's strengths has become interchangeable with their 'assets' and the 'assets' in their community. The language of the market dominates because an asset is defined as, 'a thing of value, especially property, that a person or company own and that can be used or sold to pay debts' (*Oxford Learner's Dictionary*, 2022). 'Asset' also stands in direct contrast to liability, which is, of course how many survivors experience themselves in mainstream services – liabilities to be contained and controlled. Strengths-based practice must be attuned to the nuances and power of language, which can marginalise or empower. Language must be analysed within the political and cultural context in which it emerges and where it is then used and circulated.

The strengths-based practice handbook claims that strengths-based practice is 'aligned with risk enablement' and positive risk-taking, in collaboration with service users (Department of Health, 2019). Yet, within mental health practice, the risk agenda suggests the opposite. First, in the context of austerity, assessing risk is overwhelmingly concerned with the allocation of resources, and second it is about containing and controlling those perceived to be dangerous. As budgets are cut and austerity has taken hold, the concept of risk as the main criterion for eligibility has dominated assessment (Lymbery and Postle, 2015). For those suffering from mental health difficulties this is Hobson's choice – to be labelled with a 'severe and enduring' chronic mental health diagnosis with a gloomy prognosis or not to be 'risky' or 'ill' enough to meet the criteria for secondary mental health services. Those suffering from severe depression and anxiety often do not meet the eligibility criteria despite the deleterious effect on quality of life.

Consideration of risk is at the forefront of all mental health assessments. The risk agenda has moved the responsibility for risk from the state to the individual. This is evident in another enabler of strengths-based practice, personalisation, where the service user is cast in the role of employer. Within mental health, risk is dangerous and requires containment, not only adding to the stigma for individuals and communities but also pushing the policing and social control aspects of containing risk further up the agenda. The worlds of social care and social control, once so distinct, have seeped into each other, and this is justified through an apparently common language of morality and individual responsibility. There has been a shift away from support in community resources to a more punitive and heavy-handed approach for all those perceived to be on the margins. Community treatment orders (CTO) (Mental Health Law Online, 2021) are possibly the most controversial and contested 'section' of the Mental Health Act (1983 (Legislation.gov.uk, 2014). 'Patients' are hospitalised repeatedly against their will if they disengage from their treatment plan. These CTOs are considered, by many, to be coercive and punitive, and have been dubbed 'psychiatric asbos' by their critics because punishment has replaced care (Hunter, 2013). For practitioners working with somebody on a CTO their role is not dissimilar to that of a detective. Inevitably when workers end up taking on the role of a detective, surveillance and mutual suspicion can become the norm of the working day.

Punitive Personal Independence Payments

Another factor that both creates and perpetuates mental distress and social exclusion and hence mitigates the potential benefits of strengths-based practice is the increasingly punitive benefits system, particularly the introduction of Personal Independence Payments (PIP) and Employment and Support Allowance (ESA).

In 2013 PIP replaced the Disability Living Allowance. As part of the austerity agenda, PIP is designed to reduce the number of claimants and to save money. Applying for PIP is a lengthy and stressful experience; the criteria are heavily weighted to those with physical health difficulties, and, if awarded, claimants are only eligible for a fixed period which is subject to review. In 2017 the High Court found that part of the rules governing PIP were unlawful and breached human rights by discriminating against people with mental health problems (*Rf v. Secretary of State*, 2017). PIP perpetuates feelings of invalidation as one service claimant articulates: 'you go with the full intention of telling them how you are as an individual but I really got the feeling that they thought I was lying' (Machin and McCormack, 2021).

Those applying for ESA are subjected to Work Capability Assessments and Work Focused Interventions as well as sanctions around compliance and behaviour. ESA exacerbates mental distress by using 'behavioural psychology' (Lavalette and Moth, 2017). Dubbed 'psycho-compulsion', such practices seek to impose 'psychological explanations for unemployment together with mandatory activities intended to modify beliefs, attitude, disposition or personality in order to activate the unemployed' (Lavalette and Moth, 2017, p 10). Unemployment then is framed as individual deficiency and calls into question people's moral worth. While ESA is ostensibly a benefit to get people back into work, Moth and Lavalette's research revealed that those who claim it are penalised, and interviews have revealed 'surveillance traps' where claimants are watched by cameras in the waiting area, depression and anxiety are downplayed and the staff completing the assessments have very little, if any knowledge of mental health difficulties and take a procedural 'tick box' approach to eligibility (Lavalette and Moth, 2017). Distress caused by the eligibility criteria, both in terms of plunging people into poverty and discrediting their condition, cannot be overestimated:

> In my recovery I've never felt so ashamed, so excluded and so out of synch with how I've been treated by the benefits system and my shame and the sense is that you're not worthy predominantly comes from how we access our benefits systems [...] the system that's supposed to be helping us to feel less ashamed and more included is excluding us and knocking us back to miles gone back to centuries ago. I was thinking it's a bit like Charles Dicken's times, isn't it, worse, you know, food banks and everything. (Lavalette and Moth, 2017, p 22)

This culture of blame and shame frames mental health difficulties as being self-inflicted in nature and increases stigma, social exclusion and marginalisation. 'Those mired in welfare dependency are framed as a burdensome weight serving to impede, with their "negative" and "workshy" attitudes and lifestyles, the journey to economic "recovery"' (Garrett, 2018, p 78).

All in the mind

In 2018 Vicki Nash, head of policy and campaigns for MIND explained that many people still do not feel supported by mental health services. She stressed the 'urgent need for a cross-government strategy that recognises the huge impact of housing, benefits, employment and other aspects of people's lives on their mental health' (CQC, 2018). Social work's professional roots in social justice are undermined when the ugly reality of social inequality, widespread deprivation and poverty are papered over. Support networks for mental health appear to operate through a binary opposition of inclusion and exclusion. Those with mental health difficulties are considered troubling and troubled because they are perceived to be not participating and, more significantly, not contributing to society or the economy. Poverty becomes contiguous with social exclusion and, in turn, social exclusion becomes criminalised. To be effective, strengths-based practice must not sidestep a sense of collective responsibility:

> We must stress again that seeking to work with individuals' lived experience is a positive approach, but it is clearly an approach which stresses the role of the individual away from the collective responsibility of the state and that can be said to not address the structural explanations of poverty, class and gender which all influence the person and their experience. (Cummins et al, 2020, p 94)

Arcs of resistance: 'opening the window'

There is a need to challenge the pathology of mental illness and to understand, at least in part, mental distress as symptomatic of a political culture that excludes and discriminates. While there is an irreconcilable conflict between neo-liberal imperatives and strengths-based practice, there are spaces where harnessing strengths and promoting recovery become a real possibility. Perhaps it is the spaces outside of clinical criteria where strengths-based practice can become meaningful and practitioners have a genuine opportunity to practice in a manner set out by the Chief Social Worker, Lyn Romeo, where it is possible to apply 'imagination, creativity and curiosity to working in partnership with individuals and their carers, acknowledging the centrality of people's own expertise about their experience and needs' (Department of Health, 2011). Voluntary sector organisations are 'perceived ... as taking a holistic view of people's needs, focusing on their strengths and aspirations and being less constrained by clinical thresholds' (Centre for Mental Health, 2019).

There are, outside of statutory provision, sites of resistance where conceptions of mental distress are reframed. The remainder of this chapter will focus on one such example. Arts for Recovery in the Community (Arc) is based in Stockport in the north-west of England. Arc offers creative activities and support for adults and some young people suffering from or recovering from poor mental health. Their 'mission' is to 'offer high impact creative experiences, skills and opportunities which promote individual and communal wellbeing, reaching the most vulnerable within communities, recognising the value of creativity to self-worth, resilience and confidence' (Arts for Recovery in the Community, 2021). Arc is part of the long-established tradition of thinking about the relationship between creativity and mental health. Arc illustrates that hegemonies are not completed projects and provides a space which quietly challenges the 'responsibility' agenda.

Many participants come to Arc with their stories told for them. Some of the people who attend Arc are seeking sanctuary from structures which have only compounded feelings of paranoia, lack of agency, worthlessness and, in many cases, utter alienation. They also come with a multitude of complex issues that penetrate every area of their life: poverty, housing issues, struggles with benefits, involvement with children's social care and trauma. Many have been discriminated against and oppressed by the structures discussed in the first part of this chapter, structures which should be there to support them. Many have been reminded again and again about their lack of ability to live life well or make the right decisions. They have often internalised the message that they are the authors of their own misfortune.

Addressing social exclusion and working alongside participants to rebuild fractured lives is what places like Arc do best. The stigmatising effect of mental distress can be challenged by offering a space where new meanings can be generated, different roles can be explored safely and confidence can be rebuilt. Places like Arc have a different formulation of mental distress: people usually demonstrate resilience rather than pathology, and everybody has the right to self-determination and the opportunity to turn potential into reality and a belief that recovery from mental distress can be transformative. People who come to Arc are participants, not patients or service users. In mainstream mental health provision there are not the resources or the time for people to receive more holistic support or to address what are often perceived through the medical model of mental health as secondary issues – creating relationships, meanings and values – and this is what Arc addresses through a shared humanity which encourages creative exploration and curiosity. Jacqui Wood, Artistic Director of Arc, explains their vision:

> at its heart it is a really simple idea ... we acknowledge people need to feel connected – to each other, to their place, to their self – in order to feel mentally healthy. We offer creative ways to connect and these processes are exploratory, emotional, tangible and ultimately affirming. Being creative, a person can find an opportunity, share their story and feel validated and listened to, often by making something beautiful. It is both an individual and a communal experience. (Wood, 2022)

If being connected and feeling validated are essential for both the process and the outcome of strengths-based practice, then more attention needs to be paid to secondary issues. Strengths-based guidance recognises the role isolation plays in mental distress: 'Reducing isolation and building supportive social networks and relationships promotes good mental health and recovery as well as preventing mental health problems' (Department of Health, 2011). Many participants at Arc cite loneliness as one of the most debilitating aspects of their lives. Addressing loneliness is relatively easy. As one participant commented on joining Arc: 'It's saved me from being very lonely … it's like opening the window.' According to an all-parliamentary group inquiry, 'At least one third of GP appointments are, in part, due to isolation' (All-Parliamentary Group on Arts, Health and Wellbeing, 2017). Clearly loneliness creates and exacerbates mental health difficulties and social exclusion. Loneliness is a logical product of a rampant individualism which sees communities decimated and ideas of collective responsibility lost. Loneliness is not a personal deficit; it is a symptom of a culture that excludes. An organisation like Arc can tackle loneliness because it is not procedural and it is not tasked with fulfilling key performance indicators (KPIs) which become the marker of good practice and success within mental health teams. KPIs take away the autonomy and professional discretion of individual workers as well as the time and benefits brought about by a meaningful relationship between service user and professional which is so important to strengths-based practice (Moth, 2020).

Arc has a broad referral base, including referrals directly from hospital and from secondary care. However, many of Arc's referrals come through a social prescriber who refers or signposts through primary care. Over the past few years, a growing evidence base has emerged to show the benefits of social prescribing, particularly in terms of addressing loneliness and promoting connectivity: 'Through social prescribing and community resilience programmes, creative arts can have a significant impact on reducing isolation and enabling wellbeing in communities (All-Party Parliamentary Group on Arts, 2017). NHS England Policy's (2019) mission is to embed social prescribing into primary care, employing more social prescriber link workers with the aim of successfully referring 900,000 people by 2023/24 (National Health Service, 2019). However, the focus on primary care means that, for most in secondary care, interventions remain procedural, and risk-led.

The evidence base clearly indicates that arts-based community projects are enablers of strengths-based practice: 'the potential contribution of the arts to health and wellbeing has, as yet, been all too little realised. Too often, arts programmes for health are temporary and provision is uneven across the country' (All-Parliamentary Group, 2017). Given the evidence and the potential financial benefits, it is striking that there are still so few projects and even fewer that are supported financially through public funds. For the financial year 2021–2022, 44 per cent of Arc's income was generated from public funds. Despite the evident savings, there is no long-term financial commitment from the state and the expectation is that the majority of annual income will be generated independently. State withdrawal 'aided by the logic of the market is believed to prompt private individuals and non-state bodies to be more "active"' (Baker and Brown, 2012, p 20).

'A human-shaped space'

As discussed earlier, the concept of responsibility within mental health provision takes on an ethical dimension because it 'valorises certain kinds of desirable conduct. It foregrounds a focus on subjects as reflexive, rational consumers and an increasing moral emphasis on citizens as duty-owing members of communities' (Baker and Brown, 2012, p 15). Relations with each other within these communities are mediated by the state. Spaces like Arc cannot be regulated or policed in quite the same way; the opportunity for self-education and self-realisation through creativity, it could be argued, is not only not valued by the state but is a little threatening to the status quo. In an interview, author and professor of political economy William Davies makes a pertinent point about what he describes as the 'phenomenon of safe spaces' (Bailes, 2017). In the world of contemporary capitalism, there are no 'sanctuaries from economic competition' (Bailes, 2017). In terms of mental health provision, this is evident with the personalisation agenda and it is evident with state benefit provision. The lack of sanctuaries has created a need for safe spaces which provide 'the possibility of being somewhere where vulnerability is accepted' (Bailes, 2017).

Case studies: Lynne and David

The importance of space is mentioned time and again by participants – both the physical literal space and the space they are given in terms of time: time to talk, to connect, and time to be vulnerable. Jacqui Wood, Artistic Director of Arc, explains the importance of space: 'Arc provides a space – a human-shaped space, welcoming, friendly, warm. Inspiring and yet challenging. A space to create. A space to connect. A space to feel better' (Wood, 2022).

A former participant, Lynne Robinson, also explains the importance of space:

> It felt like a safe space. I was scared of meeting people but the people in the group were going through the same feelings. I met people from different walks of life. The space was calm. It felt like a family. We were never told to leave. We sat and ate our lunch together. We learnt not to be frightened to talk to each other we learnt to laugh. We could sit and look at our exhibits and feel proud while we drank our coffee. Being able to sit and have a coffee or join the singing group was so important. If I felt vulnerable one day I couldn't go in a coffee shop, it would be too hard but at Arc somebody would come and speak to me. (Robinson, 2022)

Lynne, like others, has also experienced another type of space, a space that is connected with being disconnected and disregarded. Another participant who was part of a creative writing group wrote the following about her PIP appeal:

> I can't concentrate and I can't focus. I don't want to leave the house but I have to go to a PIP appeal. I have to sit in a cramped, stuffy waiting room with

a security guard and someone is angry. A young woman is crying. Numbers come up on the board and people shuffle in. I feel disconnected and start panicking. There's a thick glass screen between us and them. I get told by them – with a bang on the glass – that I can't have my hot drink in the waiting room and have to take it outside. 'Could be used as a weapon apparently', someone says. After an hour I go up to the counter. 'How long will I wait?' 'I don't know' says the muffled voice behind the shatterproof glass. 'He's gone on his lunch break now.'

This surreal and disconnected space is testimony to the 'othering' of those seen as 'undeserving'. Any meaningful application of strengths-based practice involves mitigating the inclusion and exclusion criteria discussed earlier in this chapter. This can be partly achieved by creating spaces which validate, spaces which are conducive to recovery and create a genuine opportunity to reframe experiences. For one participant, their feeling of exclusion was mitigated through artistic expression: 'I don't want to sit and look at other people living their lives. I want to live mine. I do my painting and I don't feel that I'm in a box left out of this world. I feel like I'm creative and I count.'

David is a former Arc participant and now a trustee. For him space and creative exploration were paramount to his recovery, as was the concept of transformative suffering.

> At Arc it was OK not to be OK. These days, being creative is actively discouraged in society – it's devalued. Productivity is what's seen as important. If it doesn't have a monetary value attached to it, it isn't seen as worthwhile. Arc taught me that it was about the process of doing art that was important and not the end result. This was very liberating for me. I stopped caring about what people might think of my finished piece and just enjoyed getting lost in the process of creating something. We don't always need an end result and I discovered myself through realising this. It gave me a freedom to experiment and express myself without judgement. Arc has been integral to my recovery and confidence.

When David first came to Arc, he had split up from his wife, lost his job and was diagnosed with clinical depression. Over the next couple of years he battled with alcoholism, spent a period of time homeless and sleeping in his car and, most painful of all, his school-age children could no longer live with him. He had no motivation, no goals and experienced what he called 'an abandonment of hope' (Milligan-Croft, 2022). Five years on and David is a trustee for Arc and is working as a technical instructor delivering, among other things, art sessions on an adult acute mental health ward. David is an artist and writer. His poem below, written just before he became very ill, captures the grief and despair of a lost time.

SOMETIMES, I GO UPSTAIRS
David Milligan-Croft

Sometimes, you might hear a bang,
Like something has been knocked over
And you shout out,
'Hey! What are you two up to?'

Sometimes, you go upstairs,
You know, to check on the girls.
To make sure they haven't kicked off
Their duvets, or fallen out of bed.

But, when you go up,
You realise they're not there anymore.
And, for a moment,
You thought life was like it was before.

Through his journey David gained insight into the transformative potential of creativity in a space outside of 'productivity'.

Lynne also stresses the importance of creativity, but just as important is access to cultural life which supported her to feel 'valued' and included:

> It wasn't just about art. We went out: we were part of projects. We did Bells for Peace at Manchester Cathedral, we went to the ballet, art galleries and museums. There was no way on this earth that I could have gone to the theatre without support. It's the interaction and being supported to access certain spaces that was important. A string quartet from the Camerata came to Arc. We felt cultured, we dressed up, eating our lunch and listening to music. We felt valued and special. (Robinson, 2022)

Lynne's testimony provides evidence that a strengths-based approach can work in the right environment. Art, in all its forms, provides an alternative lens through which to view the world. Yet many people do not have access to the arts, and this is because those who are excluded from mainstream middle-class society are misrecognised in cultural spaces like galleries and theatres. If people are responsible for their 'failures', then they are made to feel equally underserving of opportunities and this includes access to the arts.

Both Lynne's and David's testimonies highlight a process of recovery from a political culture that, at the very least, exacerbated mental distress because it excluded and stigmatised them. Lynne found the structures that should have been there to support her threatening:

> I felt judged. I didn't open up because I didn't trust anybody. I felt patronised and scared that social services would take George, my son, from me. I was

scared of the bank, housing benefit applications. Before I was ill I had a good job but I forgot how to be independent. I felt a bad mum. I wasn't. I was a mum who was struggling … I rediscovered myself at Arc. (Robinson, 2022)

Places like Arc provide the space to reconfigure oneself in a space that, while not outside of neo-liberal ideology, is at least a space of collective responsibility where people are not scrutinised, diagnosed, labelled, objectified. Importantly, all participants have medical anonymity; they are not viewed as people in mental distress. Being 'well' is not about the presence or absence of symptoms. Suffering can be transformative in spaces where social inclusion and human rights are at the centre of practice. 'The important task for the individual under neoliberal ideology is a process of reconfiguring the self, such that emotions – particularly those that might disrupt productivity or consumption, for example grief, anger or misery – are construed as something to be self-managed, privatised and constrained' (Baker and Brown, 2012, p 17).

'When I could stop feeling I was to blame, I gained confidence. When I gained confidence I could find my place in the world. I could find my strengths' (Robinson, 2022).

Conclusion

A narrow focus on service user's strengths in direct practice cannot compensate for a more robust approach which recognises that assessment and intervention are political activities where metaphors of deficits, dysfunction and pathologies still dominate. The medical model, the risk agenda and the benefits system perpetuate mental distress, stigma and social exclusion, which makes it challenging to practise effectively in a strengths–based manner. As it stands, strengths–based practice and its 'enablers' function as a political smokescreen; problems of neo-liberalism and austerity are reconfigured as personal responsibilities while government responsibility is diverted. In such an environment a truly restorative strengths–based practice struggles to establish itself. It is perhaps for this reason that the evidence base is so scant: 'We found that many social workers and social care professionals we met fundamentally supported a strengths–based approach within adult social work and social care but often found it difficult to demonstrate, evidence and practise such an approach in practice' (Department of Health and Social Care, 2019, p 23). However, there are chinks of light. Parliamentary groups recognise the contribution of arts–based interventions to strengths–based practice and could influence a shift in culture where spaces like Arc and mainstream provision become more aligned:

The arts have an amazing ability to bring people together, enabling us to find strength in ourselves and each other. By connecting through creativity to people and place, we support each other, and develop a genuine sense of belonging. This has a profound impact on our mental health. (Arts for Recovery in the Community, 2021)

Key learning points

- The potential of strengths-based practice within mainstream mental health provision is undermined by a neo-liberal culture.

- Mental health is often framed in terms of individual morality.

- Mental distress is exacerbated by social inequality and social exclusion.

- There is alternative support available which tackles stigma and prioritises social inclusion.

- Arts-based interventions have a valuable contribution to make within strengths-based practice.

Further reading

For more detail about Arc and arts-based programmes: https://arc-centre.org

Baker, C., Crone, D.M., Hughes, S., James. D., Loughren, E.A. and Sumner, R.C. (2020) 'Factors associated with attendance, engagement and wellbeing change in an arts on prescription intervention', *Journal of Public Health*, 42(1): 8–95.

Gallant, G., Hamilton-Hinch, B., Litwiller, F. and White, C. (2019) *'Removing the Thorns': The Role of the Arts in Recovery for People with Mental Health Challenges.* [online] Available from: https://doi.org/10.1080/17533015.2017.1413397

For more information about the impact of neo-liberalism on perceptions of mental health:

Lavalette, M. and Moth, R. (2017) *Social Protection and Labour Market Policies for Vulnerable Groups from a Social Investment Perspective: The Case of Welfare Recipients with Mental Health Needs in England.* RE-inVEST working paper series D5.1, Liverpool: Hope University/Leuven: HIVA-KU Leuven.

Moth, R. (2020) *Understanding Mental Distress: Knowledge Practice and Neoliberal Reform in Community Mental Health Services*, Bristol: Policy Press.

10

People with lived experience of strengths-based approaches

Deanna Edwards, Kate Parkinson and People with Lived Experience

Introduction

This chapter acknowledges the importance of hearing directly from the people with lived experience of strength-based and other social work approaches. It will consider why these voices are important and address how practitioners and services can involve those people in service development and delivery, what we can learn from seeking the views of those with experience of services and how we can address the dearth of experience-led voices in social care services.

While it is desirable to hear from people involved in all areas covered in this text, for brevity and for practical reasons this has not been possible. What we can learn from these gaps is explored later in the chapter.

In order to safeguard the identity of other people involved in these narratives, some names and identifying details have been omitted and changed and personal life events have not been shared in any detail.

Why involve people with lived experience?

At the heart of the strengths perspective is the practice of building upon the strengths of the people to whom we are providing services. To this end practitioners and services need to engage and build relationships with these people. This will involve hearing their voices, their perspectives, their strengths and their concerns as well as those of professionals. Good communication is therefore a central tenet of this approach. If strengths-based practice is to be authentic, it requires a commitment to empowerment, engaging with users of services and listening to their voices. In many of these chapters the reader is introduced to current research informing practice, but to be truly needs-led a service must listen to the voices of those, often under-represented, individuals and families who use the service. It is only these voices that can tell us the truth about the efficacy of these services, how they can be improved, what works and what doesn't. That said, it needs to be recognised that this chapter will not meet this ideal for reasons outlined below, by hearing the voices of people with lived experience. The ideal needs to be achieved by robust research that involves them as well as authentic discourse and their involvement in service development and delivery. It is acknowledged here that the voices presented in this chapter are in all probability subject to a participant bias or demand characteristics (Robson, 2002) from the people who responded to the call to be involved. This means those contributors may be more likely to write about positive experiences of their involvement in strengths-based practice; these people are also more likely to agree to become involved with the project. Nevertheless, this does not make their voices less valuable; what they have to say can still help to shape both current and future practice, and this will be addressed later in the chapter. Since strengths-based approaches were born out of a desire to counter a deficit approach (Saleebey, 2002) this positive spin may indeed be desirable. It must also be noted here that conversations with people with lived experience took place during the COVID-19 pandemic in 2021–2022. This will have undoubtedly altered the way services operated and the way in which people perceived the service. This is noted in the text when directly observed.

As discussed in the introductory chapter, one of the central tenets of the approach is that we serve people best by collaborating with them, and to this end the approach requires social work to do so, which in turn leads to a conclusion that practitioners and researchers need to involve people who use services in those services. This of course involves listening to their voices about the efficacy of those services.

In addition to this, those working in the field have a responsibility to uphold social work values. Social Work England's first professional standard requires social workers to: 'Promote the rights, strengths and well-being of people, families and communities which requires us to recognise them as experts in their own lives' (www.socialworkengland.org.uk/standards/professional-standard).

The Professional Capabilities Framework (PCF) requires social workers in England and Wales to contribute to the development of organisations and services, and working with people with lived experience in this development can be a productive way forward (https://www.basw.co.uk/professional-deve lopment/professional-capabilities-framework-pcf/the-pcf).

People with lived experiences of 'traditional social work' practice

Before we progress to consider how people with lived experience perceive some of the strengths-based approaches covered in this book, it is useful to consider how traditional social work is viewed by those who have been recipients. Of course, when doing this it is difficult to assess (unless stated) whether these social workers are utilising a strengths approach, and so this section at best presents an overview of how generic social work is experienced.

Kam (2019) argues that those people who use social work services are the most suitable to communicate what is effective social work practice and what qualities a social worker should have. Kam goes on to argue that these personal qualities include an acknowledgement of social work as a vocation and not just a job, building effective relationships and being an ally. He also goes on to say that a focus upon strengths and abilities rather than on problems and deficits was viewed more positively. This was coupled with seeing the person with lived experience as the expert in their own life. Similarly, Ylvisaker (2011) argued that 'good social work involves empathy, sensitivity and opportunities allowing clients to voice their own concern' (p 203). McLaughlin (2016) agrees that social workers were valued for such qualities and specifically for emotional and practical support but warns that the role has become increasingly driven by procedures and targets, leaving less time to focus upon these important skills.

It is interesting and perhaps unsurprising that the perception of child protection social workers is somewhat mixed, given the statutory nature of much of this involvement. Buckley, Carr and Whelan (2010) found that, while people found the process 'intimidating and stressful', the 'development of good relationships between workers and [people with lived experience] could compensate for the harsher aspects of involvement with child protection' (p 101). They argued that multiple stereotypes of child protection, such as social workers being powerful and removing children, persist alongside shame and stigma about these services being involved with their family. The fear of losing children was very real, and families felt they were 'under surveillance' (p 109). Frustrations were experienced when social workers were unreliable, didn't turn up on time or didn't return calls, and families felt that they would be judged if their behaviour was as inconsistent and unreliable. However, social workers who were warm, friendly and relaxed were perceived as supportive. People using child protection services wanted these qualities alongside reliability, transparency, experience and expertise.

In terms of the views of children and young people, research suggests that their experiences are again mixed, especially in relation to child protection services. Bell (2002) found similar results to those described above in that children wanted a relationship of trust with a social worker, an experienced echoed by Cossar et al (2011). Buckley et al (2010) argued that good relationships can to an extent counteract the intimidating and stressful nature of child protection for children and young people. Jobe and Gorin (2013) interviewed young people involved in child protection and found that one of their main frustrations was an inconsistent relationship with a social worker, frequent changes when passed between services and when social workers leave or are off sick. Another complaint they had was about not being informed what was happening to them and that social workers listened more to adults than to young people.

One person who was interviewed for this chapter agrees with some of the fear that young people have of social workers. Talking about a young person, she said,

> 'I think the phrase social worker can frighten somebody young because she automatically thinks she is being ripped away from her family.'

Because of ethical considerations young people were not spoken to directly for this chapter, so we hear more from the voices of adults involved with social care services. As indicated in the research cited above, views of social workers were mixed. One person interviewed felt that the social workers involved with their relative were constantly checking up on them and dictating how they lived their life. She felt the messages they were given included

> 'we don't think you're doing that right, we suggest you do this and we want you to do that.'
> 'you must do that.'

She suggested that it was hard for the family to go from no involvement to

> 'someone's on your case all of the time'.

From the perspective of this interviewee the social worker was young, inexperienced and taking her advice from a 'textbook and not 'day-to-day real life'. She describes how

> 'what frustrates us is that H thinks she knows it all and actually she thinks we don't know anything. Actually H doesn't know about the situation really, she's only young and only knows what she thinks she knows.'

Another interviewee had similar views saying that there was a general resentment about the intrusion. K felt that, while she was co-operating with the requirement to do a parenting course, there was little recognition of the difficulty of raising three small children and she shouldn't be 'told' how to raise her own kids.

> 'I don't mistreat them, they're always clothed nice, they're not short of things.'

She went on to say of her social worker,

> 'You've not struggled to get three kids to school when it's pouring with rain and I've got no money and I'm struggling with this and I'm struggling with that and you think its so easy to write it down on paper and this is how you should be doing it and it's not like that.'

Mica's views were that she was looking forward to a time when there are no social workers in her family's life. She had mixed experience but said that her current social worker has taken time to get to know them and has done an assessment based on 'as she saw things today rather than on the past'.

She also commented that she doesn't just 'look at a textbook' but that she does 'take it from a parent's point of view as well'. Her perspectives on child protection conferences she attended were less positive.

'I just felt like everyone was picking on me ... they were just pecking me and pecking me and they made me think I wasn't good enough. I was sat thinking I can't do right for doing wrong here, honestly it felt like that. It was literally all these professionals and they were all just on at me. I just thought I'm gonna lose my kids.'

One person who had experienced significant domestic abuse said that she felt that she was being blamed rather than the perpetrator.

'no-one said what I was good at, it was all based around I hadn't kept the kids safe even though he'd [father of children] done all the DV [domestic violence] I had to prove myself to social services.'

There were also issues with social workers being difficult to contact (for example, 'it took six weeks for anyone to get back to me', 'I have been trying to get hold of someone for eight weeks') and with people being so afraid of the social worker that they told the children, 'Don't tell the social worker.' Mica said that in her household they even have a joke that 'The kids have odd socks on and we say, "Don't tell the social worker"'.

She gives the following advice:

'If they'd just come in and said right OK you've been through a shit time, you've had all this happen and all this happen and yes alright maybe you shouldn't have gone that way but let's work on it. If they'd have come in and done that instead of picking on me – they've probably worn me down more than I was.'

Stacey offers a counter-perspective describing her current social worker as 'amazing' and, like Mica, she argues that this is because the worker considers the present situation rather than the past.

'She was normal: "I'm not gonna read any reports, I'm going to make up my own mind, I'm going to start afresh".

She'd come in and play with the kids and it was like having a friend in the house.'

Key learning points

In summary these interviews suggest that child protection is stressful and difficult and that social workers can be perceived as judgemental and unsupportive. However, social workers who focus upon the present, who support families rather than criticise them, develop relationships and are realistic rather than 'textbook', are viewed positively.

Stacey went on to say that the social worker had no expectation that the house would be tidy and that if the toys were out and washing up and washing was around, then this was positive proof that she was playing with the kids, feeding them and washing their clothes. This was supported by another interviewee, who said that she wasn't 'marked down' for having a messy house and that her social worker 'mucks in and helps out'.

Involving people with lived experience in generic strengths-based social work

This section attempts to acknowledge that some of the strengths-based work that social workers do falls under the umbrella of 'generic strengths-based work'. This means that it is not tied to a specific type of approach/theoretical perspective or model such as Signs of Safety or a narrative approach. Indeed, in the UK some local authorities have described their overall signature style or dominant philosophy as strengths-based. For example, Leeds City Council Adult Social Care has a 'strengths-based social care board' and has introduced strengths-based working throughout its adult services (https://www.local.gov.uk/casestudies/leeds-city-coun cil-strengths-based-working). Similarly, the Social Care Institute for Excellence (SCIE) lists a number of strengths-based projects that operate as a generic strengths-based service. One such project is the Growing Futures project in Doncaster, which is a service for children, young people and their families established in 2015. It particularly uses a strengths-based approach in working with families who have been impacted by domestic abuse. This involves providing a Domestic Abuse Navigator (known as a DAN) to work intensively with such families to support, provide practice advice and help to advocate and educate. Feedback about DAN workers has been positive and has included the following piece:

> '[She] has been more giving us, like, solutions, to, you know, if you think there's an incident about to happen or you feel that you are getting frustrated, type thing, she's shown us different ways of going about dealing with it.' (http://www.scie.org.uk/strengths-based-app roaches/young-people#casestudies, [Accessed 6 December 2021])

A number of individuals who utlilised the Growing Futures project were consulted about their views in relation to the service. They were overwhelmingly positive about the service in a focus group-type meeting, stating that the service was 'amazing' and 'life-saving'. The service manager also attended this meeting and maintained their strengths-based stance by reinforcing to the women who used the service that it was they who were 'amazing' and reminding them of their incredible strength and resilience in the face of difficult life experiences. Two of the women form the service agreed to discuss the service individually. These women, Mica and Stacey, were incredibly generous with their time and open to sharing their experiences. While their personal stories will not be shared for reasons of confidentiality, they had both had a DAN worker whom they found to be positive, helpful and supportive. Mica said of her DAN worker:

'she was brilliant, she was absolutely lovely, to be honest she helped me learn a lot more about the domestic abuse, we did a lot of work together by breaking it down. She helped me realise there was a lot more to it.'

Key learning points

There is a focus on two things here: the building of a relationship of trust and the emphasis on working in partnership in terms of Mica's assertion that they worked 'together'.

Stacey argued that the work was also effective because it wasn't rushed and time was taken to support her:

'She works at my pace there was no rush, just support, always support.'

She added that the worker helped her to build back her self-confidence by reinforcing that she has strengths and capabilities:

'It's reinstating that self-worth and self-confidence just make you feel worth knowing, that you can do it, that you have got support out there, having that empowerment back.'

This was reinforced by encouragement and positive affirmations:

'She reassured me. If I did something positive it was praised, it was "you're doing really well".'

These positive affirmative statements weren't just made by the DAN worker, though, and Stacey recognises their importance throughout the child protection process. They are, she said, particularly memorable among the messages of what she had not got right and the feelings of being told what to do and what not to do. In among this she particularly remembered the words of a police officer at a child protection conference. This officer told Stacey that

'I absolutely commend you for what you've done, there's not a lot of women who could do it pregnant.'

Stacey said that this meant so much and has stayed with her.

135

Mica was equally enthusiastic and emphasised different qualities, particularly those of calmness and having a non-judgemental attitude:

> 'She was really calm, she never came in and said, "You've done this, you've done that, you should have done this, you should have done that." She never judged me.'

This approach worked, and Mica said that the DAN worker had helped her to change for the better and helped her to change her perspective on how relationships should be. Mica added that her worker was available and supportive, which made her feel like she was working with someone who wanted to do the job and who wanted to work with her:

> 'She spoke to me like a human rather than a case. I could ring her whenever I wanted to, and she'd text me just to check in that I was OK. I actually felt like she wanted to help rather than just being told to.'

Stacey, Mica and the other women who attended the focus group emphasised how valuable they found the service, how its ethos is based upon building positive, supportive relationships, using affirmations, with staff being available and, as one person said, 'on my side'. One might therefore argue that the success of the service rests upon these central tenets.

Family Group Conferences

The origins of Family Group Conferences (FGCs) are strongly intertwined with the rights of people with lived experience (Connolly, 1994), and some of their key principles are about empowerment and being family-led (Edwards in Edwards and Parkinson, 2018). As a result, one would expect that FGCs also have a history of consulting with and involving people with lived experience. However, as Edwards has pointed out (Edwards and Parkinson, 2018), this work has often been sporadic and piecemeal, although there has often been a visible presence of the voices of people with lived experience at FGC events and conferences. Anecdotal evidence from FGC co-ordinators also suggests that UK practice has sometimes also employed 'family members' as co-ordinators, and Edwards cites the story of Brian and Zoe, who were employed by an FGC service following their own families' FGC. In the Netherlands an FGC is called an Eigen Kracht-conference, which in translation places the emphasis on 'using the own strengths and resources of people to make a plan and make decisions for the future and thus keep the directorship of their lives in their own hands' (https://www.eigen-kracht.nl). The process is facilitated by an independent co-ordinator who is a community member and a citizen volunteer rather than a 'professional' co-ordinator (Wachtel, 2015). This is designed to give more ownership of the process to families, as co-ordinators only facilitate a few FGCs per year alongside their other work, making the process more community-led.

While it is evident from research that families are more positive about FGCs than traditional statutory processes (Holland et al, 2005), if strengths-led processes are to be embedded in mainstream social work practice and to realise Eigen Kracht's vision of keeping people's 'directorship of their lives', we must continue both to listen to and to involve people with lived experience in both FGC delivery and development.

For the purposes of this chapter, four people were consulted about their experiences of being part of an FGC as a family member. All of these family members were involved in children and family FGCs, which are much more widespread in the UK than adult FGCs. None of them was the parent of the child/children involved in the FGC but they were all wider family members or friends invited by the child and/or parent to attend the FGC. Three out of four interviewed attended the FGC, but one (Kirsten) did not wish to attend and had her views presented at the meeting by an advocate. Her reasons for not attending were complex, but she was concerned about potential conflict at the meeting:

> 'When I was going to it I was frightened of it. I was nervous, I'd not had one before and I didn't know what it was. When it was described to me, I thought it was a brilliant idea but I was wary.'

It is important to acknowledge that without extensive preparation family members may well be apprehensive about attending an FGC, particularly the potential for conflict in private family time. Tuckman's (1965) group work theory which outlines the stages of a group as 'storming, norming, performing' may be evident here, and the 'storming' stage, if not planned, may leave family members feeling exposed. Kirsten was grateful to have the option to have her views represented. For Kirsten it was important that her views were represented accurately 'word for word'. Of her advocate she said:

> 'They listened and it was your wording that was the most important thing, that it's your wording. Anything I said she typed up and sent to me and said, "This is what I'm going to read out in the meeting is this alright", so it's your thoughts.'

This chapter recognises that the person or people who are the subject of the meeting may feel differently about the FGC from other wider family, as D says they are more invested in the process. D comments that:

> 'It was OK I think because I'm a little bit further back from the situation – it's not me directly that's involved in it, the main parties may have found it … intimidating.'

However, wider family are central to the success of the process, and involving them can make a difference in the outcome. S sums this up when he describes that he was unaware of the full extent of the issues until the FGC:

> 'Sometimes we don't know what you want us to do because we're away from the core of the matter, we're family but we don't see them every day.'

D agrees that

> 'if you're not telling us that you need support or you're struggling with something, we're not actually aware.'

From this it can be argued that one of the central strengths of the FGC is that it involves the wider family in the solutions to the presenting issues. Central to this is the concept of the family making a plan, during private planning time. This plan might be quite mundane, as C describes it:

> 'The plan was just everyday routine really, for instance, R's sister to take her to Brownies.'

However, D cautions that plans are all very well but

> 'You can't always plan your life on a piece of paper.'

She adds that

> 'The plan is good in theory but its not always easy to stick to a plan, the plan being the children must be here at a certain time then if they go to grandparents the plan would be that I would take them ... sometimes it's difficult, some people are working, you know I work full-time. When I'm free they're doing something else or they just wanna play, they don't wanna be confined to doing what the plan says.'

S adds that despite feeling that 'overall it's successful' and that the family 'have done some things on the plan' it is 'quite easy to drift off plan'. Kirsten is more optimistic, saying that

> 'We all agreed to it and the plan was stuck to. We couldn't not stick to it because we were all involved in looking after A [child].'

She continued that the process was 'brilliant' and 'sorted everything out', although she agreed that Tuckman's 'storming' stage definitely occurred, saying that,

'Initially it took a little bit of time for the steam to calm down.'

The only negative feature, she felt, was that

'It is something that I've not heard of and to me even now I don't hear of this, it seems quite hidden … it's not promoted enough.'

Others agreed that the FGC was positive and they were glad to be involved. C said:

'You want a good outcome for them and you feel like you've got to play your part to get to the stage where the social worker is not involved in their day-to-day life'.

D agrees that it was good to be involved and that she would recommend FGCs to other families as 'worth trying';

'Everybody had their say, everybody said, "We would do this, we would do that, what support would you need?".'

She adds that as social work intervention is 'not as intense now, that has to be a good thing'. She does, however, feel that children could have had more involvement and could at least have attended the review. Kirsten agrees that we need to ensure that young people's voices are heard, and while the young person attended the meeting that she was involved with, she cautioned that

'She did have a voice but she was a bit pressured over what to say; she wasn't in the right frame of mind.'

She does however add that this approach was 'softer for her' than traditional social work approaches. In using FGCs, professionals need to guard against 'paying lip service' to the involvement of children and young people and ensure that there are policies in place (including advocacy) to ensure their voices are heard. For a fuller discussion of this see Laws and Kirby (2008).

Key learning points

Family members' views of FGCs may be more heard than other areas of social work, but the comments from those family members above leave no room for complacency. FGCs are family-led and professionals must continue to explore these voices in policy and practice.

Solution-focused practice

As the name suggests, solution-focused practice emphasises both strengths and a focus upon problem-solving, with an assumption that the person with lived experience has the resources to do this. It is not widely used in social work practice, although Corcoran and Pillai (2009) argue that it has a number of compatibilities with social work, particularly social work that emphasises a strengths-based approach. They argue that it is applicable in a variety of settings, especially crisis intervention and child protection. The issue is that solution-based practice is largely seen as therapeutic, and indeed solution-focused brief therapy is widely used in a variety of settings. However, solution-focused approaches have influenced both FGCs and Signs of Safety (Connolly, 2006; Sheehan et al, 2018).

As this approach is less widely utilised, feedback from people with lived experience was not forthcoming. That said, feedback about Signs of Safety was not forthcoming either and that is more widely utilised, particularly in children's services. Reasons for this may be explained by the settings in which it is used. As Corcoran and Pillai (2009) have previously noted, those receiving social work services have complex needs and are often managing crisis. Therefore, asking them to contribute to 'feedback', however well-meaning, might be a step too far. Both researchers and services need to give thought to how to reach such people, as their contribution to the debate is undoubtably invaluable.

For this chapter we were able to obtain feedback from the perspective of clients of a small private practice run by a social worker. Clearly, like all feedback in this chapter, it will be subject to participant bias since the practitioner may have selected people who:

- are likely to give positive feedback;
- have completed their therapeutic journey;
- had sought intervention voluntarily, unlike many recipients of social work services who may be 'involuntary' clients. (Bukhari et al, 2021)

To this end, this feedback is selective and will not represent a cross-section of people. However, as has been acknowledged elsewhere in this chapter, this does not invalidate the experiences of these people or lessen the importance and impact of their voices. Kirsty was incredibly articulate when she wrote:

> 'When I began my solution-focused counselling I entered with a level of scepticism, having throughout the years experienced different versions of counselling to different levels of success.'

She went on to say that many of these had dwelt on the past and that the solution-focused approach finally felt 'the right fit':

'I have never valued dwelling on past events longer than to acknowledge they happened so having a support that helped me to unlock some workable and comfortable solutions … was perfect.'

In terms of taking this forward, Kirsty felt that the time-limited nature of the therapy, far from being a disadvantage, left her with tools to take forward:

'I ended my counselling after a fairly short amount of sessions as I felt I had all the tools I needed to start to build a more positive outlook.'

She gave some examples of how she had moved forward by 'putting into practice the things we discussed', including a work promotion and the 'best-performing year I have ever had at work'.

Jill was even more positive, saying that

'It is no exaggeration to say that solution-focused counselling has changed my life … I have walked into a session feeling at my utter lowest and halfway through my mindset switches and I leave optimistic, motivated and with a completely different attitude towards my problems.'

While she describes the therapist as using a kind of 'magic', she acknowledges that actually he simply asks the right questions to 'enable me to find the solutions myself'. She adds:

'Apparently they are in my head all along but without the help of solution-focused practice I would struggle to find them.'

P agrees that solution-focused practice enabled them to find the 'tools' to manage a busy life. P was struggling with 'a busy job, a demanding thesis and an exciting but terrifying house move'. They make similar points to Kirsty and worried that therapy would be time-consuming and focused on the past:

'I had the … understanding that reaching out for help would involve loads of sessions chatting about my childhood and what not, and what I really wanted help to solve the problems I was experiencing at the time and SF did exactly that.'

They acknowledged that solution-focused practice helped to 'feed my brain the right diet' and gave them the 'tools to tackle' their presenting issues.

These brief snapshots help us to form the impression of solution-focused practice as an approach that provides tools for people to continue to use, once their (time-limited) sessions are at an end.

Conclusion

This chapter has indicated that much work still needs to be done to listen to voices of people with lived experience of social work services. Despite a significant amount of publicity and in excess of 100 strengths-based services contacted, it was difficult to get people to interview for this chapter. This, it seems, would indicate that consultation with people with lived experience by these agencies is either in its infancy or non-existent. This is of concern since the very essence of strengths-based practice is about putting these people at the centre of practice, which should include consultation with the individuals involved. Of course, it is entirely possible that this consultation is taking place at some level but without fanfare or public acknowledgement. However, more of it is needed and, when consultation is taking place, a greater focus needs to be place on promoting it and ensuring that people with lived experience are aware that it is happening.

Shelter has recognised this and has suggested that that there are three priorities if people with lived experience are meaningfully involved in social work services:

- the development of statements and policies to reflect a commitment to the involvement of people with lived experience;
- practical support to people with lived experience to enable them to engage;
- genuine engagement at a strategic planning level.

In addition to these important points, people with lived experience need to be involved not only in service delivery and development but also in social work education and research.

Our final words go to Stacey, who brilliantly argues:

> 'You need to remember we are living, we are humans, we are not numbers, we are families that are suffering. Don't look down your nose at us, don't judge us. Most of us didn't choose to be in this situation. Don't come in and tell us what to do. We are struggling. Sometimes things happen in life, sometimes we make mistakes. We need help, we need support, we need to feel like we are human. You've got to let us trust you. Sometimes we are told not to trust anyone, you need to get to know your family before you start working.
>
> Everybody's got potential.'

Acknowledgements
This chapter was a collaborative effort and would be meaningless without the voices of people with lived experience. Some of these people wished to remain anonymous and some wanted their names recorded. How their names are recorded is in accordance with their wishes and the order in which they appear in this chapter. Those who wished to remain anonymous are represented by

an initial which is not their own. Heartfelt thanks go to the following chapter authors: Mica, Stacey, K, Kirsten, D, C, S, Kirsty, Jill, P.

This chapter would also not be possible without the support of a number of services and practitioners. Thanks therefore go to: Alicia Lee and the Growing Futures project; Melanie Davidson, Ursula Lane and the Doncaster Family Group Conference Service; Donna Havill and the Oldham Family Group decision-making service; Amy Udall and Laura Burke and the Salford Family Group Conference Service; and Bryan Thornton, Solution-Focus Sheffield.

Further reading

Beresford, P. (2012) *Social Care, Service Users and User Involvement*, London and Philadelphia: Jessica Kingsley.

McLaughlin, H., Duffy, J., McKeever, B. and Sadd, J. (eds) (2018) *Service User Involvement in Social Work Education*, London and New York: Routledge.

11

Conclusion

Deanna Edwards and Kate Parkinson

This book has focused upon strengths-based social work, its uses, efficacy, evidence base and practice. While it has not attempted to cover all aspects of practice and applicability of a strengths approach, it has covered some of the commonly used strengths-led areas of practice. These are: solution-focused approaches, Family Group Conferences, Signs of Safety, multisystemic therapy and narrative approaches. It has also looked at some generic strengths-based practice in both adult services and mental health services. Where there are gaps, this is often because little has been written about these approaches or where they are under-funded or under-utilised. It has also attempted to give an overview of both the philosophy and the theoretical underpinning of strengths-based approaches and their roots in advocacy and empowerment and their growth as a reaction to 'deficit'-led social work approaches.

The strengths perspective is not new and as a philosophy has probably been around for centuries. As an approach to social work, it emerged in the 1980s as a response to what Saleebey (1992) describes as 'deficit'-led approaches which focus upon pathologies and problems. Instead, he argues the focus should be on the CPRs of the individual the social worker is working with. These are:

C – competence, capacities, courage;
P – promise, positive expectations;
R – resilience, reserves, resources.

This book has therefore attempted to capture some of the ways in which these strengths are both recognised in and applied with the people who social workers work to support.

Arguably the most important chapter in this book, given the nature of its subject, is Chapter 10, which was written with people with lived experience of social work services. In this chapter we heard from people who have experienced both strengths-based and other approaches as well as about social work that they consider to be good and social work that they consider to be unhelpful. The main lesson we learned from the people who have been on the receiving end of social work services is that the quality of the worker is of paramount importance. People emphasised not only the importance of working with strengths but also the importance of building strong and trusting relationships. As Jobe and Gorin (2013) have acknowledged, stereotypes of social workers abound, and frequent changes of worker and unreliable practice are not helpful in dispelling these images. Chapter 10 showed us that not only do people with lived experience value social workers who focus on strengths and, as Stacey put it, 'what we can do and not what we can't', they also value workers with whom they can build honest, trusting and long-lasting relationships. To this end practitioners, employers and policy makers need to take heed of the recruitment and retainment crisis in social work, to be able to implement strengths-based practice. They also need to acknowledge the funding crisis that exists in social care so workers can be resourced to support people with lived experience effectively. One of the critiques of a strengths-based approach is that it puts the onus for finding resources back onto families. However, finding strengths should not be about expecting families to find their own solutions. True strengths-based practice is about working in partnership with people. This takes time and resources and hence requires appropriate funding.

Slasberg and Beresford ask in the title of their 2017 paper if strengths-based approaches are social care's latest elixir or the next false dawn? One might argue that this depends on some of the factors discussed above. Whether this approach is successful and useful will depend upon whether we can recruit and retain reliable, talented well-trained experts in strengths-based practice and whether these experts can be afforded the time and space to build effective relationships with the people they work with. This is, of course, centrally about people with lived experience; however, it must also be recognised that these relationships also need to happen elsewhere – with wider family and friends and with other agencies and workers that may be involved. Therefore, to be effective, strengths-based practice must be placed hand in hand with both relationship-based practice and systemic practice. Only then can it perhaps live up to its potential as an elixir for truly empowering social work.

References

Abdullah S. (2015) 'An Islamic perspective for strengths-based social work with Muslim clients', *Journal of Social Work Practice*, 29(2): 163–172.

Adams, R. (2008) (4th edn) *Empowerment, Participation and Social Work*, Basingstoke: Palgrave Macmillan.

Adams, P. and Chandler, S. (2004) 'Responsive regulation in child welfare: systemic challenges to mainstreaming the family group conference', *Journal of Sociology and Social Welfare*, 31(1): 93–116.

Ahmed, A. (2015) *Retiring to Spain: Women's Narratives of Nostalgia, Belonging and Community*, Bristol: Policy Press.

Ahmed, A. and Rogers, M. (2017) 'Polly's story: using structural narrative analysis to understand a trans migration journey', *Qualitative Social Work*, 16(2): 224–239.

All-Party Parliamentary Group on Arts, Health and Wellbeing: Inquiry (2017) *Creative Health: The Arts for Health and Wellbeing: The Short Report*. Available from: https://www.culturehealthandwellbeing.org.uk/appg-inquiry/Publications/Creative_Health_The_Short_Report.pdf (culturehealthandwellbeing.org.uk) [Accessed 7 January 2022].

Anderson, M. and Parkinson, K. (2018) 'Balancing justice and welfare needs in Family Group Conferences for children with harmful sexual behavior: the HSB–FGC framework', *Journal of Child Sexual Abuse*, 27(5): 490–509, doi: 10.1080/10538712.2018.1477217.

Anthony, W.A. (1993) 'Recovery from mental illness: the guiding vision of the mental health system in the 1990s', *Psychosocial Rehabilitation Journal*, 16(4): 11–22.

Arts for Recovery in the Community. (2021) Annual Report and Financial Statement for the Year Ended 31 March 2021–2022. Available from: https://drive.google.com/file/d/1TkeeRc73FZxAhizttHktBxs0GnYI_ePY/view [Accessed 4 May 2022].

Ashley, C. (ed.) (2006) *The Family Group Conference Toolkit: A Practical Guide for Setting Up and Running an FGC Service*, London: Family Rights Group.

Ashley, C. (ed.) (2011) *Working with Risky Fathers: Fathers Matter*, vol. 3, *Research Findings on Working with Domestically Abusive Fathers and Their Involvement with Children's Social Care Services*, London: The Family Rights Group.

Ashley, C. and Nixon, P. (eds) (2007) *Family Group Conferences: Where Next?*, London: Family Rights Group.

Asthana, S., Callaghan, L., Elston, J., Gradinger, F. and Husk, S. (2019) 'Social prescribing: where is the evidence?', *British Journal of General Practice*. Available from: doi:https//doi.org/10.3399/bjgp19X00325 [Accessed 13 April 2022].

Attlee, C. (1920) *The Social Worker*, London: Bell.

Backwith, D. (2015) *Social Work Poverty and Social Exclusion*, Maidenhead: Open University Press.

Baginsky, M., Hickman, B., Harris, J., Manthorpe, J., Sanders, M., O'Higgins, A., Schoenwald, E. and Clayton, V. (2020) *Evaluation of MTM's Signs of Safety Pilots Evaluation Report*, London: Department for Education.

Baginsky, M., Hickman, B., Moriarty, J. and Manthorpe, J. (2020) 'Working with Signs of Safety: parents' perception of change', *Child and Family Social Work*, 25(1): 154–164.

Baginsky, M., Ixer, G. and Manthorpe, J. (2021) 'Practice frameworks in children's services in England: an attempt to steer social work back on course?', *Practice: Social Work in Action*, 33(1): 3–19.

Baginsky, M., Moriarty, J., Manthorpe, J., Beecham, J. and Hickman, B. (2017) *Evaluation of Signs of Safety in 10 Pilots*, London: Department for Education.

Baginsky, M., Moriarty, J. and Manthorpe, J. (2019) 'Signs of Safety: lessons learnt from evaluations', *Journal of Children's Services*, 14(2): 107–123.

Baginsky, M., Manthorpe, J. and Moriarty, J. (2021) 'The framework for the assessment of children in need and their families and signs of safety: competing or complementary frameworks?', *The British Journal of Social Work*, 51(7): 2571–2589.

Bailes, J. (2017) 'Mental health and neoliberalism: an interview with William Davies', *Counterpunch*. Available from: https://www.counterpunch.org/2017/10/18/mental-health-and-neoliberalism-an-interview-with-william-davies/ [Accessed 6 April 2022].

Baker, C., Crone, D.M., Hughes, S., James. D., Loughren, E.A. and Sumner, R.C. (2020) 'Factors associated with attendance, engagement and wellbeing change in an arts on prescription intervention', *Journal of Public Health*, 42(1): 8–95.

Baker, S. and Brown, B.J. (2012) *Responsible Citizens: Individuals, Health and Policy under Neoliberalism*, London: Anthem Press.

Bakhtin, M.M. (1986) *Speech Genres and Other Late Essays*, Austin, TX: University of Texas Press.

Baldwin, C. (2013) *Narrative Social Work*, Bristol: Policy Press.

Baldwin, L. and Raikes, B. (2019) *Seen and Heard: 100 Poems by Parents and Children Affected by Imprisonment*, Hook: Waterside Press.

Ban, P. (2005) 'Aboriginal child placement principle and family group conferences', *Australian Social Work*, 58: 384–394, doi:10.1111/j.1447–0748. 2005.00234.x.

Barclay, P.M. (1982) *Social Workers: Their Role and Tasks*, London: Bedford Square Press.

Barn, R. and Das, C. (2016) 'Family Group Conferences and cultural competence in social work', *British Journal of Social Work*, 46(4): 942–959, doi: 10.1093/bjsw/bcu105

Barnsdale, L. and Walker, M. (2007) *Examining the Use and Impact of Family Group Conferencing*, Edinburgh: Scottish Executive.

Baron, S., Stanley, T., Colomina, C. and Pereira, T. (2019) *Strengths-Based Approach: Practice Framework and Practice Handbook*, London: Department of Health and Social Care.

Barringer, A., Hunter, B., Salina, D. and Jason, L. (2016) 'Empowerment and social support: implications for practice and programming among minority women with substance abuse and criminal justice histories', *The Journal of Behavioural Health Science and Research*, 44(1): 75–78.

Barthes, R. (1977) 'Introduction to the structural analysis of narrative', in R. Barthes (ed.) *Image-Music-Text*, London: Fontana Press, pp 235–272.

BASW (2014) *Code of Ethics*. Available from: https://www.basw.co.uk/resources/basw-code-ethics-social-work [Accessed 20 June 2022].

BASW (n.d.) https://www.basw.co.uk/resources/person-centred-care-made-simple.

Bell, M. (2002) 'Promoting children's rights through the use of relationships', *Child and Family Social Work*, 7: 1–11.

Bennett, E., Dayson, C. and Painter, J. (2020) 'Social prescribing for patients of secondary mental health services: emotional, psychological and social wellbeing outcomes', *Journal of Public Mental Health*, 19(4): 271–279.

Berg, I.K. (1994) *Family-Based Services: A Solution-Focused Approach*, New York: Norton.

Berg, I.K. and Kelly, S. (2000) *Building Solutions in Child Protective Services*, New York: Norton.

Berg, I.K. and Miller, S. (1992) *Working with the Problem Drinker*, New York: Norton.

Berg, I.K. and Reuss, N. (1997). *Solutions Step by Step: A Substance Abuse Treatment Manual*, New York: Norton.

Berg, I.K. and Steiner, T. (2003) *Children's Solution Work*, New York: Norton.

Berger, P.L. and Luckmann, T. (1966) *The Social Construction of Reality: A Treatise in the Sociology of Knowledge*, Garden City, NY: Anchor Books.

Beyebach M., Neipp M.-C., Solanes-Puchol, Á. and Martín-del-Río, B. (2021) 'Bibliometric differences between WEIRD and non-WEIRD countries in the outcome research on solution-focused brief therapy', *Frontiers in Psychology*, 17 November. Available from: frontiersin.org/articles/10.3389/fpsyg.2021.754885/full [Accessed 19 May 2022].

Blundo, B. (2014) 'Group supervision in child protective service: utilizing the miracle question', *Journal of Solution Focused Practices*, 1(1): 46–60. Available from: https://digitalscholarship.unlv.edu/journalsfp/vol1/iss1/6/ [Accessed 18 May 2022].

Bogo, M., Herschman, J., Johnstone, M., Tsang, T. and Lee, E (2019) 'Honouring the voice of the client in clinical social work practice: negotiating with epistemic injustice', *Social Work*, 64(1): 29–40 [online]. Available from: 10.1093/sw/swy050

Booker, C. (2004) *The Seven Basic Plots,* London: Continuum Books.

Booth, J. (2019) 'Empowering disadvantaged communities in the UK: missing the potential of co-production', *Social Change*, 49(2): 276–292.

Borduin, C.M., Quetsch, L.B., Johnides, B.D. and Dopp, A.R. (2021) 'Long-term effects of multisystemic therapy for problem sexual behaviours: a 24.9 year follow-up to a randomised clinical trial', *Journal of Consulting and Clinical Psychology*, 89(5): 393–405.

Bottrell, D. (2009) 'Understanding "marginal: perspectives: towards a social theory of resilience', *Qualitative Social Work*, 8(3): 321–339, doi:10.1177/1473325009337840

Boulden, W.T. (2009) 'The behavior intervention support team program: underlying theories', *Reclaiming Children and Youth*, 19(1): 17–21.

Bourdieu, P. (1977) *Outline of a Theory of Practice*, trans. R. Nice, Cambridge Studies in Social and Cultural Anthropology, Cambridge: Cambridge University Press, doi:10.1017/CBO9780511812507.

Bourdieu, P. (1998) *Acts of Resistance against the Tyranny of the Market*, New York: The New Press.

Brady, B. and Miller, M. (2009) *Barnardos Family Welfare Conference Project, South Tipperary: Evaluation Report*. Galway: The Child and Family Research Unit, NUI Galway.

Braye, S., Orr, D. and Preston-Shoot, M. (2011) 'Conceptualising and responding to self-neglect: challenges for adult safeguarding', *Journal of Adult Protection*, 13(4): 182–193.

Broadhurst, K. and Mason, C. (2014) 'Social work beyond the VDU: foregrounding "co-presence" in situated practice: why face-to-face practice matters', *The British Journal of Social Work*, 44(3): 578–595.

Brodsky, A.E. and Cattaneo, L.B. (2013) 'A transconceptual model of empowerment and resilience: divergence, convergence and interactions in kindred community concepts', *American Journal of Community Psychology*, 52(3–4): 333–346, doi: 10.1007/s10464–013–9599-x

Bronfenbrenner, U. (1979) *The Ecology of Human Development*, Cambridge, MA: Harvard University Press.

Brown, L. and Levitt, J. (1979) 'A methodology for problem system identification', *Social Case Work*, 60: 408–415.

Browne Olson, K. (2009) 'Family group conferencing and child protection mediation: essential tools for prioritizing family engagement in child welfare cases', *Family Court Review*, 47(1): 53–68.

Buckley, H., Carr, N. and Whelan, S. (2010) '"Like walking on eggshells": service user views and expectations of the child protection system', *Child and Family Social Work*, 16(1): 101–110.

Bukhari, F., Alketbi, R., Rashid, S., Ahmed, A. and Shakir, K. (2021) 'Challenges in dealing with involuntary clients', *Cogent Social Sciences*, 7(1): 1–15.

Bunn, A. (2013) *Signs of Safety in England: An NSPCC Commissioned Report on the Signs of Safety Model in Child Protection*, London: NSPCC.

Burack-Weiss, A., Lawrence, L.S. and Mijangos, L.B. (eds) (2017) *Narrative in Social Work Practice: The Power and Possibility of Story*, New York: Columbia University Press.

Burnham, J.B. (1984) *Family Therapy*, London: Tavistock.

Bushe, G.R. (2013). 'The appreciative inquiry model', in E.H. Kessler (ed.) *Encyclopedia of Management Theory*, vol. 1, Thousand Oaks, CA: Sage Publications, pp 41–44.

Butler, L. and Manthorpe, J. (2016) 'Putting people at the centre: facilitating making safeguarding personal approaches in the context of the Care Act 2014', *The Journal of Adult Protection*, 14(4): 204–213.

Cade, B. and O'Hanlon, B. (1993) *A Brief Guide to Brief Therapy*, New York: Norton.

Caiels, J., Milne, A. and Beadle-Brown, J. (2020) *Taking a Strengths-Based Approach to Social Work and Social Care: A Literature Review*, London: National Institute for Health Research.

Camic, P.M., Chatterjee, H.J. and Thomson, L.J. (2015) *Social Prescribing: A Review of Community Referral Schemes*, London: University College London.

Canda, E.R. (2006) 'The significance of spirituality for resilient response to chronic illness: a qualitative study of adults with cystic fibrosis', in D. Saleebey (ed) *The Strengths Perspective in Social Work Practice* (4th edn), Boston, MA: Allyn & Bacon, pp 61–75.

Care Act (2014). Available at: https://www.legislation.gov.uk/ukpga/2014/23/contents/enacted [Accessed 4 April 2022].

Care Quality Commission (2018) *National Survey Highlights Decline in People's Experience of Community Mental Health Services*. Available from: https://www.cqc.org.uk/news/releases/national-survey-highlights-decline-peoples-experiences-community-mental-health [Accessed 4 April 2022].

Carey, M. (2015) 'The limits of cultural competence: an indigenous studies perspective', *Higher Education Research & Development*, 34(5): 828–840, doi: 10.1080/07294360.2015.1011097

Carroll, L. (1865) *Alice's Adventures in Wonderland*, London: Macmillan.

Centre for Mental Health. (2019) *Arm in Arm*. Available from: https://www.centreformentalhealth.org.uk/publications/arm-arm [Accessed 6 April 2022].

Centre for Welfare Reform (2012) *Resource Allocation System*. Available from: http://www.centreforwelfarereform.org/library/by-az/resource-allocation-system-ras.html [Accessed 9 February 2023].

Chassot, C.S. and Mendes, F. (2014) 'The experience of mental distress and recovery among people involved with the service user/survivor movement', *Health: An Interdisciplinary Journal for the Social Study of Health, Illness and Medicine*, 19(4): 372–378.

Chatzidakis, A., Hakim, J., Littler, J., Rottenberg, C. and Segal, L. (2020) *The Care Manifesto*, London: Verso Books.

Children Act (1989). Available at: https://www.legislation.gov.uk/ukpga/1989/41/contents.

Children (Leaving Care) Act (2000). Available at: https://www.legislation.gov.uk/ukpga/2000/35/section/3.

Children, Young People and their Families Act (1989), Available from: https://www.refworld.org/docid/3ae6b5d10.html [Accessed 10 February 2023].

Christie, C. (2011) Commission on the Future Delivery of Public Services. Available from: https://www.gov.scot/publications/commission-future-delivery-public-services/ [Accessed 9 February 2023].

Christman, J. (2004) 'Relational autonomy, liberal, individualism and the social constitution of selves', *Philosophical Studies*, 117(1–2): 143–164.

Cocker, C., Cooper, A., Holmes, D. and Bateman, F. (2021) 'Transitional safeguarding: presenting the case for developing making safeguarding personal for young people in England', *Journal of Adult Protection*, 22(3): 144–157.

Cohen, J.A., Mannarino, A.P. and Deblinger, E. (2017) (2nd edn) *Treating Trauma and Traumatic Grief in Children and Adolescents*, New York: The Guilford Press.

Coleman, J.S. (1990) *Foundations of Social Theory*, Cambridge, MA: Belknap Press of Harvard University.

Connolly, M. (1994) 'An act of empowerment: the Children, Young Persons and their Families Act (1989)', *British Journal of Social Work*, 24: 87–100.

Connolly, M. (2006) 'Fifteen years of family group conferencing: coordinators talk about their experiences in Aotearoa New Zealand', *The British Journal of Social Work*, 36(4): 523–540.

Connolly, M. (2007) 'Practice frameworks: conceptual maps to guide interventions in child welfare', *The British Journal of Social Work*, 37(5): 825–837.

Connolly, M. and Healy, K. (2009) 'Social work practice theories and frameworks', in M. Connolly and L. Harms (eds) *Social Work: Contexts and Practice*, Melbourne: Oxford University Press.

Connolly, M. and Morris, K. (2011) *Understanding Child and Family Welfare: Statutory Responses to Children at Risk*, London: Bloomsbury.

Cooper, A., Cocker, C. and Briggs, M. (2018) 'Making safeguarding personal and social work practice with older adults: findings from local-authority survey data in England', *The British Journal of Social Work*, 48: 1014–1032.

Corcoran, J. and Pillai, V. (2009) 'A review of the research on solution-focused therapy', *The British Journal of Social Work*, 39(2): 234–242.

Cossar, J., Brandom, M. and Jordan, P. (2011) *'Don't Make Assumptions' Children and Young People's Views of the Child Protection System and Messages for Change*. London: Office of the Children's Commissioner.

Cowden, S. and Singh, G. (2017) 'Community cohesion, communitarianism and neoliberalism', *Critical Social Policy*, 37(2): 268–286.

Cowger, C.D. (1998) 'Clientism and clientification: impediments to strengths-based social work practice', *The Journal of Sociology and Social Welfare*, 25(1): 25–37.

Cowger, C.D. and Snively, C.A. (2002) 'Assessing client strengths', in A.R. Roberts and C.J. Greene (eds) *Social Workers' Desk Reference*, New York: Oxford University Press, pp 221–225.

Crampton, D. (2007) 'Research review: family group decision-making: a promising practice in need of more programme theory and research', *Child & Family Social Work*, 12(2): 202–209.

Crow, G., Marsh, P. and Holton, E. (2004) 'Supporting pupils, schools and families: An evaluation of the Hampshire family group conferences in education project', University of Sheffield, England and Hampshire County Council, Winchester, England.

Cruwys, T., Stewart, B., Buckley, L., Gumley, J. and Scholz, B. (2020) 'The recovery model in chronic mental health: a community-based investigation of social identity processes', *Psychiatry Research*, 291: 113–241.

Cummins, I., Parkinson, K. and Pollock, S. (eds) (2020) *Social Work and Society: Political and Ideological Perspectives*, Bristol: Policy Press.

Curtis, N.M., Ronan, K.R. and Borduin, C.M. (2004) 'Multisystemic treatment: a meta-analysis of outcome studies', *Journal of Family Psychology*, 18(3): 411.

Dalrymple, J. (2002) 'Family Group Conferences and youth advocacy: the participation of children and young people in family decision making', *European Journal of Social Work*, 5(3): 287–299.

Davis, M. (1986) 'Brief therapy: focused solution development', *Family Process*, 25(2): 207–221.

Department for Education (2018) *Working Together to Safeguard Children: A Guide to Inter-Agency Working to Safeguard and Promote the Welfare of Children*, London: HM Government. Available from: https://assets.publishing.serv ice.gov.uk/government/uploads/system/uploads/attachment_data/file/942 454/Working_together_to_safeguard_children_inter_agency_guidance.pdf [Accessed 26 October 2021].

Department of Health (2002) *Fair Access to Care Services: Guidance on Eligibility Criteria for Adult Care Services,* LAC (2002)13, London: Department of Health.

Department of Health and Social Care (2011) *No Health without Mental Health: A Cross-Government Outcomes Strategy*. Available from: https://assets.publishing. service.gov.uk/government/uploads/system/uploads/attachment_data/ file/213761/dh_124058.pdf [Accessed 9 February 2023].

Department of Health and Social Care (2014) *Care and Support Statutory Guidance: Issued under the Care Act 2014*, London: Department of Health.

Department of Health and Social Care (2015) *Knowledge and Skills Statement for Social Workers in Adult Services*. Available from: https://assets.publishing.service. gov.uk/government/uploads/system/uploads/attachment_data/file/411957/ KSS.pdf [Accessed 4 January 2022].

Department of Health and Social Care (2017) *Strengths-Based Social Work Practice with Adults: Roundtable Report*, London: Department of Health.

Department of Health and Social Care (2019) *Strengths-Based Approach: Practice Framework and Practice Handbook* [online]. Available from: https://assets. publishing.service.gov.uk/government/uploads/system/uploads/attachment_ data/file/778134/stengths-based-approach-practice-framework-and-handbook. pdf [Accessed 9 February 2023].

De Jong, P. and Berg, I.K. (2002) (2nd edn) *Interviewing for Solutions*, Pacific Grove, CA: Brooks/Cole.

De Jong, P. and Berg, I.K. (2008) (3rd edn) *Interviewing for Solutions*, Belmont, CA: Thompson.

de Shazer, S. (1982) *Patterns of Brief Family Therapy: An Ecosystemic Approach*, New York: The Guilford Press.

de Shazer, S. (1985) *Keys to Solution in Brief Therapy*, New York: Norton.

de Shazer, S. (1988) *Clues: Investigating Solutions in Brief Therapy*, New York: Norton.

de Shazer, S. (1991) *Putting Difference to Work*, New York: Norton.

de Shazer, S. (1994) *Words Were Originally Magic*, New York: Norton.

de Shazer, S., Berg, I.K., Lipchik, E., Nunnally, E., Molnar, A., Gingerich, W. and Weiner-Davis, M. (1986) 'Brief therapy: focused solution development', *Family Process*, 25(2): 207–221. doi: 10.1111/j.1545-5300.1986.00207.x.

Dias, P.C. and Cadime, I. (2017) 'Protective factors and resilience in adolescence: The mediating role of self-regulation, *Psicología Educativa*, 23 (1): 37–43, doi.org/10.1016/j.pse.2016.09.003.

Donovan, C. and Hester, M. (2014) *Domestic Violence and Sexuality: What's Love Got to Do with It?*, Bristol: Policy Press.

Douglas, E.M., McCarthy, S.C. and Serino, P.A. (2014) 'Does a social work degree predict practice orientation? Measuring strengths-based practice among child welfare workers with the strengths-based practices inventory', *Journal of Social Work Education*, 50(2): 219–233.

Duncan, B.L. and Miller, S.D. (2000) *The Heroic Client: Doing Client-Directed Outcome-Informed Therapy*, San Francisco, CA: Jossey-Bass.

Durlauf, Steven N. and Fafchamps, Marcel (2005) 'Social capital', in P. Aghion and S. Durlauf (eds) *Handbook of Economic Growth*, vol. 1, Amsterdam: Elsevier, pp 1639–1699.

Eassom, E., Giacco, D., Dirik, A. and Priebe, S. (2014) 'Implementing family involvement in the treatment of patients with psychosis: a systematic review of facilitating and hindering factors', *BMJ Open*, 4(10): e006108, doi: 10.1136/bmjopen-2014–006108.

EBTA (2022) *Research List*. Available from: ebta.eu/definition-and-research/ [Accessed 19 May 2022].

Edwards, R., Franklin, J. and Holland, J. (2006) *Assessing Social Capital: Concept, Policy and Practice*, Newcastle upon Tyne: Cambridge Scholars Press.

Edwards, D. and Parkinson, K. (eds) (2018) *Family Group Conferences in Social Work: Involving Families in Social Care Decision Making*, Bristol: Policy Press.

Egan, G. (2018) (11th edn) *The Skilled Helper*, Boston, MA: Cengage.

Ellis, D. A., Naar-King, S., Chen, X., Moltz, K., Cunningham, P. B. and Idalski-Carcone, A. (2012) 'Multisystemic therapy compared to telephone support for youth with poorly controlled diabetes: findings from a randomized controlled trial', *Annals of Behavioral Medicine*, 44: 207–215.

Family Rights Group (2015) Data on the Number of Local Authorities with a FGC Service, Family Rights Group, London. (Unpublished).

Featherstone, B. and White, S. (2014) *Re-Imagining Child Protection: Towards Humane Social Work with Families*, Bristol: Policy Press.

Featherstone, B., Gupta, A., Morris, K. and Warner, J. (2018) '"Let's stop feeding the risk monster": towards a social model of child protection', *Families, Relationships and Societies*, 7(1): 7–22.

Feldon, P. (2016) 'The Care Act (What do we think of it so far?)', *Professional Social Work Magazine*, May: 28–29.

Feldon, P. (2017) 'Luke Davey's unsuccessful judicial review against Oxfordshire: a social work perspective', British Association of Social Work (online). Available from: https://www.basw.co.uk/system/files/resources/basw_62044-3_0.pdf [Accessed 5 January 2022].

Ferguson, I. (2007) *Reclaiming Social Work: Challenging Neo-Liberalism and Promoting Social Justice*, London: SAGE.

Ferguson, I. (2017) *Politics of the Mind: Marxism and Mental Distress*, London: Bookmarks Publications.

Fisch, R., Weakland, J. and Segal, L. (1982) *The Tactics of Change: Doing Therapy Briefly*, San Francisco, CA: Jossey-Bass.

Fisher, M. (2014) 'Good for Nothing', *The Occupied Times* [online], https://theoc cupiedtimes.org/?p=12841 [Accessed 21 July 2021].

Foa, E.B., Hembree, E.A., Rothbaum B.O. and Rauch, S.A.M. (2019) (2nd edn) *Prolonged Exposure Therapy for PTSD: Emotional Processing of Traumatic Experiences*, New York: Oxford University Press.

Fook, J. (2012) *Social Work: A Critical Approach to Practice*, London: SAGE.

Foot, J. (2012) *What Makes Us Healthy? An Asset Approach in Practice: Evidence, Action, Evaluation*, London: Jane Foot. Available from: http://www.thinklocal actpersonal.org.uk/_library/Resources/BCC/Evidence/what_makes_us_h ealthy.pdf [Accessed 9 February 2023].

Forrester, D., Westkale, D., McCann, M., Thurnham, A., Shefer, G., Glynn, G. and Killian, M. (2013) *Reclaiming Social Work? An Evaluation of Systemic Units as an Approach to Delivering Children's Services. Final Report of a Comparative Study of Practice and the Factors Shaping It in Three Local Authorities*, Luton: University of Bedfordshire.

Fox, D. (2008) 'Family group conferencing and evidence-based practice: what works?', *Research, Policy and Planning*, 26(3): 157–167.

Fox, D.J. (2015) 'Power relations in advocacy approaches in family group conferencing with children and young people', London: London Metropolitan University. Available from: http://repository.londonmet. ac.uk/896/1/FoxDarrell_ PowerRelationsInAdvocacyApproaches.pdf [Accessed 9 February 2023].

Fox, S. and Ashmore, Z. (2011) 'An introduction to multisystemic therapy in England', *Forensic Update*, 103: 49–53.

Fox, S. and Ashmore, Z. (2014) 'Multisystemic therapy as an intervention for young people on the edge of care', *The British Journal of Social Work*, 45(7): 1–17.

Freire, P. and Ramos, M.B. (1970) *Pedagogy of the Oppressed*, New York, Seabury Press.

Freuchte, K. (2011) 'Community capitals: social capital' [fact sheet]. Available from: https://openprairie.sdstate.edu/cgi/viewcontent.cgi?article=1520&cont ext=extension_ extra [Accessed 9 February 2023].

Frost, N. and Elmer, S. (2008) *An Evaluation of South Leeds Family Group Conference Service*, Leeds: Leeds Metropolitan University (unpublished).

Gallant, G., Hamilton-Hinch, B., Litwiller, F. and White, C. (2019) *'Removing the Thorns': The Role of the Arts in Recovery for People with Mental Health Challenges* [online]. Available from: https://doi.org/10.1080/17533015.2017.1413397.

Garrett, Paul Michael (2016) 'Questioning tales of "ordinary magic": "resilience" and neo-liberal reasoning', *The British Journal of Social Work*, 4(7): 1909–1925, https://doi.org/10.1093/bjsw/bcv017.

Garrett, P.M. (2018) *Welfare Words: Critical Social Work and Social Policy*, London: Sage.

George, E., Iveson, C. and Ratner, H. (1990) *Problem to Solution*, London: BT Press.

Gergen, K.J. (1985) 'The social constructionist movement in modern psychology', *American Psychologist*, 40(3): 266–275, https://doi.org/10.1037/0003-066X.40.3.266

Gergen, K.J. (1994) *Realities and Relationships: Soundings in Social Construction,* Cambridge, MA: Harvard University Press.

Gergen, K.J. (2001) 'Psychological science in a postmodern context', *American Psychologist*, 56(10): 803–813, https://doi.org/10.1037/0003-066X.56.10.803

Gilbert, J. (2014) *Common Ground Democracy and Collectivity in an Age of Individualisation,* London: Pluto Books.

Gingerich, W., de Shazer, S. and Weiner-Davis, M. (1988) 'Constructing change: a research view of interviewing', in E. Lipchik (ed.) *Interviewing,* Rockville, MD: Aspen, pp 21–32.

Gingerich, W. and Peterson, L. (2013) 'Effectiveness of solution-focused brief therapy: a systematic qualitative review of controlled outcome studies', *Research on Social Work Practice*, 23(3): 266–283.

Gitterman, A. (2009) (2nd edn) 'The life model', in A. Roberts (ed.) *Social Workers' Desk Reference,* New York: Oxford University Press, pp 231–234.

Glicken, M.D. (2004) *Using the Strengths Perspective in Social Work Practice: A Positive Approach for the Helping Professions,* Boston, MA: Pearson Education.

Gollins, T., Fox, A., Walker, B., Romeo., Thomas, J. and Woodham, G. (2016) *Developing a Wellbeing and Strengths-Based Approach to Social Work Practice: Changing Culture,* London: Think Local Act Personal.

Goodman, S. and Trowler, I. (2012) *Social Work Reclaimed: Innovative Frameworks for Child and Family Social Work Practice,* London: Jessica Kingsley.

Gorska, S., Forsyth, K., Prior, S., Irvine, L. and Haughey, P. (2016) 'Family Group Conferencing in dementia care: an exploration of opportunities and challenges', *International Psychogeriatrics*, 28(2): 233–246.

Gray, M. (2011) 'Back to basics: a critique of the strengths perspective in social work', *Families in Society: The Journal of Contemporary Human Services*, 91(1): 5–11.

Gray, M. and Allegritti, L. (2003) 'Towards culturally sensitive social work practice: re-examining cross-cultural social work', *Social Work: A Professional Journal for the Social Worker*, 39(4): 312–325.

Green, B.L, McAllister, C.L. and Tarte, J.M. (2004) 'The strengths-based practices inventory: a tool for measuring strengths-based service delivery in early childhood and family support programmes', *Families in Society*, 85: 326–334.

Greenberg, L.S. and Pinsof, W.M. (1986) *The Psychotherapeutic Process: A Research Handbook,* New York: Guilford Press.

Greene, G.J, Lee, M.Y. and Hoffpauir, S. (2005) 'The languages of empowerment and strengths in clinical social work: a constructivist perspective', *Families in Society*, 86(2): 267–277, doi:10.1606/1044-3894.2465

Greene, G. and Lee, M.Y. (2011) *Solution-Oriented Social Work Practice: An Integrative Approach to Working with Client Strengths,* New York: Oxford University Press.

Greene, R.R. (ed.) (1999) *Resiliency: An Integrated Approach to Practice, Policy, and Research*, Washington, DC: NASW Press.

Grothaus, T., McAuliffe, G. and Craigen, L. (2012) 'Infusing cultural competence and advocacy into strength-based counseling', *The Journal of Humanistic Counseling*, 51: 51–65, https://doi.org/10.1002/j.2161-1939.2012.00005.x

Gubrium, J.F. and Holstein, J.A. (2009) *Analyzing Narrative Reality*, Thousand Oaks, CA: Sage Publications Inc.

Guo, W. and Tsui, M. (2010) 'From resilience to resistance: a reconstruction of the strengths perspective in social work practice', *International Social Work*, 53(2): 233–245, doi:10.1177/0020872809355391

Hall, S. (2011) 'The neo-liberal revolution', *Cultural Studies*, 25(6): 705–728.

Hammond, W. and Zimmerman, R. (2012) *A Strengths-Based Perspective*, Available from: https://shed-thelight.webs.com/documents/RSL_STRENGTH_BA SED_PERSPECTIVE.pdf [Accessed 9 February 2023].

Harawitz, C. (2006) 'Theoretical perspectives: conflict theory versus ecological and family systems-driven models of practice', Available from http://www. exit0.com/cheryl/fgc/theorecticalperspectives.pdf [Accessed 9 February 2023].

Harder, L. (2013) *Evaluation of Aboriginal Collective Decision Making Projects*, Vancouver: The Law Foundation of British Columbia.

Harris, J. (2002) 'Caring for citizenship', *The British Journal of Social Work*, 32: 267–281.

Harris, N. (2008) *Family Group Conferencing in Australia 15 Years On*, Melbourne: Australian Institute of Family Studies.

Hartman, A. (1995) 'Diagrammatic assessment of family relationships', *Families in Society*, 76: 111–112.

Hayden, C. (2009) 'Family Group Conferences: are they an effective and viable way of working with attendance and behaviour problems in schools?', *British Journal of Educational Research*, 35(2): 205–220.

Hayes, D. and Houston, S. (2007) '"Lifeworld", "system" and Family Group Conferences: Habermas's contribution to discourse in child protection', *The British Journal of Social Work*, 37(6): 987–1006.

Healy, K. (2005) *Social Work Theories in Context: Creating Frameworks for Practice*, Basingstoke: Palgrave Macmillan.

Healy, K. (2014) (2nd edn) *Social Work Theories in Context: Creating Frameworks for Practice*, Basingstoke: Palgrave.

Hebert, S., Bor, W., Swenson, C.C. and Boyle, C. (2014) 'Improving collaboration: a qualitative assessment of inter-agency collaboration between a pilot Multisystemic Therapy Child Abuse and Neglect (MST-CAN) program and a child protection team', *Australasian Psychiatry*, Available from: http://apy.sagepub.com/content/ early/2014/06/18/1039856214539572 [Accessed 9 February 2023].

Hengeller, S.W. (2017) 'Multi systemic therapy', in *The Encyclopaedia of Juvenile Delinquency and Justice*, Hoboken, NJ: Wiley, pp 1–5.

Henggeler, S.W., Rodick, J.D., Borduin, C.M., Hanson, C.L., Watson, S.M. and Urey, J.R. (1986) 'Multisystemic treatment of juvenile offenders: effects on adolescent behavior and family interaction', *Developmental Psychology*, 22(1): 132.

Henggeler, S.W. and Borduin, C.M. (1990) *Family Therapy and Beyond: A Multisystemic Approach to Treating the Behavior Problems of Children and Adolescents*, Pacific Grove, CA: Brooks/Cole.

Henggeler, S.W., Rowland, M.R., Randall, J., Ward, D., Pickrel, S.G., Cunningham, P.B., Miller, S.L., Edwards, J.E., Zealberg, J., Hand, L. and Santos, A.B. (1999) 'Home-based multisystemic therapy as an alternative to the hospitalization of youth in psychiatric crisis: clinical outcomes', *Journal of the American Academy of Child & Adolescent Psychiatry*, 38: 1331–1339.

Henggeler, S.W., Schoenwald, S.K., Borduin, C.M., Rowland, M.D. and Cunningham, P.B. (2009) (2nd edn) *Multisystemic Therapy for Children and Adolescents*, New York and London: The Guilford Press.

Hepworth, D.H. and Larsen, J. (1990) (3rd edn) *Direct Social Work Practice: Theory and Skills*, Belmont, CA: Wadsworth.

HM Government (2018) *Working Together to Safeguard Children: A Guide to Inter-Agency Working to Safeguard and Promote the Welfare of Children*, London: Department of Education.

Hodge, D.R. and Nadir, A. (2008) 'Moving toward culturally competent practice with Muslims: modifying cognitive therapy with Islamic tenets', *Social Work*, 53(1): 31–41.

Holland, S., Scourfield, J., O Neill, S. and Pithouse, A. (2005) 'Democratising the family and the state? The case of Family Group Conferences in child welfare', *Journal of Social Policy*, 34(1): 59–77.

Hollingworth, L., Allen-Meares, P., Shanks, T. and Gant, L. (2009) 'Using the miracle question in community engagement and planning', *Families in Society*, 90(3): 332–335.

Horan, H. and Dalrymple, J. (2003) 'Promoting the participation rights of children and young people in family group conferences', *Practice*, 15(2): 5–13.

Horner, N. (2019) *What Is Social Work?: Contexts and Perspective*, London: Sage.

Houston, S. (2016) 'Beyond individualism: social work and social identity', *British Journal of Social Work*, 46(2), 532–548.

Hunter, D. (2013) 'Are Community Treatment Orders on the way out?'. Available from: https://psuchmatter.wordpress.com/ [Accessed 27 February 2023].

International Federation of Social Workers (IFSW) (2014) *Global Definition of Social Work*, [online] Available from: https://www.ifsw.org/what-is-social-work/global-definition-of-social-work/ [Accessed 20 June 2022].

Itzhaky, H. and Bustin, E. (2002) 'Strengths and pathological perspectives in community social work', *Journal of Community Practice*, 10(3): 61–73.

Jirek, J.L. (2017) 'Narrative reconstruction and post-traumatic growth among trauma survivors: the importance of narrative in social work research and practice', *Qualitative Social Work*, 16(2): 166–188.

Jobe, A. and Gorin, S. (2013) '"If kids don't feel safe, they don't do anything": young people's views on seeking and receiving help from children's social care services in England', *Child and Family Social Work*, 18(4): 429–438.

Johnson, Y.M. and Munch, S. (2009) 'Fundamental contradictions in cultural competence', *Social Work*, 54(3): 220–231.

Jordan, B. (1979) *Helping in Social Work*, London: Routledge and Kegan Paul.

Jordan, B. (2004) 'Emancipatory social work? Opportunity or oxymoron', *British Journal of Social Work*, 34: 5–19.

Jordan, C. and Franklin, C. (1995) *Clinical Assessment for Social Workers: Qualitative and Quantitative Methods*, Chicago, IL: Lyceum.

Kam, P.K. (2019) '"Social work is not just a job": the qualities of social workers from the perspective of service users', *Journal of Social Work*, 20(6): 775–796.

Kam, P.K. (2021) 'Strengthening the empowerment approach in social work practice: an EPS model', *Journal of Social Work*, 21(3): 329–352, doi:10.1177/1468017320911348.

Kaplan, L. and Girard, J. (1994) *Strengthening High-Risk Families: A Handbook for Practitioners*, New York: Lexington Books.

Keddell, E. (2009) 'Narrative as identity: postmodernism, multiple ethnicities, and narrative practice approaches in social work', *Journal of Ethnic & Cultural Diversity in Social Work*, 18(3): 221–241.

Keddell, E. (2014) 'Theorising the signs of safety approach to child protection social work: positioning, codes and power', *Children and Youth Services Review*, 47: 70–77.

Kelly, B.L. and Gates, T.G. (2010) 'Using the strengths perspective in the social work interview with young adults who have experienced childhood sexual abuse', *Social Work in Mental Health*, 8(5): 421–437, https://doi.org/10.1080/15332981003744438

Kemp, S.P., Marcenko, M.O., Lyons S.J. and Kruzich, J.M. (2014) 'Strengths-based practice and parental engagement in child welfare services: an empirical examination', *Children and Youth Services Review*, 47: 27–35.

Kemp, T. (2007) *Family Welfare Conferences – The Wexford Experience: An Evaluation of Barnardos Family Welfare Conference Project*, London: Barnardos.

Kim, J., Jordan, S., Franklin, C. and Froerer, A. (2019) 'Is solution-focused brief therapy evidence-based? An update 10 years later', *Families in Society*, 100(2): 127–138.

Konradt, D.C. (2020) (3rd edn) 'The strengths perspective', in B. Teater (ed.), *An Introduction to Applying Social Work Theories and Methods*, Maidenhead: McGraw Hill, pp 36–46.

Korman, H., De Jong, P. and Smock Jordan, S. (2020) 'Steve de Shazer's theory development', *Journal of Solution Focused Practices*, 4(2): 47–70. Available from: https://digitalscholarship.unlv.edu/journalsfp/vol4/iss2/5/ [Accessed 21 February 2023].

Laird, S.E, Morris, K., Archard, P. and Clawson, R. (2018) 'Changing practice: the possibilities and limits for reshaping social work practice', *Qualitative Social Work*, 17(4): 577–593, doi:10.1177/1473325016688371

Laird, S.E. and Tedam, P. (2019) *Cultural Diversity in Child Protection: Cultural Competence in Practice*, London: Bloomsbury.

Lavalette, M. and Moth, R. (2017) *Social Protection and Labour Market Policies for Vulnerable Groups from a Social Investment Perspective. The Case of Welfare Recipients with Mental Health Needs in England*. RE-inVEST working paper series D5.1, Liverpool: Hope University/Leuven: HIVA-KU Leuven.

Laws, S. and Kirby, P. (2008) 'At the table or under the table? A comparative study of professional and informal advocacy for children in Family Group Conferences', in C.M. Oliver and J. Dalrymple (eds) *Developing Advocacy for Children and Young People: Current Issues in Research, Policy and Practice*, London: Jessica Kingsley, pp 81–98.

Legislation.gov.uk. (2014) *Mental Health Act 1983*, Available from: https://www.legislation.gov.uk/ukpga/1983/20/contents [Accessed 3 February 2023].

Letourneau, E.J., Henggeler, S.W., Borduin, C.M., Schewe, P.A., McCart, M.R., Chapman, J.E. and Saldana, L. (2009) 'Multisystemic therapy for juvenile sexual offenders: 1-year results from a randomized effectiveness trial', *Journal of Family Psychology*, 23: 89–102.

Ling, C. and Dale, A. (2014) 'Agency and social capital: characteristics and dynamics', *Community Development Journal*, 49(1): 4–20. https://www.jstor.org/stable/26166134.

Lipchik, E. (1988) 'Interviewing with a constructive ear', *Dulwich Centre Newsletter*, Winter: 3–7.

Lipchik, E., Derks, J., Lacourt, M. and Nunnally, E. (2012) 'The evolution of solution focused brief therapy', in C. Franklin, T. Trepper, W. Gingerich and E. McCollum (eds) *Solution-Focused Brief Therapy: A Handbook of Evidence-Based Practice*, New York: Oxford University Press, pp 3–19.

Litchfield, M.M., Gatowski, S.I. and Dobbin, S.A. (2003) 'Improving outcomes for families: results of an evaluation of Miami's Family Decision Making program', *Protecting Children*, 18: 48–51.

Littell, J.H., Pigott, T.D., Nilsen, K.H., Green, S.J. and Montgomery, O.L.K. (2021) 'Multisystemic Therapy for social, and behavioural problems in youth age 10–17: an updated systematic review and meta-analysis', *Campbell Systematic Reviews*, 17(4), https://doi.org/10.1002/cl2.1158.

Littell, J.H., Popa, M. and Forsythe, B. (2005) 'Multisystemic therapy for social, emotional, and behavioral problems in youth aged 10–17', Campbell Systematic Reviews, Available from: https://onlinelibrary.wiley.com/doi/10.4073/csr.2005.1.

Löfholm, C.A., Eichas, K. and Sundell, K. (2014) 'The Swedish implementation of Multisystemic Therapy for adolescents: does treatment experience predict treatment adherence?', *Journal of Clinical Child & Adolescent Psychology*, 43(4): 643–655.

Love, C., Burford, G. and Hudson, J. (2000) 'Family group conferencing: cultural origins, sharing, and appropriation – a Māori reflection', in *Family Group Conferencing: New Directions in Community-Centered Child and Family Practice*, New York: Aldine De Gruyter.

Luthar, S.S., Cicchetti, D. and Becker, B. (2000) 'The construct of resilience: a critical evaluation and guidelines for future work', *Child Development*, 71(3), 543–562, https://doi.org/10.1111/1467–8624.00164

Lymbery, M. and Postle, K. (2015) *Social Work and the Transformation of Adult Care: Perpetuating a Distorted Vision?*, Bristol: Policy Press.

Macdonald, A. (2011) (2nd edn) *Solution-Focused Therapy: Theory, Research and Practice*, London: Sage.

Macfarlane, A.H. and Anglem, J. (2014) *Evaluation of Family Group Conference Practice & Outcomes*, Christchurch, New Zealand: Te Awatea Violence Research Centre, University of Canterbury.

Machin, R. and McCormack, F. (2021) 'The impact of the transition to personal independence payment on claimants with mental health problems', *Disability and Society*, doi:10.1080/09687599.2021.1972409

MacLeod, M.A. and Emejulu, A. (2014) 'Neoliberalism with a community face? A critical analysis of asset-based community development in Scotland', *Journal of Community Practice*, 22(4): 430–450.

Making Safeguarding Personal Toolkit: Practice Toolkit Handbook (2019) London: Local Government Association.

Malinen, T. (2002) *From Thinktank to New Therapy: The Process of Solution-Focused Theory and Practice Development*. Available from: http://www.tathata.fi/artik_eng/thinktank.htm [Accessed 18 May 2022].

Manthey, T.J., Knowles, B., Asher, D. and Wahab, S. (2011) 'Strengths-based practice and motivational interviewing', *Advances in Social Work*, 12(2): 126–151.

Manthorpe, J. and Rapaport, J. (2020) *NIHR SSCR Methods Review 26: Researching Family Group Conferences in Adult Services*, London: NIHR School for Social Care Research.

Mapp, S., McPherson, J., Androff, D. and Gatenio Gabel, S. (2019) 'Social Work Is a Human Rights Profession', *Social Work*, 64(3): 259–269.

Marmot, M. (2003) 'Self esteem and health', *BMJ*, 327(7415): 574–575, doi: 10.1136/bmj.327.7415.574

McGoldrick, M. and Gerson, R. (1985) *Genograms in Family Assessment*, New York: Norton.

McGowan, J. (2020) 'Recognition for social work is especially meaningful during the COVID-19 pandemic', British Association of Social Work, Available from: https://www.basw.co.uk/media/news/2020/apr/recognition-social-work-especially-meaningful-during-covid-19-pandemic [Accessed 18 May 2022].

McKenzie, L. (2015) *Getting By: Estates, Class and Culture in Austerity Britain*, Bristol: Policy Press.

McLaughlin, J. (2016) 'Social work in acute hospital settings in Northern Ireland: The views of service users, carers and multi-disciplinary professionals', *Journal of Social Work*, 16(2): 135–154.

McMillen, J.C., Morris, L. and Sherraden, M. (2004) 'Ending social work's grudge match: Problems versus strengths', *Families in Society: The Journal of Contemporary Social Services*, 85(3): 317–325.

McMorris, B., Beckman, K., Shea, G., Baumgartner, J. and Eggert, R. (2013) *Applying Restorative Justice Practices to Minneapolis Public Schools Students Recommended for Possible Expulsion*, Minneapolis, MN: University of Minnesota.

Mental Health Law Online (2021) Community Treatment Orders. Available from: https://www.mentalhealthlaw.co.uk/Community_Treatment_Order [Accessed 3 February 2023].

Merkel-Holguin, Lisa (2004) 'Sharing power with the people: family group conferencing as a democratic experiment', *The Journal of Sociology & Social Welfare*, 31(1). Available from: https://scholarworks.wmich.edu/jssw/vol31/iss1/10 [Accessed 18 May 2022].

Metze, R.N, Abma T.A. and Kwekkeboom R.H. (2013) 'Family group conferencing: a theoretical underpinning', *Health Care Analysis*, 23(2): 165–180, doi: 10.1007/s10728-013-0263-2

Meyer, S. (2015) 'Double listening and the danger of a single story', *Wisdom in Education,* 5(2), article 4. Available from: https://scholarworks.lib.csusb.edu/wie/vol5/iss2/4 [Accessed 18 May 2022].

Mezey, G., Robinson, F., Campbell, R., Gillard, S., Macdonald, G., Meyer, D., Bonell, C. and White S. (2015) 'Challenges to undertaking randomised trials with looked after children in social care settings', *Trials*, 16(206), doi: 10.1186/s13063-015-0708-z

Milligan-Croft, D. (2022) Interview with David Milligan-Croft [unpublished], 16 February.

Milner, J., Myers, S. and O'Byrne, P. (2020) (5th edn) *Assessment in Social Work*, London: Macmillan.

Min, T.O.N.G. (2011) 'The client-centered integrative strengths-based approach: Ending longstanding conflict between social work values and practice', *Canadian Social Science*, 7(2): 15–22.

Mitchell, M. (2020) 'Reimagining child welfare outcomes: learning from family group conferencing', *Child and Family Social Work*, 25(2): 211–220, https://doi.org/10.1111/cfs.12676.

Mohaupt, S. (2009) 'Resilience and social exclusion', *Social Policy and Society*, 8(1): 63–71.

Morgan, A. and Ziglio, E. (2007) 'Revitalising the evidence base for public health: an assets model', *Promotion and Education*, 14(2): 17–22.

Morris, K. and Connolly, M. (2012) 'Family decision making in child welfare: challenges in developing a knowledge base for practice', *Child Abuse Review*, 21(1): 41–52.

Moth, R. (2018) '"The Business End": neoliberal policy reforms and biomedical residualism in frontline community mental health practice in England', *Competition and Change*, 24(2): 133–153, Available from: https://doi.org/10.1177/1024529418813833 [Accessed 4 April 2022].

Moth R. (2020) *Understanding Mental Distress: Knowledge Practice and Neoliberal Reform in Community Mental Health Services*, Bristol: Policy Press.

MST Services (2021) *Research at a Glance*, https://info.mstservices.com/researchataglance [Accessed 9 February 2023].

Muench, K., Diaz, C. and Wright, Rebecca (2017) 'Children and parent participation in child protection conferences: a study in one English local authority', *Child Care in Practice*, 23(1): 49–63, doi:10.1080/13575279.2015.1126227.

Munro, E. (2011) *The Munro Review of Child Protection: Final Report, a Child Centred System*, London: Department for Education.

Munro, E., Turnell, A. and Murphy, T. (2016) *You Can't Grow Roses in Concrete: Action Research Report Signs of Safety English Innovations Project.* Perth: Munro, Turnell and Murphy, Available from: https://knowledgebank. signsofsafety.net/resources/signs-of-safety-research/research-articles/you-can-t-grow-roses-in-concrete [Accessed 9 February 2023].

Myers, S., 2008. *Solution-Focused Approaches*, Lyme Regis: Russell House.

Naar-King, S., Ellis, D., Kolmodin, K., Cunningham, P., Jen, K.C., Saelens, B., et al (2009) 'A randomized pilot study of multisystemic therapy targeting obesity in African-American adolescents', *Journal of Adolescent Health*, 45(4), 417–419.

National Health Service (2019) *Social Prescribing*, Available from: https://www. england.nhs.uk/personalisedcare/social-prescribing/ [Accessed 1 May 2022].

National Institute for Health and Care Excellence (2019) *Evidence for Strengths and Asset Based Outcomes*, Available from: https://www.nice.org.uk/about/ nice-communities/social-care/quick-guides/evidence-for-strengths-and-asset-based-outcomes [Accessed 6 January 2022].

National Institute for Health and Care Excellence (NICE) (2020) *Evidence for Strengths and Asset-Based Outcomes*, Available from: https://www.nice.org.uk/ about/nice-communities/social-care/quick-guides/evidence-for-strengths-and-asset-based-outcomes [Accessed 9 February 2023].

NICE (National Institute for Health and Social Care Excellence) (2011) *Service user experience in adult mental health: improving the experience of care for people using adult NHS mental health services*, Available from: https://www.nice.org.uk/ guidance/ cg136/chapter/1-guidance [Accessed 4 July 2022].

Nygård, R.H. and Saus, M. (2019) 'Is Family Group Conferencing a culturally adequate method outside the origin of New Zealand? A systematic review', *Social Work and Social Sciences Review*, 20(1): 78–108, https://doi.org/10.1921/ swssr.v20i1.1164

O'Brien, V. and Alohen, H. (2015) *Pathways and Outcomes: A Study of 335 Referrals to the Family Welfare Conference (FWC) in Dublin, 2011–2013*, Dublin: University College.

Olsson, T.M., Långström, N., Skoog, T., Löfholm, C.A., Leander, L., Brolund, A., Ringborg, A., Nykänen, P., Syversson, A. and Sundell, K. (2021) 'Systematic review and meta-analysis of noninstitutional psychosocial interventions to prevent juvenile criminal recidivism', *Journal of Consulting and Clinical Psychology*, 89(6): 514–527.

ONS (2001) *Social Capital: A Review of the Literature*. Available from: www.statistics. gov.uk/socialcapital/downloads/soccaplitreview.pdf [Accessed 9 February 2023].

Oxford Learner's Dictionary (2022) 'Asset', Available from: https://www.oxfordlearners dictionaries.com/definition/english/asset?q=asset [Accessed 11 April 2022].

Ozbay, F., Fitterling, H., Charney, D. and Southwick, S. (2008) 'Social support and resilience to stress across the life span: a neurobiologic framework', *Current Psychiatry Reports*, 10(4): 304–310.

Pakura, S. (2003) 'A review of the family group conference service 13 years on', *Social Work Review*, 15(3): 3–7.

Pardeck, J.A., Murphy, J.W. and Meinert, R. (1998) (1st edn) *Postmodernism, Religion, and the Future of Social Work*, London: Routledge. https://doi.org/10.4324/9780203047514

Park, N. and Peterson, C. (2006) 'Moral competence and character strengths among adolescents: the development and validation of the Values in Action Inventory of Strengths for Youth', *Journal of Adolescence*, 29: 891–910.

Parkinson, K. (2018) 'The theoretical context for FGCs', in D. Edwards and K. Parkinson (eds) *Family Group Conferences in Social Work: Involving Families in Social Care Decision Making*, Bristol: Policy Press, pp 15–34.

Parkinson, K. (2020) 'Family Group Conferences: An Analysis of Their Application in Social Work Safeguarding Practice', PhD thesis (unpublished), University of Salford.

Parkinson, K., Pollock, S. and Edwards, D. (2018) 'Family Group Conferences: an opportunity to re-frame responses to the abuse of older people', *British Journal of Social Work*, 48(4): 1109–1126, https://doi.org/10.1093/bjsw/bcy048

Partners4Change (n.d.) 'The key to the door of a new way of working', Available from: http://partners4change.co.uk/the-three-conversations/ [Accessed 4 January 2022].

Parton, N. and O'Byrne, P. (2000) *Constructive Social Work: Towards a New Practice*, Basingstoke: Palgrave Macmillan.

Pattoni, L. (2012) *Strengths Based Approaches for Working with Individuals*, Insight 16, Glasgow: Iriss.

Pease, B. (2002) 'Rethinking empowerment: a postmodern reappraisal for emancipatory practice', *The British Journal of Social Work*, 32(2): 135–147. http://www.jstor.org/stable/23716754

Pennell, J. (2003) 'Are we following key FGC practices? Views of conference participants', *Protecting Children*, 18(1–2): 16–21.

Pennell, J. and Burford, G. (2000) 'Family group decision making: protecting women and children', *Child Welfare*, 79(2): 131–158.

Perry, C. (2021) 'Change agents, not gatekeepers – a timely reminder of social work's value', *Professional Social Work* (December 2021–January 2022): 18–19, Available from: https://www.basw.co.uk/resources/psw-magazine/psw-online/change-agents-not-gatekeepers-timely-reminder-social-works-value [Accessed 18 May 2022].

Pollock, S., Parkinson, K. and Cummins, I. (eds) (2019) *Social Work and Society: Political and Ideological Perspectives*, London: Policy Press.

Pon, G. (2009) 'Cultural competency as new racism: an ontology of forgetting', *Journal of Progressive Human Services*, 20(1): 59–71, https://doi.org/10.1080/10428230902871173.

Poulin, J. (ed) (2000) *Collaborative Social Work: Strengths Based Generalist Practice*, Itasca, IL: F.E. Peacock.

Pulla, V. (2017) 'Strengths-based approach in social work: a distinct ethical advantage', *International Journal of Innovation, Creativity and Change*, 3(2): 97–114.

Pulla, V. and Kay, A. (2016) 'Response to a strengths-based approach to social work in schools: an Indian school in Dubai', *International Social Work*, 60(6): 1–15.

Rapaport, J., Poirier-Baiani, G. and Manthorpe, J. (2019) 'Social work in the Canadian province of New Brunswick: reflections on family group conferencing', *Practice: Social Work in Action*, 31(4): 291–302, https://doi.org/10.1080/09503153.2018.1563588

Rapp, C.A. and Chamberlain, R. (1985) 'Case management services for the chronically mentally ill', *Social Work*, 30: 417–422.

Rapp, C.A. and Goscha, R.J. (2006) (2nd edn) *The Strengths Model Case Management with Psychiatric Disabilities*, Oxford: Oxford University Press.

Rapp, C.A., Saleebey, D. and Sullivan, W.P. (2005) 'The future of the Strengths Perspective', *Advances in Social Work*, 6(1): 79–90.

Rapp, C., Saleebey, D. and Sullivan, P.W. (2008) 'The future of strengths-based social work practice', *Social Work*, 6(1).

Reekers, S.E., Dijkstra, S., Stams, G.J.J., Asscher, J.J. and Creemers, H.E. (2018) 'Signs of effectiveness of Signs of Safety? A pilot study', *Children and Youth Services Review*, 91: 177–184.

Rees Centre (2017) *Children's Social Care Innovation Programme: Final Evaluation Report*, London: DfE.

Revell, L. (2019) 'Exploring Narratives of Neglect in Social Work Practice with Children and Families: Whose Narratives? What Neglect?', PhD thesis, University of Hull.

RF v. Secretary of State for Work and Pensions (2017) England and Wales High Court. Available from: https://commonslibrary.parliament.uk/research-briefings/cbp-7911/ [Accessed 10 February 2023].

Robbins, S.P., Chatterjee, P. and Canda, E.R. (1998) *Contemporary Human Behavior Theory: A Critical Perspective for Social Work*, Boston, MA: Allyn and Bacon.

Robinson, L. (2022) Interview with Lynne Robinson [unpublished], 5 March.

Robinson, L.J., Schmid, A.A. and Siles, M.E. (2002) 'Is social capital really capital?', *Review of Social Economy*, 60(1): 1–21, doi: 10.1080/00346760110127074.

Robson, C. (2002) (2nd edn) *Real World Research*, Oxford: Blackwell.

Rogers, C. (1951) *Client Centred Therapy: Its Current Practice, Implications and Theory*, London: Constable.

Rogers, M. and Cooper, J. (2020) (2nd edn) 'Systems theory and an ecological approach', in M. Rogers, D. Whitaker, D. Edmondson and D. Peach (eds) *Developing Skills and Knowledge for Social Work Practice*, London: Sage, pp 251–258.

Rogers, M. and Taylor, R. (2019) 'Overcoming barriers: exploring specialist interventions for supporting older women to escape domestic violence and abuse', in H. Bows (ed.) *Violence against Older Women*, vol. 2, *Responses*, Basingstoke: Palgrave Macmillan, pp 79–100.

Rollnick, S. and Miller, W.R. (1995) 'What is motivational interviewing?' *Behavioural and Cognitive Psychotherapy*, 23(4): 325–334.

Romeo, L. (2017) *Strengths-Based Social Work Practice with Adults: Roundtable Report*, London: Department of Health.

Roscoe, K.D. and Madoc, I. (2009) 'Critical social work practice a narrative approach', *International Journal of Narrative Practice*, 1(1): 9–18.

Rose, S. (2021) *Creating a Culture of Resilience for Social Workers*, Insight 58, Glasgow: Iriss.

Rutter, M. (1987) 'Psychosocial resilience and protective mechanisms', *American Journal of Orthopsychiatry*, 57: 316–331, https://doi.org/10.1111/j.1939-0025.1987.tb03541.x

Sahin, F. (2006) 'Implications of social constructionism for social work', *Asia Pacific Journal of Social Work and Development*, 16(1): 57–65, https://doi.org/10.1080/21650993.2006.9755992.

Saleebey, D. (1996) 'The strengths perspective in social work practice: extensions and cautions', *Social Work*, 41: 296–305.

Saleebey, D. (2002) (3rd edn) *The Strengths Perspective in Social Work Practice*, Boston, MA: Allyn and Bacon.

Saleebey, D. (2006) (4th edn) *The Strengths Perspective in Social Work Practice*, New York: Longman.

Saleebey, D. (2009) (5th edn) *The Strengths Perspective in Social Work Practice*, Boston, MA: Allyn and Bacon.

Saleebey, D. (2013) 'Power in the people', in D. Saleebey (ed.) *Social Work*, London: Routledge, pp 196–205.

Salveron, M., Bromfield, L., Kirika, C., Simmons, J., Murphy, T. and Turnell, A. (2015) 'Changing the way we do child protection': the implementation of Signs of Safety® within the Western Australia Department for Child Protection and Family Support', *Children and Youth Services Review*, 48: 126–139.

Sawyer, A.M. and Borduin, C.M. (2011) 'Effects of MST through midlife: a 21.9-year follow up to a randomized clinical trial with serious and violent juvenile offenders', *Journal of Consulting and Clinical Psychology*, 79: 643–652.

Sawyer, R.Q. and Lohrbach, S. (2008) *Olmsted County Child and Family Services: Family Involvement Strategies*, Rochester, MN: Olmsted County Child and Family Services.

Schaeffer, C.M. and Borduin, C.M. (2005) 'Long-term follow-up to a randomized clinical trial of multisystemic therapy with serious and violent juvenile offenders', *Consulting and Clinical Psychology*, 73(3): 69–91.

Schaeffer, C., Swenson, C.C. and Powell, J.S. (2021) 'Multisystemic Therapy – Building Stronger Families (MST-BSF): substance misuse, child neglect, and parenting outcomes from an 18-month randomized effectiveness trial', *Child Abuse and Neglect*, 122, https://doi.org/10.1016/j.chiabu.2021.105379

SCIE (2018) *Strengths-Based Social Care for Children, Young People and Their Families*. SCIE highlights no. 5, Leeds: SCIE, Leeds City Council and Shared Lives Plus, Available from: https://www.scie.org.uk/strengths-based-approaches/young-people [Accessed 10 February 2023].

Sheehan, L., O'Donnell, C., Brand, S.L., Forrester, D., Addiss, S., El-Banna, A., Kemp, A. and Nurmatov, U. (2018a) *Signs of Safety: A Mixed Methods Systematic Review*, Cardiff: Cardiff University.

Sheehan, L., O'Donnell, C., Brand, S.L., Forrester, D., Addiss, S., El-Banna, A., Kemp, A. and Nurmatov, U. (2018b) *Signs of Safety: Findings from a Mixed-Methods Systematic Review Focussed on Reducing the Need for Children to Be in Care*, London: What Works Centre for Children's Social Care.

Shennan, G. (2019a) (2nd edn) *Solution-Focused Practice: Effective Communication to Facilitate Change,* London: Bloomsbury.

Shennan, G. (2019b) 'Solution-focused practice in social work', in M. Payne and E. Reith-Hall (eds) *The Routledge Handbook of Social Work Theory*, London: Routledge, pp 224–235.

Shennan, G. (2020) 'What's in a word? Exceptions, instances, assets and unique outcomes', *Guy's blog*. Available from: guyshennan.com/post/what-s-in-a-word-exceptions-instances-assets-and-unique-outcomes [Accessed 18 May 2022].

Siegal, H.A., Rapp, R.C., Kelliher, C.W. and Fisher, J.H. (1995) 'The strengths perspective of case management: a promising inpatient substance abuse treatment enhancement', *Journal of Psychoactive Drugs*, 27(1): 67–72.

Skeggs, B. (2014) 'Values beyond value? Is anything beyond the logic of capital?', *British Journal of Sociology*, 65(1): 1–21.

Skrypek, M., Idzelis, M. and Pecora, P.J. (2012) *Signs of Safety in Minnesota: Parents, Perceptions of Signs of Safety Child Protection Experience*, St Paul, MN: Wilder Research.

Slasberg, C. and Beresford, P. (2017) 'Strengths-based practice: social care's latest elixir or the next false dawn?', *Disability & Society*, 32(2): 269–273.

Smock, S.A., Trepper, T.S., Wetchler, J.L., McCollum, E.E., Ray, R., and Pierce, K. (2008) 'Solution-focused group therapy for Level I substance abusers', *Journal of Marital and Family Therapy*, 34(1): 107–120.

Social Work England (2019) *Professional Standards*. Available from: https://www.socialworkengland.org.uk/standards/professional-standards/ [Accessed 5 January 2022].

Sparkes, A. (2012) 'The strengths model: a recovery-oriented approach to mental health services', *The British Journal of Social Work*, 42(1): 190–192. Available from: https://doi.org/10.1093/bjsw/bcr193 [Accessed 6 January 2022].

Stanley, T. and Mills, R. (2014) '"Signs of Safety" practice at the health and children's social care interface', *Practice*, 26(1): 23–36.

Staudt, M., Howard, M.O. and Drake, B. (2001) 'The operationalization, implementation and effectiveness of the strengths perspective: a review of empirical studies', *Journal of Social Service Research*, 27(30): 1–21.

Stuck, M.B., Rocco, T.S. and Albormoz, C.A. (2011) 'Exploring employee engagement from the employee perspective: implications for HRD', *Journal of European Industrial Training*, 3(4): 300–325.

Swenson, C.C., Schaeffer, C., Henggeler, S.W., Faldowski, R. and Mayhew, A.M. (2010) 'Multisystemic therapy for child abuse and neglect: a randomized effectiveness trial', *Journal of Family Psychology*, 24: 497–507.

Szasz, T. (1961) *The Myth of Mental Illness: Foundations of a Theory of Personal Conduct*, New York: Harper and Row.

Teater, B. (2014, *Contemporary Social Work Practice: A Handbook for Students*, Maidenhead: McGraw-Hill Education (UK).

Tedam, P. (2013) 'Developing cultural competence', in A. Bartoli (ed) Anti-racism in Social Work Practice, St Albans: Critical Publishing, pp 48–65.

Tengland, P.A. (2008) 'Empowerment: a conceptual discussion', *Health Care Analysis*, 16(2):77–96, doi: 10.1007/s10728-007-0067-3

Thackrah, R.D. and Thompson, S.C. (2013) 'Refining the concept of cultural competence: building on decades of progress', *The Medical Journal of Australia*, 199(1): 35–38.

The Health Foundation (2014) *Person-Centred Care Made Simple*, London: The Health Foundation.

Thompson, N. (2016) *Anti-Discriminatory Practice: Equality, Diversity and Social Justice*, Basingstoke: Palgrave Macmillan.

Titcomb, A. and LeCroy, C. (2003) 'Evaluation of Arizona's family group decision making program: protecting children, promising results, potential new directions', *International FGDM Research and Evaluation in Child Welfare*, 18(1–2): 58–64.

Toros, K. (2019) 'Miracle question promotes open communication and positive interaction between clients and practitioners', *International Social Work*, 62(2): 483–486.

Trupin, E.J., Kerns, S.E.U., Walker, S.C., DeRobertis, M.T. and Stewart, D.G. (2011) 'Family integrated transitions: a promising program for juvenile offenders with co-occurring disorders', *Journal of Child & Adolescent Substance Abuse*, 20: 421–436.

Tuckman, B. (1965) 'Developmental sequences in small groups', *Psychological Bulletin*, 63(6): 384–399.

Turnell, A. and Edwards, S. (1997) 'Aspiring to partnership: the Signs of Safety approach to child protection', *Child Abuse Review*, 6(3): 179–190.

Turnell, A. and Edwards, S. (1999) *Signs of Safety: A Solution and Safety Oriented Approach to Child Protection*, New York: Norton.

Turnell, A. and Essex, S. (2006) *Working with 'Denied' Child Abuse: The Resolutions Approach*, Buckingham: Open University Press.

Turnell, A. and Murphy, E. (2017) (4th edn) *Signs of Safety: A Comprehensive Briefing Paper*, East Perth: Resolutions Consultancy.

Tuten, L.M., Jones, H.E., Schaeffer, C.M. and Stitzer, M.L. (2012) *Reinforcement Based Treatment for Substance Use Disorders: A Comprehensive Behavioral Approach*, Washington, DC: American Psychological Association.

UKASFP (2021) Accreditation: Detailed assessment criteria, Available from: ukasfp.site-ym.com/page/Accredcriteria [Accessed 18 May 2022].

Van Breda, A. D. (2018) 'A critical review of resilience theory and its relevance for social work', *Social Work/Maatskaplike Werk*, 54(1): 1–18, doi:10.15270/54-1-611.

van der Stouwe T., Asscher, J.J., Stams, G., Deković, M. and van der Laan, P.H. (2014) 'The effectiveness of Multisystemic Therapy (MST): a meta-analysis', *Clinical Psychology Review*, 34: 468–481.

Verney, S.P., Avila, M., Espinosa, P.R., Cholka, C.B., Benson, J.G., Baloo, A. and Pozernick, C.D. (2016) 'Culturally sensitive assessments as a strength-based approach to wellness in Native communities: a community-based participatory research project', *American Indian and Alaska Native Mental Health Research*, 23(3): 271–292, doi: 10.5820/aian.2303.2016.271

Waites, C., Macgowan, M.J., Pennell, J., Carlton-LaNey, I. and Weil, M. (2004) 'Increasing the cultural responsiveness of Family Group Conferencing', *Social Work*, 49(2): 291–300, https://doi.org/10.1093/sw/49.2.291

Walker, L. (2005) 'A cohort study of 'Ohana conferencing in child abuse and neglect cases', *Protecting Children,* 19(4): 36–46.

Walker, S. (2012) *Effective Social Work with Children, Young People and Their Families: Putting Systems Theory into Practice*, London: Sage.

Walsh, F. (2015) (3rd edn) *Strengthening Family Resilience*, New York: The Guilford Press.

Wachtel, T. (2015) 'New Dutch laws put family power first', *IIRP News*, https://www.iirp.edu/news/new-dutch-law-puts-family-power-first [Accessed 9 Februrary 2023].

Weakland, J., Fisch, R., Watzlawick, P. and Bodin, A. (1974) 'Brief therapy: focused problem resolution', *Family Process*, 13(2): 141–168.

Webb, J., Schirato, T. and Danaher, G. (2002) *Understanding Bourdieu*, Crows Nest, NSW: Allen & Unwin.

Webb, S.A. (2001) 'Some considerations on the validity of evidence-based practice in social work', *The British Journal of Social Work*, 31(1): 57–79, https://doi.org/10.1093/bjsw/31.1.57

Weick, A., Rapp, C., Sullivan, W. and Kisthard, W. (1989) 'A strengths perspective for social work practice', *Social Work*, 34(4): 350–354.

Weiner-Davis, M., de Shazer, S. and Gingerich, W. (1987, 'Building on pretreatment change to construct the therapeutic solution: an exploratory study', *Journal of Marital and Family Therapy*, 13(4): 359–363.

What Works (n.d.) https://whatworks-csc.org.uk/evidence/evidence-store/intervention/family-group-conferencing/ [Accessed 9 June 2020].

Wheeler, J. (2003) 'Solution-focused practice in social work', in B. O'Connell and S. Palmer (eds) *Handbook of Solution-Focused Therapy*, London: Sage, pp 106–117.

White, C., Bell, J. and Revell, L. (2022) 'Signs of Safety and the paradox of simplicity: insights from research with social work students', *Practice*, doi: 10.1080/09503153.2022.2045009

White, J. (2020) *Terraformed: Young Black Lives in the Inner City*, London: Repeater Books.

White, M. and Epston, E. (1990) *Narrative Means to Therapeutic Ends*, London: Norton.

Wigan Council (2019) *The Deal 2030*, Available from: https://www.wigan.gov.uk/Council/Strategies-Plans-and-Policies/Deal-2030.aspx [Accessed 1 August 2021].

Williams, A. (2019) 'Family support services delivered using a restorative approach: a framework for relationship and strengths-based whole family practice', *Child and Family Social Work*, 24: 555–564.

Wood, J. (2022) Email correspondence with Jacqui Wood (unpublished), 4 April.

Word of Mouth (2022) 'Nathan Filer on the ways we talk about mental health', BBC Radio 4, 3 May, Available from: https://www.bbc.co.uk/programmes/m0016xjw [Accessed 9 February 2023].

Yeung, S., Castleden, H. and Pictou Landing First Nation (2020) '"We all know each other": a strengths-based approach to understanding social capital in Pictou Landing First Nation', *Research Papers*, 15(1), Available from: https://jps.library.utoronto.ca/index.php/ijih/article/view/34057 [Accessed 9 February 2023].

Ylvisaker, S. (2011) 'Tales from the sequestered room: client experiences of social work in Norway and Sweden', *Journal of Social Work*, 13(2): 203–220.

Index

Page numbers in **bold** refer to tables.

A

Abdullah, S. 8
ADASS (Association of Directors of Adult Social
     Services) 106, 107
adult social work and social care 99–100, 112
   1990 National Health Service and
        Community Care Act 101
   2014 Care Act 9, 99, 100, 101–2, 105, 106,
        108–9, 112
   asset-based approaches 99, 100, 109, 111
   austerity measures and 99, 101, 102, 112–13
   benefits and success of 106, 107–8, 113
   critical appraisal 99, 102–3, 104, 109–12
   Davey case: *R (Davey) v. Oxfordshire
        CC* 108–9, 112
   empowerment 101
   FACS criteria (Fair Access to Care
        Services) 101
   FGCs 39, 46, 48–9, 104, 108
   key learning points 112–13
   KSS (Knowledge and Skills Statement for
        Adults) 104
   LAC (Local Area Co-ordination) 104
   MSP (Making Safeguarding Personal) 99,
        103, 106–8
   narrative approaches with adults 95–7
   neoliberalism and 101, 109–10, 111–12, 113
   Northern Ireland 100
   peer-reviewed evidence 102–3, 106, 107, 113
   RAS 101
   SCIE 9
   Scotland 100
   Shared Lives 104
   solution-focused practice 35
   SoS 60–1, 108
   strengths-based approaches 8, 9, 21, 99–102,
        112, 134, 145
   strengths-based approaches in practice 104
   strengths-based framework for adult social
        work 103–4
   terminology 99–100
   Three Conversations approach 99, 100,
        105–6, 107, 112
   UK 103, 112
   Wigan Deal 109–10, 111–12
   see also Care Act

advocacy 101, 145
   FGCs 41, 139
   MSP 107
agency 11, 14
   MST 71, 73
   narrative approaches 93
   solution-focused practice 32–3
Ahmed, A. and Rogers, M. 86
Allegritti, L. 19
Allen, Ruth 102
Anthony, W.A. 116
antisocial behaviour 71, 72, 107
Arc (Arts for Recovery in the Community) 121–4
   as 'human-shaped space' 124–7
   see also mental health services
assessment 59–60, 78, 90
   assessment tools for strengths-based
        approaches 5–6, 7, 43, 95
   biopsychosocial assessment forms 5
   CAF (common assessment framework) 91
   Care Act assessment model 91, 102, 105, 109
   ecomaps 5, 95
   genograms 5, 95
   holistic assessment 9
   mental health assessments 119
   MST 73, 78
   narrative approaches 91–2, 97
   neoliberalism and social workers as care
        co-ordinators 101
   SoS 60–1, 67
   worksheets 5–6
asset-based approaches 99, 100, 109, 111
   asset, definition of 118
asylum seekers and refugees (UK) 111
Attlee, Clement 26
austerity measures (UK)
   2014 Care Act and 99, 102
   adult social work and social care 99, 101,
        102, 112–13
   individual responsibility and 116, 117
   mental health services 116, 117, 119, 120, 127
Australia 55–6
autonomy
   empowerment and 44
   FGCs 44–5

people with lived experience 16
relational autonomy 44
social workers and 101

B
Backwith, D. 116, 117
Baginsky, M. 67
Bailes, J. 124
Bailey, Lauren 55–69
Baker, S. and Brown, B.J. 116, 117, 118, 123, 124, 127
Bakhtin, M.M. 87
balance of power
    equal balance in social work 8
    FGCs 40, 43–4
    problem-focused approach and power imbalances 2
    strengths-based approaches and 2–3, 14
Baldwin, C. 85, 86
Baldwin, L. and Raikes, B. 97
Barclay Report (1982) 100
Barn, R. and Das, C. 47
Baron, Samantha 103
Barringer, A. 44
Barthes, Roland 85
BASW (British Association of Social Workers) 3, 21, 102
Bell, M. 131
Berg, Insoo Kim 3, 6, 28, 29, 36
Berger, P.L. and Luckmann, T. 13
BFTC (Brief Family Therapy Center, USA) 26–7, 28, 29, 37
Bogo, M. 118
Booker, C. 86
Booth, J. 112
Bottrell, D. 16–17
Boulden, W.T. 7
Bourdieu, P. 14, 111
Broadhurst, K. and Mason, C. 91
Brodsky, A.E. and Cattaneo, L.B. 45
Bronfenbrenner, U.: concentric model of social environment 18, 45–6, 72
Brown, L. and Levitt, J. 5
Buckley, H., Carr, N. and Whelan, S. 131
Burack-Weiss, A. 93
Burnham, J.B. 89

C
Cade, B. and O'Hanlon, B. 25, 28
Canda, E.R. 6
Care Act (2014) 21, 78
    adult social work and social care 9, 99, 100, 101–2, 105, 106, 108–9, 112
    asset-based approaches 99
    austerity measures and 99, 102
    Care Act assessment model 91, 102, 105, 109
    Care and Support Statutory Guidance 102, 106
    Davey case: *R (Davey) v. Oxfordshire CC* 108–9
    MSP (Making Safeguarding Personal) 99, 106
    personalisation agenda 117
    SCIE 9, 102
    Section 1 109
    Section 8 105
    Section 42 102, 105, 107
    strengths-based approaches 1, 9, 99, 101–2, 117
    Three Conversations approach 105
    'wellbeing principle' 9, 99, 102, 108
Chamberlain, R. 2
Chassot, C.S. and Mendes, F. 115–16
Chatzidakis, A. 110
child protection
    2011 Munro Review 9, 56, 67
    child deaths 57
    child protection conferences 6, 132–3
    child protection social workers 131–4
    criticism 59
    FGCs 39, 41, 44, 48, 50
    key learning points 133
    Māori children 6, 19, 39
    SoS 6, 55–7, 67, 68
Child Protection Register 78
children
    FGCs 41, 46, 48, 49
    MSP 108
    narrative approaches with 93–5
    SoS 55
    'Working Together to Safeguard Children', UK 76
    see also MST-CAN
Children Act (1989) 9, 21, 51, 108
Children and Families Services: strengths-based approaches with 1, 9
children's services
    MST 77
    solution-focused practice 29, 31, 35, 56, 140
    SoS 60, 67, 140
    strengths-based approaches 9, 21–2
Cocker, C. 108
Cognitive Behaviour Therapy 7, 76, 77, 82
    Trauma-Focused Cognitive Behavioural Therapy 76

Index

community social work 99–100, 112
    1963 Seebohm Report 100
    1982 Barclay Report 100
Connolly, M. and Healy, K. 103
Cooper, A. 107–8
Cooper, Jennifer 85–98
Corcoran, J. and Pillai, V. 140
Cossar, J. 131
COVID-19 pandemic 52, 100, 130
Cowger, C.D 4, 8
culturally appropriate social work
    practice 19–20, 23
    criticism 20, 47
    FGCs 19, 46–7
    narrative approaches 19
Cummins, I. 121

D

Davey, Luke: *R (Davey) v. Oxfordshire
    CC* 108–9, 112
Davies, William 124
De Jong, P. 3
de Shazer, Steve 6, 28, 29–30
deficit-led approaches 11, 13, 101, 145
    shift to a strengths-based model 2, 4, 42,
      106, 116, 117, 130–1
domestic abuse 133, 134–5
    DAN (Domestic Abuse
      Navigator) 134–5, 136
    master narratives vs counter-narratives 88
    see also MST-CAN
Douglas, E.M., McCarthy, S.C. and Serino,
    P.A. 4, 7

E

EBTA (European Brief Therapy Association) 36
ecological systems theory/systemic practice 5,
    18–19, 22
    ecomaps 5, 95
    FGCs 45–6
    MST 72, 73, 83
    narrative approaches and 89, 97
Edmondson, Anne 71–83
Edwards, Deanna 1–10, 11–23, 39–54,
    129–43, 145–6
Edwards, Steve 6, 55–6
Egan, G. 5
empowerment 17–18
    adult social work and social care 101
    autonomy and 44
    disempowering nature of social care
      processes 14

FGCs 43–5, 136
    'imposed empowerment' 44
    MST 71, 73, 76, 77–8
    narrative approaches 95, 98
    neoliberalism and 8, 110
    problem-focused approach 18
    relational empowerment 44
    resilience and 45
    'responsibility in the guise of
      empowerment' 8, 110
    social work practice and 17
    SoS 59, 67
    strengths-based approaches 2, 3, 7, 79,
      110–11, 129, 145
    strengths-based practitioner/user
      relationship 12, 17–18
Essex Divisional Based Intervention Team 35

F

family-led decision-making models 22
    see also FGCs
family services 7–8, 9
Feldon, P. 109
Ferguson, I. 109, 117
FGCs (Family Group Conferences) 1, 9, 20,
    39, 53
    adult social work and social care 39, 46,
      48–9, 104, 108
    advocacy 41, 139
    alternative names for 22
    autonomy 44–5
    benefits and success of 46, 48, 49, 50,
      53, 138–9
    case study 39, 50–3
    child protection 39, 41, 44, 48, 50
    children and young people 41, 46, 48,
      49, 139
    co-ordinators 40, 41, 136–7
    criticism 22, 44, 47, 49–50
    culturally appropriate social work
      practice 19, 46–7
    definition of 6, 39–42
    ecological systems theory 45–6
    empowerment theory 43–5, 136
    family/extra-familial relationships and social
      capital/networks 15, 16, 45
    as family-led decision-making model 22,
      39–40, 41–2, 53, 136, 139
    family's choice to engage or not with FGC
      process 43, 44
    as global practice 39, 43, 47
    hope 43

key learning points 53, 139
language 40, 47
Māori people and 6, 19, 39, 47
the Netherlands 136–7
New Zealand 6, 19, 22, 39, 49
people with lived experience of 136–9
research findings 47–9
resilience 45
social work theory and practice 43–7, 53
as strengths-based approach 6, 22, 39, 42–3,
 53, 145
UK 39, 43, 44, 47, 48, 136, 137
venues for 40, 47
FGC process
 1. preparation stage 40–1, 51–2
 2. information-giving stage 41, 52
 3. private family time 41–2, 52, 53,
  137, 138
 4. agreeing a family plan 42, 52, 138
 5. reviewing the plan 42, 52–3
Fisch, R., Weakland, J. and Segal, L. 25
Fisher, M. 110
Fleming, Mhairi 71–83
Fox, Simone 71–83

G
Garrett, P.M. 16, 110, 120
generic strengths-based social work 134–6, 145
Gergen, K.J. 13
Gilbert, J. 111, 112
Gingerich, W. and Peterson, L. 36
Glicken, M.D. 2
Golden, Will 39–54
Gollins, T. 111
Goscha, R.J. 12
Gray, M. 8, 19, 109, 110
Green, B.L., McAllister, C.L. and Tarte, J.M. 7
Greene, G.J, Lee, M.Y. and Hoffpauir, S. 17
Growing Futures project, Doncaster 134
Guo, W. and Tsui, M. 18

H
Hammond, W. and Zimmerman, R. 16
Harawitz, C. 45
Harris, J. 68, 157
health services 7
Hengeller, S.W. 6
Hepworth, D.H. and Larsen, J. 5
Hickman, B. 67, 68
Holland, S. 44
hope
 FGCs 43

solution-focused practice 30–1, 37
strengths-based approaches 2, 3, 9, 12,
 43, 78
Houston, S. 110
Hunter, Tony 102

I
IFSW (International Federation of Social
 Work) 20–1, 22
Ireland
 MST 76–7, 78, 82
 MST-FIT 77

J
Jirek, J.L. 95
Jobe, A. and Gorin, S. 131, 145
Johnson, Y.M. and Munch, S. 20
Jordan, B. 110

K
Kam, P.K. 130
Kaplan, L. and Girard, J. 17
Kay, A. 7
Keddell, E. 19
Kemp, S.P. 8
Kim, J. 36
Kisthard, W. 11
Korman, H. 28

L
language
 FGCs and 40, 47
 mental health care and 118–19
 narrative and narrative approaches 85, 91
 social constructionism and 13
 SoS and 64
 strengths-based approaches and 4–6, 13
Lavalette, M. and Moth, R. 120
Leeds City Council Adult Social Care 134
LGA (Local Government Association) 106, 107
Ling, C. and Dale, A. 14
Littell, J.H. 72
Love, C. 47

M
MacLeod, M.A. and Emejulu, A. 110
Manthorpe, J. 48, 67–8
Māori people and FGCs 6, 19,
 39, 47
Mapp, S. 21
McLaughlin, J. 131
medical model 13, 115, 117, 127

mental health
 2011 *No Health without Mental Health* 116
 dementia 95–7
 loneliness and 112, 123
 social exclusion and 117, 119, 120, 121, 122, 123, 127, 128
 social inequality and 116, 121, 128
 stigma associated with mental distress 115–16, 117, 122, 126, 128
Mental Health Act (1983) 51, 119
mental health services 48–9, 115, 127
 2014 NICE guidance, UK 21, 117
 Arc 121–7
 austerity measures and 116, 117, 119, 120, 127
 blame and shame culture 120, 127
 case studies 115, 124–7
 collective responsibility 117, 121, 123, 127
 CTO (Community Treatment Orders) 119
 ESA (Employment and Support Allowance) 119
 key learning points 128
 KPIs (Key Performance Indicators) 123
 language and 118–19
 medical model 115, 117, 127
 mental health assessments 119
 narrative approaches 95–7
 neoliberalism, individual responsibility and 115, 116–17, 119, 127, 128
 pathology of mental distress 115–16, 117–18, 121
 PIP (Personal Independence Payments) 119–20
 recovery, definition of 115–16, 117
 risk agenda 115, 119
 social prescribing 123
 state benefits eligibility criteria 115, 120
 strengths-based approaches 7, 11–12, 115, 117–19, 121, 122–3, 125, 127, 145
 survivors 115–16, 117–18
 see also mental health
Mental Research Institute, Palo Alto (California, USA) 26
Metze, R.N, Abma T.A. and Kwekkeboom R.H. 18, 43, 44, 45
Meyer, S. 34
Milligan-Croft, David 115, 125–6
Mills, R. 67
minority groups 14, 19, 47
Mitchell, M. 49
Mohaupt, S. 16
Morgan,A. and Ziglio, E. 3
Moriarty, J. 67–8

Morris, K. and Connolly, M. 47
motivational interviewing 7, 8
MSP (Making Safeguarding Personal) 99, 103, 106–8
MST (multisystemic therapy) 2, 82
 adaptations of 71, 73, 82
 agency 71, 73
 aim of 71
 antisocial behaviour 71, 72
 assessment 73, 78
 benefits and success of 71–2, 81, 82
 case study 79–81
 children's services 77
 definition of 6, 71, 82
 development of 71–2
 ecological systems theory 72, 73, 83
 empowerment 71, 73, 76, 77–8
 family-focused therapeutic intervention 6, 73
 'fit circle' 73
 as global practice 71, 82
 home-based therapeutic intervention 6, 72–3, 74
 Ireland 76–7, 78, 82
 key learning points 82–3
 MST team 72, 77
 overview of 72–3
 referrals to 77–8
 research on 71–2, 82
 Scotland 78
 as strengths-based approach 6, 71, 75, 77, 78–9, 82, 83, 145
 substance misuse and 71, 75–6, 79, 81
 theoretical orientation 73
 treatment principles 73, **74**, 78
 UK 72, 76–7, 78–9, 82
 USA 71, 82
 young people 6, 71, 78
 Wales 77
 workforce and social work context 77
MST-CAN (MST for child abuse and neglect) 71, 82
 case study 81–2
 communication between MST-CAN team and children's social workers 77
 effectiveness 73–4
 evidenced-based interventions 75, 76
 goals 75
 MST team 74
 referrals to 74–5
 standard MST/MST-CAN comparison 74
 UK 76

MST-FIT (MST-Family Integrated
    Transitions) 71, 77
Munro Review of Child Protection (2011) 9,
    56, 67
Murphy, E. 56
Myers, Steve 55–69

N
narrative
    concepts and methods 86–7
    key learning points 88
    language and 85
    narrative turn 85
    plurality 85
    as subjective account 89
narrative approaches 2, 85–6, 97
    adult social work and social care 95–7
    agency 93
    assessments 91–2, 97
    authorship and audience 87
    biographical work 93–5
    case studies 92, 95–6
    characters and characterisation 86–7
    culturally appropriate social work practice 19
    definition of 6–7, 85, 98
    development of narrative approaches in social
        work 89–90
    'double listening' 34
    ecological systems theory 89, 97
    empowerment 95, 98
    externalising the problem 92–3
    genre/formats for narrative 87
    'Hackney Model' 89
    interpretation of narratives 90, 98
    key learning points 98
    language 91
    master- and counter-narratives 86, 87–9, 90,
        92, 93, 97
    mental health care 95–7
    narrative identity 90
    narrative questioning 93
    narrative therapy 89
    people with lived experience as storyteller 85
    plots 86
    polyphony and heteroglossia 87
    sense-making process 85, 87, 89, 97
    social work with family and social
        networks 97
    storytelling 6–7, 87, 98
    as strengths-based approach 6, 91, 97,
        98, 145
    using a narrative approach in practice 90

narrative approaches with children and young
    people 93–5
    later-life letters 94–5
    life-story books 94
    parallel stories 94
    pathway planning 95
    therapeutic stories 94
narrative approaches with adults 95–7
    life-story work 96
    one-page profiles 96
    reminiscence groups 96–7
Nash, Vicki 121
National Health Service and Community Care
    Act (1990) 101
National Institute for Health Research 103
neoliberalism 127
    communities, fragmentation of 111, 113
    empowerment and 8, 110
    individual responsibility/responsibilisation 8,
        16–17, 109–10, 111–12
    mental health services and individual
        responsibility 115, 116–17, 119, 127, 128
    resilience and 16–17
    strengths-based approaches and 8, 16–17, 109–10,
        111–12, 113, 115, 117, 117, 127, 128
    UK political ideology 101
    Wigan Deal 109–10, 111–12
the Netherlands 136–7
New Zealand 6, 19, 22, 39, 49
    see also Māori people
Newman, Sam 105
Northern Ireland
    2013 Health and Social Care (reform) Act 100
    adult social work and social care 100
Nygård, R.H. and Saus, M. 47

P
Pakura, S. 49
Parkinson, Kate 1–10, 11–23, 39–54, 129–43, 145–6
Partners4Change 99, 105–6
Pattoni, L. 9
people with lived experience 1, 2, 10, 129–30,
    142, 145, 146
    autonomy 16
    decision-making 16, 18
    empowerment 17
    as experts in their own life 19, 21, 85, 91–2,
        105, 107, 109, 131
    FGCs 136–9
    key learning points 133, 135, 139
    people with lived experiences of 'generic
        strengths-based social work' 134–6

people with lived experiences of 'traditional social work' practice 130–4
self-esteem 16
solution-focused practice 140–1
as storytellers 85
see also strengths-based practitioners/users relationship
Pollock, Sarah 99–113
postmodernism 12–13
Poulin, J. 5–6
problem-focused approach 2, 11, 18
Prolonged Exposure Therapy 76
Pulla, V. 7, 17, 21

R
Rapaport, J. 48
Rapp, C.A. 2, 11, 12, 42–3
RAS ('resource allocation system') 101
resilience 7, 15–17
  'bouncing back' 15, 16, 45
  criticism 16–17
  definition 15, 45
  empowerment and 45
  FGCs 45
  neoliberalism and 16–17
  protective factors 15, 16
  social network and 16, 45
  spirituality and 6
  strengths-based approaches 2, 3, 11, 13
  vulnerability factors 15
responsibility
  collective responsibility 117, 121, 123, 127
  empowerment and 8, 110
  neoliberalism and individual responsibility 8, 16–17, 109–10, 111–12
  neoliberalism, mental health services and individual responsibility 115, 116–17, 119, 127, 128
restorative approach 7–8, 9
Revell, L. 67
Robinson, Lynne 115, 124–7
Rogers, C. 3
Rogers, Michaela 85–98
Romeo, Lyn 9, 99, 101, 102, 121
Roscoe, K.D. and Madoc, I. 6–7
Roundtable Report (2017) 102, 103
Rutter, M. 16, 45

S
Saleebey, Dennis 4, 11, 12, 14, 42–3, 118
  CPRs 3, 145
  defining the issues 5

definition of strengths-based approach 2–3
empowerment 17
resilience 15
SCIE (Social Care Institute for Excellence, UK) 9
  2014 Care Act 9, 102
  generic strengths-based work 134
  strengths-based approach, definition of 12
  strengths-based practitioners 10
Scotland
  2007 Adult Support and Protection Act 100
  2013 Social Care (self-directed support) Act 100
  2016 Carers Act 78
  adult social work and social care 100
  MST 78
Seebohm Report (1963) 100
Shennan, Guy 25–38
Skeggs, B. 110
Slasberg, C. and Beresford, P. 8, 146
Snively, C.A. 4
social capital 11, 14–15
  resilience and social networks 16, 45
social constructionism 11, 12–14
social work
  balance of power and 8
  BASW 21
  definition of 20, 26
  disempowering nature of social care processes 14
  empowerment and 17
  funding crisis in 146
  key principles for social work practice 20–2
  as 'narrative activity' 85
  rights-based social work 21
  users of social care services as poor, marginalised and disenfranchised 14
Social Work England 104, 130
social workers 130–4, 145–6
  autonomy 101
  as change agents 26
  child protection social workers 131
  importance of 145
  as moralising agents 117
  neoliberalism and social workers as care co-ordinators 101, 117
  PCF (Professional Capabilities Framework) 130
  recruitment and retainment crisis 146
  see also strengths-based practitioners
solution-focused practice 1, 8, 25–6, 36–7, 43, 56, 140
  adult social work and social care 35

benefits and usefulness of 35–6, 37, 140–1
BFTC, Milwaukee, USA 26–7, 28, 29, 37
children's services 29, 31, 35, 56, 140
clients as team 26–7
definition of 6, 140
description and agency 32–3
EBTA 36
end-of-session interventions 26, 27
exceptions to problems 6, 25–6, 27–8, 32, 34, 37
formula first session task 26–7
future focus 25, 28–9, 30
as global practice 36, 37
good fit between solution-focused practice and social work 26
hope 30–1, 37
instances 32, 33, 34, 37
key learning points 37
listening with constructive ear 34–5, 36
miracle question 26, 28–9, 31–2, 37
NSPCC toolkit 35
people with lived experience of 140–1
pre-session change 26, 27–8, 37
scaling questions 33–4
as strengths-based approach 6, 140, 145
two ways of using a solution-focused practice 29, 36–7
UK 29–30, 36, 37
UKASFP (UK Association for Solution Focused Practice) 29
see also solution-focused practice: BRIEF version
solution-focused practice: BRIEF version 29–32, 37
1. setting a direction 30–1, 37
2. describing preferred futures 31–2, 34, 37
3. describing progress and what's working 32, 37
see also solution-focused practice
SoS (Signs of Safety) 1, 55, 68
adult social work and social care 60–1, 108
assessment framework 60–1, 67
benefits of 67–8
child protection 6, 55–7, 67, 68
children 55
children's services 60, 67, 140
criticism 67–8
definition of 6, 55, 56, 60, 68
development of the approach 55–6
empowerment 59, 67
as global practice 56
'it takes a village to raise a child' 59, 60

key learning points 68
language 64
principles of 55, 57–8
research on 67–8
risk 55, 58–9, 67, 68
safety 56, 59, 68
safety plans 55, 68
scaling questions 64
as strengths-based approach 6, 8, 22, 55, 58–9, 145
Three Houses 65
UK 56, 67
vulnerability 55, 65
Western Australia 55–6
words and pictures 60
see also SoS case study
SoS case study 59–66
SoS mapping **62–3**
SoS questions **61**
SoS scaling **64**
SoS Three Houses **65**, 66
Step 2 Judgement: scaling questions 64–6
spirituality 6, 8
Stanley, Tony 67, 103
Steiner, T. 36
strengths-based approaches 2–10, 145
arts-based interventions: contribution to strengths-based practice 127, 128
assessment tools 5–6, 7, 43, 95
challenges 102, 108, 109, 118–19, 127, 146
generic strengths-based work 134–6, 145
Islam and 8
peer-reviewed evidence 102–3
in school social work setting 7
in social work practice 1, 2, 3, 4, 7, 103–4
strengths-based assessment: guidelines for 4–6
strengths-based practices inventory 7
types of 6–7
UK practice 8, 9, 12, 21, 78, 134
see also strengths-based approaches: criticism; strengths-based approaches: theoretical context; strengths-based practitioners
strengths-based approaches: criticism 79, 102, 118–19
community, sense of 111–12, 113
gendered nature of care 110–11
neoliberalism and 8, 16–17, 109–10, 111–12, 113, 115, 117, 127, 128
reduction of state support 117
responsibilisation 109–10, 111–12, 127, 146
social context 116

strengths-based approaches: theoretical context
  agency 11, 14
  balance of power 2–3, 14
  capacity and capability 2, 3
  collaborative/partnership working 3, 4, 12,
    21, 60, 102, 130, 135, 146
  CPRs 3, 145
  culturally appropriate social work
    practice 19–20, 23
  definition of the strengths-based
    approach 2–3, 12, 104
  ecological systems theory 18–19
  empowerment 2, 3, 7, 12, 17–18, 79,
    110–11, 129, 145
  four elements of 3
  as holistic and multi-disciplinary 3
  hope 2, 3, 9, 12, 43, 78
  informed/meaningful choice 12, 43
  key learning points 2, 4, 22–3
  language, power of 4–6, 13
  origins and development of the strengths-
    based approach 11–12, 100–1, 145
  as person-centred practice 3, 4, 8, 106, 107
  principles of the strengths-based approach 3,
    17, 42–3
  research on 7–8
  resilience 2, 3, 11, 13
  social capital 11, 14–15
  social constructionism 11, 12–14
  social work practice: key principles 20–2
  social work theories 17–22
  'strengths-based approach' as umbrella
    term 11, 22, 104
strengths-based practitioners 6, 7
  characteristics of 10, 136
  as facilitator 18
  as partners with expertise 12
  role of 12
  see also social workers
strengths-based practitioners/users
    relationship 12, 129, 145–6
  collaborative work 3, 4, 12, 21, 60, 102,
    130, 135, 146
  decision-making 18
  empowerment 12, 17–18
  positive, supportive relationships 136
  quality relationship as hope-inducing 12
  relationship of trust 135
  see also people with lived experience;
    strengths-based practitioners
Stuck, M.B., Rocco, T.S. and Albormoz,
    C.A. 10

substance misuse 90
  MST and 71, 75–6, 79, 81
  Reinforcement-Based Therapy 75
  solution-focused practice and 29
Sullivan, W.P. 11, 12, 42–3
systemic practice see ecological systems theory/
    systemic practice
Szasz, Thomas 116

T
Taylor, R. 88
Teater, B. 18
Tedam, P. 20
Tengland, P.A. 17–18
Three Conversations approach 99, 100, 105–6,
    107, 112
Tuckman, B. 137, 138
Turnell, Andrew 6, 55–6

U
UK (United Kingdom)
  asylum seekers and refugees in 111
  community social work 100
  FGCs 39, 43, 44, 47, 48,
    136, 137
  MST 72, 76–7, 78–9, 82
  MST-CAN 76
  MST-FIT 77
  neoliberalism 101
  social work practice 78
  solution-focused practice 29–30, 36, 37
  SoS 56, 67
  strengths-based approaches 8, 9, 12, 21,
    78, 134
UKASFP (UK Association for Solution Focused
    Practice) 29
University of Kansas: School of Social Welfare,
    USA 11
USA (United States of America)
  BFTC 26–7, 28, 29, 37
  MST 71, 82

W
Wales
  2014 Social Services and Well-Being
    Act 78
  MST 77
Walker, L. 49
Walker, S. 89, 90
Webb, J., Schirato, T. and Danaher, G. 14
Weick, A. 2, 11, 30
Weygang, Emily 115–28

White, C., Bell, J. and Revell, L. 67
White, J. 111
White, M. and Epston, E. 89
Wigan Deal 109–10, 111–12
Williams, A. 7
Withers, Alex 99–113
Wood, Jacqui 122, 124

Y
Ylvisaker, S. 131
young people
    FGCs 41, 46, 48, 49, 139
    narrative approaches with 93–5
    social workers and 131
    see also MST